SO-BYR-507

Praise for W. David Marx's
Ametora

"This is what happens when a really smart person takes on a really interesting topic. Japanese culture and fashion come shining into view."

—Grant McCracken, anthropologist
and author of *Culturematic* and *Chief Culture Officer*

"W. David Marx's *Ametora* answers the questions I had about the history and direction of menswear in Japan, and his research and analysis will undoubtedly be the authoritative word on the subject for years to come. This is a marvelously written, important, and necessary read for any student of global fashion today."

—G. Bruce Boyer, author of *True Style*

"W. David Marx's *Ametora* is a careful, complex, wildly entertaining cultural history of the highest caliber. This book will obviously be of immediate and considerable appeal to Japanophiles, classic-haberdashery connoisseurs, and other assorted fops, but its true and enormous audience ought to be anyone interested in the great hidden mechanisms of international exchange. In an age overrun with hasty jeremiads about the proliferation of global monoculture, Marx has given us quite a lot to reconsider. *Ametora* is a real pleasure."

—Gideon Lewis-Kraus, author of *A Sense of Direction*

"*Ametora* is a reflection of its author's own unique place in contemporary Japanese culture. W. David Marx is an astute writer, historian, and critic of Japanese culture and its relationship to the global youth culture. Marx's book explores the often hidden connection between Tokyo and American style that has eluded many writers before him. Less about runways, more about the urban street, this is an important documentation of the reinvention of American style."

—John C. Jay, president of Global Creative of Fast Retailing

"*Ametora* cuts through the myth, postulation, and hearsay that have long plagued the Japanese fashion origin story. David Marx has crafted the first thoroughly researched and well-written narrative that explains how Japan became the unlikely vanguards of American clothing styles. A must-read for anyone with even a passing interest in men's fashion, cultural assimilation, or otaku obsessions—*Ametora* is basically the bible of Japanese menswear."

—David Shuck, managing editor, Rawr Denim

AMETORA

AMETORA

HOW JAPAN SAVED AMERICAN STYLE

W. DAVID MARX

BASIC BOOKS
A Member of the Perseus Books Group

Published by Basic Books
A Member of the Perseus Books Group

Cover Credits:
Gray crewneck sweatshirt from Loopwheeler, made from slow-moving, vintage
    "Tsuriamiki" knitting machines discontinued from mass production in the mid-
    1960s. (Image courtesy of Loopwheeler)
Jeans are Studio D'artisan's DO-1 model, first made in 1986. The DO-1 kicked off the
    vintage reproduction boom in Japan. (Image courtesy of Studio D'artisan).
A pair of "Leisure Handsewn" shell cordovan loafers made in Massachusetts by American
    brand Alden, special ordered for Japanese retailer Beams+. (Image courtesy of Beams)

Books published by Basic Books are available at special discounts for bulk purchases
in the United States by corporations, institutions, and other organizations. For more
information, please contact the Special Markets Department at the Perseus Books Group,
2300 Chestnut Street, Suite 200, Philadelphia, PA 19103, or call (800) 810-4145, ext.
5000, or e-mail special.markets@perseusbooks.com.

Library of Congress Control Number: 2015944908
ISBN: 978–0-465-05973-7 (Hardcover)
ISBN: 978–0-465-07387-0 (eBook)

10 9 8 7 6 5 4 3 2 1

For my parents

Morris and Sally

CONTENTS

Introduction   ix

one   A Nation Without Style   1

two   The Ivy Cult   23

three   Taking Ivy to the People   49

four   The Jeans Revolution   75

five   Cataloging America   97

six   Damn Yankees   123

seven   Nouveau Riche   149

eight   From Harajuku to Everywhere   175

nine   Vintage and Replica   195

ten   Exporting Ametora   221

ACKNOWLEDGMENTS   243
NOTES AND SOURCES   245
BIBLIOGRAPHY   249
INDEX   259

INTRODUCTION

In the summer of 1964, Tokyo prepared to host thousands of foreign guests for the Olympic Games. Planners hoped to reveal a futuristic city reborn from the ashes of World War II, complete with sprawling highways, modernist stadium complexes, and elegant Western restaurants. As old-fashioned trolley cars disappeared from the streets, a sleek monorail debuted to whisk tourists into the city from Haneda Airport.

The Tokyo government paid special attention to Ginza, the crown jewel of the city, knowing that tourists would gravitate towards its luxury department stores and posh cafés. Ginza's community leaders eliminated any possible suggestion of postwar poverty, even replacing wooden garbage cans with modern plastic ones.

These cleanup efforts proceeded steadily until August, when the switchboards at Tsukiji Police Station began lighting up with frantic phone calls. Ginza shop owners reported an infestation on the main promenade, Miyuki-dōri, requiring immediate assistance from law enforcement: *There were hundreds of Japanese teenagers hanging around in strange clothing!*

Police sent reconnaissance teams to the scene, where they discovered young men wearing shirts made from thick wrinkled cloth with unusual buttons holding down the collar, suit jackets with a superfluous third button high up on the chest, loud madras and tartan plaids, shrunken chino pants or shorts with strange straps on the back, long black knee-high socks, and leather shoes with intricate broguing. The teens parted their hair in a precise seven-to-three ratio—a look requiring the use of electric hair dryers. Police soon learned that this style was called *aibii*, from the English word "Ivy."

Throughout the summer, tabloid magazines editorialized against these wayward teens in Ginza, dubbing them the Miyuki Tribe (*miyuki-zoku*). Instead of dutifully studying at home, they loitered all day in front of shops, chatted up members of the opposite sex, and squandered their fathers' hard-earned money at Ginza's menswear shops. Their pitiful parents likely had no idea about their tribal identities: the teens would sneak out of their houses dressed in proper school uniforms and then slip inside café bathrooms to change into the forbidden ensembles. The press began to call Miyuki-dōri, a street name that honored the Emperor's departure from his palace, *Oyafukō-dōri*—"street of unfilial children."

The media condemned the Miyuki Tribe not just for their apparent juvenile delinquency, but for sticking a dagger right into the heart of the national Olympic project. The 1964 Summer Games would be Japan's first moment in the global spotlight since their defeat in World War II, and would symbolize the country's full return to the international community. Japan wanted foreign visitors to get firsthand views of the country's miraculous progress in reconstruction—not disobedient teens clogging up the streets. Japanese authorities feared that American businessmen and European diplomats sauntering over to tea at the Imperial Hotel would run into an ugly spectacle of wicked teenagers in frivolous shirts with button-down collars.

Local shop owners, on the other hand, had a more direct complaint: each weekend, two thousand teens obscured window displays and gummed up the gears of commerce. During the authoritarian days of prewar Japan, the police could have simply arrested the derelict teenagers in Ginza for the most trivial of reasons. But in the new democratic Japan, the police's hands were tied. There was no legal justification to round up Miyuki Tribe members. They were just standing around and talking. However,

Police sweep Miyuki Tribe members off the street in September 1964. (©The Mainichi Newspapers)

the police, like the shopkeepers, feared that, without intervention Ginza would soon degenerate into a "hotbed of evil."

So, on the night of Saturday, September 12, 1964, with the Olympics' Opening Ceremony less than a month away, ten plain-clothes detectives ran a coordinated sweep of the Ginza streets. They stopped anyone in a button-down shirt and John F. Kennedy haircut. Two hundred teens were apprehended, with eighty-five raced back to Tsukiji jail in buses to endure a night of processing, lectures, and a visit from their distraught parents.

The next day, detectives revealed to the newspapers the Miyuki Tribe's many nefarious tricks, such as hiding cigarettes inside the pages of thick English books. Not all tribe members were wrong-doers, they admitted, but the police felt the raids were necessary to "protect these youth from *becoming* delinquents." The arrests also confirmed a worry among police that the teens' unusual interest in fashion correlated with a crisis in masculinity. Detectives recoiled at the Miyuki Tribe boys speaking in "feminine" language.

Determined to stamp out these subversive youth, the police swarmed Ginza again the next Saturday night to pick up any stragglers. Their hard-line tactics succeeded: the Miyuki Tribe disappeared from Ginza for the rest of the year, and the 1964 Tokyo Olympics went off without a hitch. Not a single foreigner returned home with lurid tales of misbehaving Japanese teenagers in shrunken cotton trousers.

ADULTS MAY HAVE DEFEATED THE MIYUKI TRIBE, BUT JAPA-nese youth would triumph in the greater war. Around the globe, from the 1960s onward, rebellious teenagers spurned parents and authorities and forged their own unique cultures, breaking free from their narrow identities as students. In Japan, the first and most important step was to replace the standard-issue school uniform with their own choice of stylish clothing. This interest in fashion started among youth from elite families, but spread to the masses in tandem with the country's miraculous economic growth and explosion of mass media. Since the Ivy takeover of Ginza, Japan has been on a fifty-year trajectory towards its current status as the world's most style-obsessed nation.

Japanese teenagers spend an inordinate amount of time, effort, money, and energy in pursuit of fashionable clothing, especially when compared to their global peers. America, with a population 2.5 times larger than Japan, has fewer than ten magazines focusing on men's style. Japan has more than fifty. Novelist William Gibson once wrote that Japanese youth shopping chain PARCO made "Fred Segal on Melrose look like an outlet store in Montana." The sale of clothing to people under the age of thirty is the primary economic activity of multiple Tokyo neighborhoods such as Harajuku, Shibuya, Aoyama, and Daikanyama. And that is just the capital: one can easily buy the top Japanese and foreign fashion brands in small shops all the way from frozen Hokkaidō to subtropical Okinawa.

For many years, the Japanese were the world's most passionate consumers of global fashion, but over the last thirty years the trade balance has shifted. Japan's designers and brands have enjoyed significant attention from overseas audiences, and now export their clothing around the world. European fashion insiders first fell in love with exotic Japanese designer apparel—the boisterous Oriental patterns of Kansai Yamamoto and Kenzō Takada, and later, the avant-garde creations of Comme des Garçons, Yohji Yamamoto, and Issey Miyake. From the 1990s on, the creative classes in America and Europe also celebrated Japanese versions of basic items like T-shirts, jeans, and oxford cloth button-downs. By the first decade of the twenty-first century, hip-hop lyrics referenced Japanese streetwear brands A Bathing Ape and Evisu as conspicuous accoutrements of a lavish lifestyle. Meanwhile, savvy shoppers in New York's Soho or London's West End came to prefer Japanese chain UNIQLO over The Gap.

Then, something even more extraordinary happened: the fashion cognoscenti started to proclaim that Japanese brands made better American-style clothing than Americans. And American youth began to crib notes on traditional American style from unauthorized scans of Japanese magazines posted on the Internet. In 2010, people around the world snapped up reprints of the rare 1965 Japanese photo collection *Take Ivy*, a documentary of student style on the Ivy League campuses. The surprising craze for the book helped popularize the idea that the Japanese—like the Arabs protecting Aristotelian physics in the Dark Ages—had safeguarded America's sartorial history while the United States spent decades making Dress Down Friday an all-week affair. Japanese consumers and brands *saved* American fashion in both meanings of the word—archiving the styles as canonical knowledge and protecting them from extinction.

Japan's excellence in fashion—especially American fashion—is now widely acknowledged the world over. But the question remains, how and why did American style come to hold this venerated place in Japanese culture?

This book provides a detailed answer, showing the exact process by which classic American clothing first entered Japan, and explores how the Japanese adaptation of that same style now influences the rest of the world. Ivy League student outfits, jeans, hippie gear, West Coast sportswear, Fifties retro, New York streetwear, and vintage workwear arrived in Japan over the course of several decades, transformed the look of Japanese society, and boomeranged back to influence global style.

This is not a book, however, about the intricacies of clothing patterns or design concepts. Our story follows the individuals responsible for introducing American clothing to Japan, as well as the youth who absorbed these American ideas into the Japanese identity. More often than not, the instigators of change were not trained designers, but entrepreneurs, importers, magazine editors, illustrators, stylists, and musicians. These pioneers faced steep challenges in sourcing products, obtaining technical know-how, and convincing skeptical retailers—and they always had to keep one step ahead of organized opposition from parents, police, and entrenched elements of the apparel industry. But thanks to clever solutions and some lucky breaks, they got their products into teenagers' hands and made tremendous profits.

While American fashion affected the clothing styles of both sexes in Japan, the United States' influence on menswear has been both greater and more constant. Since the shedding of the kimono in the postwar period, Japanese womenswear has moved to the metronome of European designer collections. Japanese men, on the other hand, only came to accept fashion as an acceptable pursuit through a growing interest in elite campus wardrobes, rugged outdoorsmanship, (sub)cultural identity, and imitations of Hollywood stars—all of which led them to America's more casual, lifestyle-grounded styles. While London's Savile Row gave Japan its basic model for prewar male dress, after 1945 the raiment of the New World offered a much more compelling vision.

With the United States taking responsibility for rebuilding Japanese society after World War II, it may seem obvious that Japanese fashion "Americanized." And Americans have long believed their own pop culture to be the center of the world: Eastern Europeans, as we all have heard, wanted rock 'n' roll and blue jeans so badly that they tore down the Iron Curtain. The intense Japanese embrace of button-down shirts, denim, and leather jackets only further proves that the world is besieged by "Coca-colonization."

But the actual history of American fashion in Japan complicates that narrative. "Americanization" in Japan has not always been a direct idolization of the United States. After the occupation of Japan ended, very few youth ever encountered actual Americans, and Japanese television, magazines, and retailers crafted idealized versions of American life purely for marketing purposes. For the most part, Japanese youth adopted American fashion in imitation of *other Japanese*. Tokyo's army of ducktail greasers in the 1970s, for example, looked more to singer Eikichi Yazawa than to Elvis Presley. America may have provided the raw forms for Japan's fashion explosion, but these items soon became decoupled from their origin. As we will see, recontextualization was essential for the true absorption of American culture into Japan.

The story of Japan's embrace, reappropriation, and exportation of American style thus stands as a highly illustrative episode of how culture globalizes. Japan's geographical and linguistic isolation in the first postwar decades limited the free flow of information from the West. This makes it unusually easy to track exactly when and how American customs entered the country, and what it took for those customs to become a part of the social fabric. Globalization is a chaotic, complex process, and as time marches forward, the cultural threads only become more entangled. The story of Japanese fashion provides the perfect test case for tracing how the initial threads tied into loops and then into knots.

More importantly, the Japanese built new and profound layers of meaning on top of American style—and in the process, protected and strengthened the original for the benefit of all. As we will see, Japanese fashion is no longer a simple copy of American clothing, but a nuanced, culturally-rich tradition of its own.

Japanese looks imported from the United States now inhabit their own genre, which I call, *Ametora*, the Japanese slang abbreviation of "American traditional." Our search for the roots of Ametora is not just a journey into the historical record—but a chance to understand why Japanese fashion moves the way it does, and how the quirks of intensely local experiences can shape culture for the rest of the world.

ONE

A Nation Without Style

The widespread adoption of American style in Japan took several decades, but the very beginning can be traced back to a single individual—Kensuke Ishizu. Ishizu was born on October 20, 1911, the second son of a prosperous paper wholesaler in the southwestern city of Okayama. 1911 happened to be the very last year of the Meiji Era, a period that marked Japan's transition from a feudal society to a modern nation-state.

For the 265 years before the start of the Meiji Era, in 1868, the Tokugawa military government enforced a *sakoku* or "closed country" policy to isolate Japan from the rest of the world. Japan's seclusion came to an end in 1854 when United States Naval Commodore Matthew Perry and his fleet of black warships demanded the country open its borders to trade. Four years later, the shogunate signed a series of "unequal treaties" with the Western powers, a humiliating capitulation that threw the country into economic and cultural chaos. Determined to get the nation back on track, reform-minded samurai took control of the government in 1868 under the banner of Emperor Meiji.

During this so-called Meiji Restoration, the country's leaders worked to adopt Western technology and lifestyles, believing that a more modern Japan could fight off additional American and European attempts at colonization. Over the next forty years, the Meiji government modified and updated every part of Japanese life—the economy, laws, military, business practices, education system, and dietary habits. Bolstered by these efforts, Japan did not just ward off imperial invaders, but, in a few decades, became an imperial power of its own.

These radical social transformations mapped directly to changes in the male wardrobe. Before the Meiji Era, members of Japan's high-ranking samurai caste wore their long hair in topknots, strolled dirt roads in robes, and demonstrated their status with two swords tucked into their belts. By the first decade of the twentieth century, the country's rulers attended bureaucratic meetings, banquets, and gala balls in three-piece suits and Napoleonic military uniforms. Imported clothing styles became a steady source of prestige.

Even before Western fashion supplanted traditional costumes, Japanese society had long used clothing as an important marker of status and position. To maintain social order, the Tokugawa military government (1603–1868) micromanaged the nation's vestments, strictly regulating materials and patterns to certain castes. For example, only the nobles and samurai—a mere 10 percent of the population—were permitted to wear silk. But not everyone followed these rules. When farmers and urban merchants began to accumulate more wealth than their samurai betters, they lined standard cotton robes with silk in an act of subversive panache.

After 1868, the Meiji government instituted a set of policies to move men into practical Western dress as part of the modernization agenda. In 1870, the Emperor cut his hair into a short Western hairstyle and donned a European-inspired military uniform. A year later, the Haircut Edict instructed all former samurai to lop off their top knots. The military meanwhile adopted Western uniforms, with the Navy imitating the British and the Army imitating the French. During the following decade, government officials such as bureaucrats, policemen, mailmen, and train conductors

Emperor Meiji in traditional costume (left) and modern military uniform (right).

would follow the military's lead in Western dress. In 1885, Tokyo's Imperial University put its pupils in black *gakuran* (or *tsume-eri*) closed square-collar jackets and matching pants—a look that has since become the classic uniform for male students.

It was not long before Western culture began to trickle down from state institutions and into the lives of Japan's upper crust. The enduring symbol of the early Meiji Era was the Rokumeikan—a French Renaissance-styled hall where Japanese elites dressed up in formal ensembles, danced the waltz, and mingled with wealthy foreigners. From the 1890s forward, urban white-collar workers wore British-style suits to work.

Kensuke Ishizu's childhood coincided with the Taishō Era, a period when the growing middle classes joined elites in adopting Western customs. Everyone consumed more meat and milk, and the most radical political factions demanded greater democratic representation. Ishizu was a product of his times, playing imported sports like baseball and preferring hamburger steaks to fish. He also exhibited a precocious interest in Western clothing. He

Kensuke Ishizu as a middle school student (left) and university student (right). (Courtesy of the Ishizu family)

wanted to wear the black gakuran jacket with gold buttons so badly that he asked his parents to transfer him to a different school far from his home. Later, in middle school, Ishizu schemed with his tailor to add flair to his uniform without breaking the dress code—square flaps on the back pockets and wider hems.

At this point in the 1920s, Japan was undergoing rapid changes in social mores. The notorious *mobo* and *moga*—"modern boys" and "modern girls"—stood at the vanguard. After the devastating 1923 Great Kantō earthquake, many Japanese women adopted practical Western dress for better disaster preparedness. Moga, by contrast, played with Western culture as style—wearing silky dresses with short bobs. Their mobo beaus slicked back long hair and wore flared wide-leg "trumpet pants." Every weekend, mobo and moga flocked to Tokyo's lavish Ginza neighborhood and strolled its well-lit brick streets. These youth liberated Western culture in Japan from the Rokumeikan model, swiping style leadership from the upper classes and taking it in unauthorized directions.

In 1929, Ishizu moved to Tokyo to attend Meiji University after promising his father he would come back to take over the family business. With an ample stipend, he transformed himself into a "man of action." He remembered later in life, "My life as a

Kensuke Ishizu (far right, top row) on his wedding day, March 1932. (Courtesy of the Ishizu family)

student was amazing. I was never once bored." He coached boxers as a cornerman, founded the school's first motorcycle club, and ran an unlicensed taxi service with a friend. In just a few short months, Ishizu had become the living embodiment of the mobo.

As part of this mobo ethos, Ishizu rejected the utilitarian gakuran school uniform and instead ordered a three-piece suit in brown-green tweed—at the cost of half a professor's monthly salary. He matched it with white-and-brown saddle shoes. Ishizu lived in this dashing outfit at all moments, even in the stifling Tokyo summers.

But the mobo/moga moment would be short-lived: worried about the rise in leftist radicals, the government reversed course on liberalization in the early 1930s. Tokyo's Metropolitan Police Department launched a campaign to clean up juvenile delinquency, pledging to close every dance hall in the city. Law enforcement swept the streets of Ginza for overly-fashionable youth. The police arrested anyone doing anything suspiciously modern—going to cinemas, drinking coffee, or even eating grilled sweet potatoes on the street.

After narrowly escaping trouble with Japan's notorious thought police, Ishizu returned to Okayama in March 1932 to marry his young bride, Masako. While most of the family dressed in traditional Japanese robes, Ishizu could not resist the opportunity for sartorial flair—he was wed in a high-collar morning coat and a custom-ordered ascot. For their honeymoon, the couple headed back to Tokyo and spent a week at the dance halls and movie theaters, enjoying the last gasp of the mobo-moga life. At the tender ages of twenty-one and twenty, Ishizu and his wife settled down in their hometown to run the decades-old paper company.

CONFINED TO OKAYAMA, ISHIZU DID ANYTHING HE COULD to escape the "boring as shit" world of paper wholesale. He patronized geisha houses at night and took glider lessons on the weekends. He assembled an extensive wardrobe of tailored suits and daydreamed about making clothes for a living.

This decadent life might have continued unabated if not for Japan's lurch towards dictatorship in the 1930s. After the invasion of Manchuria in 1931 and a right-wing pushback against political parties, a military-led government stamped out all varieties of dissent and heterodoxy. Fanatic "patriot" groups assassinated democratic politicians and attempted coup d'états. The war in China soon hit home for Ishizu: the government increased its regulations on industry to manage war supplies, forcing his wholesaling company to cap its business activity.

Luckily, things looked sunnier in Japan's colonies. By the early 1930s, the Japanese Empire controlled Taiwan, Korea, Manchuria, as well as swaths of Eastern China. In mid-1939, Ishizu's hometown friend, Teruo Ōkawa, received a letter from his older brother in the Chinese port city of Tianjin asking them to come and help run the family's successful department store, Ōkawa Yōkō. With

Kensuke Ishizu in Tianjin, China with Russian friends (left) and in front of Public Security Department (right). (Courtesy of the Ishizu family)

no work at home, Ishizu's father encouraged him to go off and try something new. Ishizu was thrilled to leave: "The young men of that era grew up with freedom. I especially needed new forms of stimulation on a daily basis and longed more and more to be over in the freewheeling Tianjin." There was also a more urgent motive to leave town: Kensuke heard whispers that his favorite geisha was pregnant. The rumors ended up being false, but Ishizu chose not to stick around to find out. In August 1939, Ishizu and his family boarded a boat and moved to Tianjin.

Tianjin, located on the East China Sea, was famous for its international flavor, with self-governed British, French, and Italian concessions incorporating their own unique architectural styles into the fabric of the city. Beyond the Chinese population and fifty thousand resident Japanese, the city hosted a diverse group of Europeans—from British country-club elites in tails to disheveled White Russian émigrés.

At the age of twenty-eight, Ishizu began a new life in China as Sales Director of the department store Ōkawa Yōkō. Ishizu was a natural salesman and delighted in dreaming up new promotions for the store. He soon took over clothing manufacture and design. When World War II got in the way of distribution routes from the home islands in 1941, Ishizu brought his tailor from Okayama and started making suits in China.

Outside of work, Ishizu did not stick with other Japanese but integrated himself into the wider international community. He picked up basic English and Russian and learned Chinese from a local geisha. He frequented British tailors to learn trade secrets, heard war news at the local Jewish club, and bet on Jai Alai in the Italian concession.

Living in Tianjin allowed Ishizu to avoid the hard times back home. After the attack on Pearl Harbor in December 1941, war in the Pacific went from a regional conflict to a full-scale military engagement with the United States. Japan mobilized for total war. While Ishizu enjoyed the European culture and comforts of Tianjin, his country systematically rolled back all Western influences from local culture. The Japanese public heard daily propaganda about the savage crimes of the "devilish Anglo-Americans." New regulations demanded that companies remove English words from brand names and even advised against writing words horizontally. Baseball avoided persecution only by replacing its foreign-derived terminology with native Japanese terms for strikes and home runs. While Ishizu wore his high-end three-piece suits, Japanese men back in Okayama lived in practical, khaki-colored uniforms called "citizen clothing" (*kokuminfuku*)—an early parallel to the Mao suit.

The war brought numerous hardships to Japan: at first, food shortages, and then, from April 1942, American bombing campaigns. Thanks to a part-time job as an instructor for military gliders, Ishizu avoided the front lines. Japan's Imperial Army ravaged the interior of China, but Tianjin saw little conflict.

By 1943, Japan's prospects for victory looked bleak, and the Ōkawa Yōkō team worried that their trade in luxury goods would appear unpatriotic. The elder Ōkawa brother decided to sell off the company and split the money between the employees. With his share of the proceeds likely to be confiscated on his return to Japan, Ishizu chose to remain in China.

Ishizu shaved his head and enlisted. Taking a cushy position as a naval attaché, he ordered himself a debonair version of the standard uniform in high-quality British serge wool. Ishizu was assigned to look over a glycerin factory but retooled the machinery to make clear soaps scented with Parisian spices. He later felt remorse about this dereliction of duties: "I was ashamed that I never did any work of use to my country. We probably lost the war because of Japanese like me."

It was in this makeshift soap factory in August 1945 that Ishizu heard the Emperor's radio broadcast announcing the Japanese surrender to Allied Forces. The Nationalist Chinese prevented any mass violence against the former occupiers, but they treated Ishizu with contempt and ransacked his factory for barrels of glycerin. Ishizu spent most of September 1945 locked in a former Japanese naval library.

Things improved in October with the arrival of the U.S. 1st Marine Division. The Marines came ashore to an impromptu victory parade, as thousands of Chinese and European expatriates stormed the streets to greet their liberators. Looking for Japanese men who could speak English, a young American, Lieutenant O'Brien, broke Ishizu out of the library. In subsequent weeks, Ishizu and O'Brien became good friends. The American regaled Ishizu with stories of his undergraduate life at Princeton—the first time Ishizu heard about something called the "Ivy League."

Through luck and cunning, the thirty-four-year-old Ishizu had managed to avoid the worst of his country's repressive fascist society and wartime violence. And even after Japan's humiliating defeat, he parlayed his cooperation with the American forces into relative material comfort. Ishizu did not taste the war's bitterness until March 15, 1946, when the Americans put him and his family on a cargo ship back to Japan. He left behind everything that could not fit in a backpack, including the modern equivalent of $27 million in cash. The Ishizus spent a week with hundreds of others on a rickety boat with shallow cots for beds and two primitive toilets. Sadly, the harsh life on the sea was not just a temporary hardship for Kensuke Ishizu and his family—this would be the new normal for the people of Japan. Ishizu's days of easy luxury were over.

At the end of March 1946, Kensuke Ishizu returned to his hometown of Okayama to find it completely burnt to the ground. American bombing campaigns leveled almost every major industrial area in Japan, leaving endless landscapes of rubble punctuated by the occasional husk of a concrete building. Ishizu's seven-year sojourn to China had protected him from this apocalyptic nightmare, but, in 1946, he could find no more respite from the war's great terror.

Postwar life was bleak. Between the aerial attacks on the mainland and overseas fighting, Japan lost around three million people—4 percent of its population. American bombs destroyed much of Japan's working infrastructure, and, in 1946, the country suffered from chronic shortages of food and other supplies. National wealth plummeted back to 1935 levels. People spent the first postwar years trying to avoid starvation, typhus, and hypothermia. Japan was also bruised on a spiritual level. The failed promise of the Japanese empire disillusioned most citizens towards traditional institutions.

Meanwhile, an American army towered over the defeated population—the first foreign occupation in Japan's long history. Indoctrinated by wartime propaganda, the Japanese populace braced for a ruthless campaign of vengeful pillaging. Before the Americans' arrival, Nobel prize-winning author Kenzaburō Ōe assumed that Americans would "rape and kill and burn everybody with flamethrowers." The Occupation troops, while nowhere near perfect, did not live up to the fears. They built up a pleasant rapport with the local population, most famously by handing out chewing gum and chocolate to children.

Nevertheless, the obvious power imbalance between Americans and Japanese generated feelings of bitterness. Healthy, well-fed, and gigantic American troops patrolled the streets, while starving, unkempt Japanese men scrounged the black markets for food. The Occupation forces made many of Japan's most famous hotels, luxury estates, and department stores off-limits to locals.

In the first year after the war, Kensuke Ishizu sold off the family business, and after taking time to rethink his life, joined the Ōkawa brothers in a new venture working for Renown, Japan's largest undergarment maker. Based on his experiences selling clothes in Tianjin, Ishizu became the menswear designer for Renown's high-end clothing showroom in Ōsaka.

The late 1940s was an odd time to manufacture expensive menswear. The vast majority of Japanese were getting rid of clothing rather than purchasing it. Food shortages in the big cities forced the urban population to travel to the countryside and trade their garments for vegetables—a shedding of layers likened to "living like a bamboo shoot." In the late 1940s, Japanese spent forty times more on food than they did on clothing. Women continued to wear the baggy, high-waisted *monpe* farming pants they wore during wartime. Men lived in their tattered army uniforms with the medals plucked off. Pilots who had been in line to perform kamikaze missions when the war ended wandered around in brown flight suits.

Even though there were no more authoritarian mandates on dress, the postwar government still campaigned for frugality and moderation. Between the U.S. stopping all commercial imports of textiles and garments to Japan and a rationing system set up in 1947, few could buy or even make new clothing. The only fresh source of shirts and pants came from boxes of used garments collected in American charity drives, most of which ended up in the black markets.

In this fashion vacuum of garment shortages and rationing, the first group in Japan to adopt Western style were the Pan Pan Girls—streetwalking prostitutes who catered to American soldiers.

As writer Kōsuke Mabuchi described, "The Pan Pan Girls were the de facto fashion leaders of the immediate postwar." Pan Pan Girls wore brightly colored American dresses and platform heels, with a signature kerchief tied around their necks. They permed their hair, caked on heavy makeup, and wore red lipstick and red nail polish. Pan Pan Girls' jackets had enormous shoulder pads in imitation of officers' wives. Prewar, Western fashion and customs had entered society through the male elite and trickled down. In a topsy-turvy social reversal, the first to wear American-style clothing in postwar Japan were women—and prostitutes at that.

As the Occupation progressed, Japanese outside the demi-monde took an interest in American culture as well. A thirty-three-page Japanese-English Conversation Manual came out within a month of the war's end and sold four million copies. 5.7 million households listened to the popular English-language radio program "Come Come English." Japanese youth tuned into Armed Forces Radio Service to hear jazz and American pop, and local language covers of standards like "Smoke Gets in Your Eyes" became hit songs. Newspapers syndicated the comic "Blondie," giving Japanese readers a window into the material comforts of American middle-class suburban life.

Even the most Occupation-weary Japanese came to admire America's sheer affluence. As historian John Dower writes, "In the years of acute hunger and scarcity, the material comfort of the Americans was simply staggering to behold." Douglas MacArthur's General Headquarters (GHQ) took over the upscale Ginza neighborhood as its base of operations, and with thousands of G.I.s and their wives out on the streets, the area became known as "Little America." The U.S. military PX ("post exchange") stocked imported goods and foodstuffs in quantities unimaginable to the starving Japanese public. Officers' wives exited the PX each day with arms wrapped around giant hams and overflowing bags of rice while famished Japanese looked on in awe.

This disparity gave a veneer of prestige to anything American, whether physical goods or cultural practices. Following the American way of life looked like a golden ticket out of despair. Prewar interest in Western culture was an aesthetic choice and status symbol—now it was also a means of self-preservation. Kensuke Ishizu had a clear business advantage in this new Japan where everyone hoped to imitate American lifestyles. Thanks to a lifelong obsession with Western culture and time spent living overseas, he understood the West and, more importantly, knew how to make and sell Western clothing.

In the course of working for Renown, Ishizu built up a network of the top sewing talent in Ōsaka. He stockpiled fabrics and zippers through a Harvard-educated soldier named Hamilton, who shopped for him at the PX. Ishizu turned out top-notch garments that got the attention of not just others in the garment industry, but also law enforcement. His product was so good that the police apprehended him for a short time on suspicion that he was illegally importing clothing from abroad.

At the end of 1949, Ishizu quit Renown to start up his own business, Ishizu Shōten ("Ishizu Store"). Although few in Japan could afford to buy new clothing, Ishizu was confident that the market would return. If someone was going to make great Western-style clothing in Japan, it was going to be him.

THE OCCUPATION DREW TO A CLOSE IN THE EARLY 1950S. Figurehead General Douglas MacArthur departed Japan in April 1951, with two hundred thousand cheering him as he made his way to the airport. The two former enemies signed the San Francisco Peace Treaty in September, which returned sovereign status to Japan in April of 1952. And, with that, American troops gradually disappeared from the landscape.

Even before the treaty, Japan's economic anxieties had begun to subside with the eruption of the Korean War in 1950. Proximity to the Korean Peninsula made Japan a key manufacturing base for the American military effort. Seventy-five percent of the country's exports went to supplying the Korean conflict. This flooded the country with cash, striking the initial match to Japan's long recovery. The Korean War boom also minted the postwar's first millionaires, rejuvenating the market for luxury goods.

These boom times encouraged the urban middle classes to throw away wartime garments and revamp their wardrobes. By the early 1950s, no one in Tokyo would be caught dead wearing old monpe farming pants, and most young women abandoned the kimono for Western dresses. Yet there were still serious challenges to clothing the nation. The government swept in to rebuild the textile industry as part of its economic recovery plan, but focused all production on exports. Mills churned out bolts of cotton fabric in huge numbers, but almost nothing remained in the country. Protectionist regulations meanwhile blocked imports of foreign clothing.

Facing this scarcity of materials, few companies attempted to mass manufacture garments for sale in the Japanese market. The shortage of textiles forced many women to make "reborn clothing" (kōseifuku), American-style items from old kimono fabric and discarded parachute nylon. The government's lifting of restrictions on imported textiles in 1949 tempered this practice in the commercial market, but even throughout the 1950s, women continued to rely on neighborhood tailors, sisters, friends, or themselves to stitch together their wardrobes from whatever scraps they could find.

As the economy improved, white-collar workers reappeared at their local tailors to order new suits. Kensuke Ishizu pursued an alternate business model—ready-to-wear clothing. Tailoring was expensive and time-consuming (one suit cost a month's salary), whereas Ishizu's off-the-rack clothing could get a larger volume of garments to an eager public. As other companies struggled to decode the secrets of American and European style, Ishizu already had a few hits up his sleeve. He pumped out saddle shoes as well as cotton flannel shirts and indigo work pants under a faux American brand called Kentucky.

Ishizu Shōten found its most profitable niche, however, in high-end sport coats for rich elites—targeting company owners

Kensuke Ishizu in Ōsaka during the early years of VAN Jacket, 1954. (Courtesy of the Ishizu family)

flush with cash from the Korean War boom. Ishizu, along with the apparel industry as a whole, enjoyed the ripple effects of a growing economy as the nouveau riche celebrated their business success with new wardrobes. Ōsaka department store Hankyū gave Ishizu Shōten its own corner, and from there, Ishizu found a loyal customer base in the wealthy families of the Ashiya suburb. As the business grew, Ishizu wanted a more memorable brand name, so he rechristened his company VAN Jacket, borrowing "VAN" from the title of a postwar comic magazine.

To grow further, Ishizu needed customers not just at the top of society but from Japan's ballooning "new middle class." One major barrier remained, though: it was taboo for men to show interest in fashion. When white-collar workers first donned Western suits in the early twentieth century, the garment was meant as a modern and sober uniform—not as a means of self-expression. Any tweaks or customization to the basic formula implied vanity. Fashion scholar Toby Slade writes, "The dominant concepts of masculinity instruct that men should not be too aware of what they wear or take too much time considering what they wear. The suit provides the answer to this modern dictate on the seriousness of masculinity; it is a uniform that can be worn every day and allows men to look good without having to consider their outfits too much and therefore becoming feminine."

Dress was simple for Japanese men. Students wore the square-collared gakuran to school. After graduation, they moved to suits, at which point they never again had to think about their clothing. If the suit's wool looked rough, a tailor would turn the fabric inside out and sew it back together. The basic male wardrobe went to extremes of conformity: a single charcoal-gray or navy-blue suit, dark tie, white shirt, and dark shoes. White shirts outsold colored ones more than 20-to-1. A striped shirt was enough to get a worker in trouble. When veteran advertising creative director Yōichi Matsumoto once wore a red vest to the office, his boss asked, "Are you going out somewhere or did you come to do your job?"

To sell designer jackets, Ishizu needed men to part with their drab, functional uniforms and celebrate the new era of Japanese prosperity through their wardrobes. Women were hitting the town in brightly-printed dresses shaped in the latest international style, but men did not want to follow their wives' leads. In fact, the blossoming of womenswear in the postwar era simply reinforced the idea that "fashion" was an exclusive plaything of the fairer sex.

And even if Japanese men warmed to self-expression through dress, Ishizu faced another hurdle: fashionable men believed that all good clothes were tailor-made. Men dismissed non-tailored garments as *tsurushi* or *tsurushinbo*—meaning "something hung up," with the sting of a racial slur. Menswear meant suits, and suits meant tailors.

To take his niche business in Western Japan nationwide, Ishizu would have to rewire the Japanese male brain to think differently about fashion. Ishizu was a powerful evangelist among his own customers, but he needed a way to mold more than one mind at a time.

IN THE EARLY 1950S, JAPANESE WOMEN COULD ENJOY A HAND-ful of fashion magazines, but they were utilitarian—pages packed full of black-and-white dressmaking patterns rather than dream catalogs of glossy photos. Men, in comparison, had only one fashion resource: the suit pattern guide *Danshi Senka*. To find sartorial inspiration, most young Japanese turned to films instead of print. In 1953, a film adaptation of a national broadcaster NHK's radio show *Kimi no Na wa* ("What Is Your Name?") sparked a fashion trend where girls wrapped shawls around their heads and neck like the film's protagonist, Machiko. The next year's debut of the classic Audrey Hepburn film *Roman Holiday* ushered the star's boyish, short hairstyle into vogue.

Yet, films mostly influenced womenswear, because Japanese society already accepted that women should follow global trends. Cinema did little to convince older men to dress up. Lacking any knowledge about fashion, men needed more than just visual inspiration. They needed detailed explanations on how to put together a basic wardrobe.

The editors of women's magazine *Fujin Gahō* came to the same conclusion in early 1954. Female readers reveling in the latest Parisian styles complained that their husbands accompanied them to parties and weddings in bland business suits. Editors believed that men needed a fashion magazine to teach them how to dress properly, at least for special occasions. But to make the magazine compelling, they wanted a charismatic figure to be the face of men's fashion. After asking around the industry, one name kept popping up—Kensuke Ishizu.

Ishizu joined the editorial team, and the quarterly publication *Otoko no Fukushoku* ("Men's Clothing") debuted in late 1954. The magazine offered fashion photography and articles, but the editorial tone was pure instruction—a textbook introduction to semi-formal wear, business wear, sportswear, and golf wear. Ishizu

婦人画報増刊 男の服飾讀本

FUJIN GAHO MEN'S FASHION
最もスマートな男の服飾の第一歩から
世界の流行をマスターする専門雑誌！

第一集

Debut issue of *Otoko no Fukushoku*, 1954. (Courtesy of Hearst Fujingahō)

and the other writers gave practical advice to fashion novices and introduced the latest styles from America, France, and England.

Ishizu did more than just help write articles; he turned *Otoko no Fukushoku* into a VAN media organ. Advertisements and clothing samples from VAN weaved in and out of the entire magazine. Ishizu would buy up the majority of each thirty-five-thousand-issue print run and sell them to VAN's retailers. He wrote so much for the first few years that he had to hide his work under playful pen names such as "*Esu Kaiya*" (Esquire) in fear that his authorship was too conspicuous.

Otoko no Fukushoku functioned as a benevolent form of menswear propaganda, molding men's minds on why and how to dress better. The magazine also worked as an industry circular for ready-to-wear retailers where they could learn about what to stock. Ishizu's sponsorship of the magazine worked miracles for his business: with VAN deeply embedded into the content, both consumers and retailers bought up more of the brand's clothes.

Once embedded within the Japanese media complex, Ishizu looked to expand his presence in the capital. In 1955, VAN opened a Tokyo office to house the company's planning division, with Ishizu's Okayama and Tianjin pal Teruo Ōkawa joining to run sales. In the new office, a select team charted fashion trends and put VAN's clothing in front of key retailers.

In 1956, the Japanese government's white paper on the economy opened with a joyous phrase—*mohaya sengo de wa nai*, "The postwar is over." In the eleven years after the war, the country had moved past the trauma of defeat and embarked upon a new trajectory towards prosperity. The Japanese were not yet wealthy, but they had moved beyond the prewar standard of living. Rubble no longer littered the landscape of major cities, and malnutrition was rare.

As the population found enough food, work, and shelter, they began to think more about what to wear. Apparel consumption per person in 1956 reached 12.3 lbs—the first time to exceed the 1937 high of 11.68 lbs. Clothing companies experienced growing revenues, and VAN was no exception. The company's strong sales allowed Ishizu to expand VAN's capital fivefold over its first four years, and the one-time thirty-person Ōsaka operation became a three-hundred-person company across two cities.

But even with the steady PR from *Otoko no Fukushoku*, Ishizu still slammed into the same wall—middle-aged men deplored off-the-rack clothing. Readers would find something they liked in *Otoko no Fukushoku,* and then ask their tailors to make copies. Ishizu resigned himself to the fact that his own generation would never like ready-to-wear clothing. But he still had a chance to influence an entirely new set of consumers: youth.

Otoko no Fukushoku always dedicated a few pages each issue to clothing for university students, but Ishizu convinced the editors to bolster its youth-oriented content. From the fifth issue forward, the magazine added a catchy English title to the cover—"Men's Club." VAN, however, did not make the right clothing for students. Ishizu family friend, Hajime "Paul" Hasegawa, remembers,

The "V-look" in *Men's Club*, 1956. (Courtesy of Hearst Fujingahō)

"VAN had a fashionable flair, but it was very niche. Most kids couldn't afford it. And, as a kid, you didn't really didn't want to stand out that much."

Ishizu wanted to make a new line of ready-to-wear clothing for younger men, but none of the contemporary trends in Japan looked right. At the time, *Otoko no Fukushoku* promoted an aggressive V-shaped silhouette—enormous shouldered jackets that tapered to a slim waist. Fashion illustrator Yasuhiko Kobayashi, an art school student at the time, remembers, "We would only see the vulgar 'bold look' in Hollywood films and on gang members." The magazine also pushed the trendy, summer-themed style of the Sun Tribe films—gaudy Hawaiian shirts and matching floral "cabana sets." Ishizu needed something newer, more subdued, and less associated with delinquency.

Looking for inspiration, Ishizu embarked on a month-long world tour in December 1959, culminating in his first visit to the United States. Growing up on European suits, Ishizu often grumbled, "There are no stylish Americans." But while in New York, Ishizu sought out a popular American fashion style often covered in *Otoko no Fukushoku*'s international reporting—"Ivy League." Ishizu knew the phrase from his American friend, Lieutenant O'Brien, back in Tianjin, and by the late 1950s, the look had moved beyond campuses and into the mainstream of American wardrobes. Yet Ishizu had qualms about the Ivy look. He told *Men's Club* in 1956, "I'm doubtful that Japanese men could wear Ivy League style well, and beyond problems with the shape, it's an era of following Europe anyway."

Despite these prejudices, Ishizu took the train down to Princeton to visit O'Brien's alma mater. The gothic architectural beauty of the campus revealed an unusual side of America to Ishizu—one not singularly obsessed with modernization. The students' fashion style was even more impressive than the buildings. Japan's elite campuses were packed with identical-looking boys in black wool uniforms, but Ivy League students dressed up for classes in a distinct, individual way. He snapped a few shots of Princeton undergraduates with his compact camera, which later illustrated his U.S. trip report for *Men's Club*. One attractive Ivy Leaguer in a blazer, undone dark necktie, white button-down shirt, gray flannel pants, and a coat slung over his shoulder became the issue's unwitting cover model. Ishizu wrote in the accompanying essay that, in Princeton, "there was nothing like that particular American flamboyance that we all have come to expect."

With this short trip to Princeton, Ishizu had identified the style he wanted Japanese youth to imitate: Ivy League fashion.

These elite, athletic students demonstrated how dapper a young man could look in ready-to-wear clothing. Compared to the bold look, the clothes looked neat and fit closely to the body. Ishizu especially liked that the style relied on natural materials such as cotton and wool, which could be worn for a long time and easily cleaned. Japanese students in the late 1950s had little pocket money, but Ivy clothing would be a good investment—durable, functional, and based on static, traditional styles.

And there was something chic about how Ivy students wore items until they disintegrated—holes in shoes, frayed collars on shirts, patches on jacket elbows. Many nouveau riche Japanese would gasp in horror at this frugality, but the old-money Ishizu saw an immediate link between Ivy League fashion and the rakish, rough look of *hei'i habō*, the early twentieth century phenomenon of elite students flaunting prestige through shabby uniforms. Ivy clothing signaled status through subtle underplay, something that Ishizu could feel in his old money blood.

Ishizu was now armed with the most ingenious idea of his entire career: using Ivy League-style clothing to develop Japan's first youth fashion market. In 1959, VAN took the first step by producing an "Ivy model" suit—a detailed copy of Brooks Brothers' classic Number One Sack Suit with a loose, dartless jacket.

Nearing the age of fifty, however, Ishizu no longer had a natural feel for youth culture nor understood what Japanese youth truly desired. For Ivy League clothing to be successful, he needed a few young employees to make the clothes they themselves wanted to wear. Ivy could be Ishizu's big break—he just needed the right people to help him seize the moment.

TWO

The Ivy Cult

ALL TOSHIYUKI KUROSU EVER WANTED WAS A SUIT. IN THE mid-1950s, the nineteen-year-old and his classmates at prestigious Keiō University shuffled onto campus each day wearing black wool gakuran uniforms, hot and cold, rain and shine. The daily repetition took its toll. Kurosu remembers, "You'd only send the gakuran to the cleaners in summer after you wore it through the whole winter. Then you'd wash it again before you wore it in fall. It was dirty, and everybody smelled sour."

Wearing a real suit would liberate Kurosu from this mundane existence. After classes, he holed up in bookstores and studied the pages of tailoring magazine *Danshi Senka*. Once he saved up enough pocket money to place an order, he asked his father to take him to the tailor. The older gentleman laughed in his face, "A college student with a suit? You must be joking."

The father's rejoinder echoed the conventional wisdom of Western clothing in Japan—white-collar businessmen wore suits, and students wore uniforms. Society expected young men to wear their gakuran up to the day they graduated, even to formal events and job interviews. The serge wool jacket, matching wool pants, and a white "cutter" button-up shirt was a

Toshiyuki Kurosu in gakuran school uniform (left) and first suit jacket (right). (Courtesy of Toshiyuki Kurosu)

four-season wardrobe. When it got hot, students could just remove the jacket.

Since youth wore their uniforms everywhere, there was no such thing as "youth fashion." Kurosu recalls, "If you went to a department store, there was the kids' section and the gentlemen's section—but absolutely nothing in-between. Stores didn't think they could sell anything made for youth, so they didn't even try."

The few young men who rejected their uniforms for stylish clothing were summarily marginalized as delinquents. Beyond Japanese society's fundamental prejudice against social deviation, parents in the postwar era felt a particular anxiety about their children wearing contemporary clothing. The strict morality of the Imperialist era collapsed after World War II in tandem with the wartime regime, and parents assumed their children would go astray in the ensuing moral vacuum. Moreover, the Occupation's promotion of democracy, freedom, and egalitarianism encouraged many youth to thumb their noses at traditional ethical codes. Adults of the era deployed the pejorative term *apure* (from the French term for "postwar," *après guerre*) to describe the teens who lost their principles in the peacetime chaos.

In the ensuing moral panic about the apure, parents monitored clothing as an early warning sign for disobedient tendencies. The black gakuran symbolized adherence to traditional Japanese values; American clothing like Hawaiian shirts or MacArthur-style aviator sunglasses implied contempt for societal norms. Adults believed that fashionable clothing foretold not just unfilial behavior, but potentially criminal minds.

The sensational "Oh, Mistake Incident" of 1950 solidified these mental associations between youth fashion and moral decay. Hiroyuki Yamagiwa, a nineteen-year-old chauffeur at Nihon University, broke into a coworker's car at knifepoint, slashed the driver, and drove off with ¥1.9 million of cash stuffed in salary envelopes. Yamagiwa then took his girlfriend on a three-day joyride. The police easily apprehended the young lovers, but the minor crime made headlines after Yamagiwa screamed out in pidgin English "Oh, mistake!" upon arrest. During police interrogation, Yamagiwa continued to drop random English words into his Japanese and also revealed a tattoo that puzzlingly said "George." With all the press coverage, "Oh, mistake" became a society-wide punchline—a pseudo-English catchphrase that perfectly symbolized postwar youth's overeager, and now, evidently indulgent embrace of American culture.

As the young lovers awaited trial, the news coverage focused heavily on their outfits. In just three days on the lam, Yamagiwa and his girlfriend spent ¥100,000—ten times a university graduate's starting monthly salary—on clothing in high-end Ginza boutiques. When they made their perp walk in front of media flashbulbs, Yamagiwa wore a gold corduroy jacket, red pocket square, dark brown gabardine pants, light brown button-up shirt with extremely long collar point, argyle socks, chocolate brown shoes, and a President Truman-style fedora. His girlfriend dressed in an elegant light brown wide-collar two-piece wool suit with yellow sweater and black heels. The couple looked like young celebrities attending a film premiere—not prison-bound juvenile offenders. For disapproving adults across Japan, the connection

The arrested couple in the "Oh mistake" incident. (©Asahi Shinbunsha)

between loose morals and American fashion could not have been any clearer.

Toshiyuki Kurosu's father surely remembered the "Oh Mistake" incident when his son asked to buy a suit. Like any good parent, he refused to enable his son's potential descent into depravity. Kurosu fortunately had an alternative way to get new duds—his jazz band. Like many of his generation, Kurosu first heard jazz on American Armed Forces radio, and as a teenager, learned to play drums. As Kurosu explains, the 1950s was an excellent time to be an amateur musician: "During the Korean War, there were all these Army camps around Tokyo, and they would always have bands playing at night. Even students or amateurs could get gigs." Kurosu and his friends used the money from their concerts to make matching uniforms in the prevailing "Hollywood" style—wide-shouldered one-button jackets worn with slim pants.

The Hollywood-style jacket satisfied Kurosu's fashion urges, but during his time on military bases, he discovered a unique suit style on African-American soldiers. "They would wear four-button suits, derby hats, and white gloves and carry really narrow umbrellas. I just thought they were incredibly cool." Back in Tokyo jazz cafés, he spied a similar style on the covers of imported records. Kurosu loved the buttoned-up look of the American soldiers and jazz musicians, but he did not know what to call it.

In the summer of 1954, Kurosu's interest in suits led him to the first issue of the Kensuke Ishizu-edited fashion magazine *Otoko no Fukushoku*. When he got to the "Dictionary of Men's Fashion Terms," he became excited by the very first entry—*aivii riigu moderu* ("Ivy League model"):

> Also called "Brooks Brothers model," this is one of America's leading styles. Sometimes called "university model" since so many of the devotees are college students or college graduates. Straight hanging. Shoulders are narrow and extremely natural, with either no pads or very little padding. Three or four buttons on the jacket; there are no two-button versions. Pants are slim and slightly tapered, commonly with no pleats. Cutting-edge, but the aim is intensely conservative—the very opposite of the equally popular "Hollywood model." These two models form the two extreme poles of current American fashion. In America, the Ivy League model is urban, often described as "the clothes worn on Madison Avenue."

This short text, without illustrations or photos, would alter the entire course of Kurosu's life. The high-button suit style he saw on military bases was none other than this "Ivy League model," a suit style *intended* for university students. Americans apparently wore these so-called Ivy suits to class—and this was considered "conservative"! Kurosu imagined a civilized world across the Pacific where proud fathers accompanied their Ivy League sons to the tailor to make suits. He decided that when he finally ordered his first suit, it was going to be an "Ivy League model."

PARENTAL FEARS ABOUT AMERICAN CULTURE WERE PERHAPS not so irrational: the jazz band got in the way of Kurosu's studies, and the university asked him to repeat freshman year. His father forced him to sell off the drum kit, but Kurosu refused to be a studious drone in the black gakuran. Looking for a new hobby, he signed up for artist Setsu Nagasawa's weekly fashion illustration seminar. At the Saturday night classes, he struck up a friendship with one of the other two men in the class, an older student-teacher named Kazuo Hozumi. A trained architect, Hozumi was legendary among Nagasawa's pupils for leaving his full-time job to become a freelance illustrator working on *Otoko no Fukushoku*.

Hozumi immediately liked Kurosu—the "modern boy from Keiō"—and they talked each week about jazz, cars, and men's fashion. *Otoko no Fukushoku* was their bible, and after the magazine ran an in-depth feature on American collegiate style in Fall 1956, both Kurosu and Hozumi became complete converts to "Ivy." Hozumi recalls the appeal, "When I first saw Ivy, I thought, this is it! It was a suit—but it looked nothing like what older Japanese men wore. No one in Japan had such slim suits with three buttons."

With few opportunities to see Ivy League clothing actually worn in Japan, other than on the occasional soldier in flashy "neo-Ivy" style, their only sources of information were the American magazines that Hozumi pilfered from the Fujingahōsha offices. In their pages, Kurosu and Hozumi continually uncovered new aspects of what made an item of clothing "Ivy." Jackets hung straight with no darts. Pants had a buckled strap on the back. They finally saw the full range of Ivy items when they located a four-page *GQ* article about Brooks Brothers.

After a year of dutiful study, Kurosu and Hozumi were eager to wear actual Ivy League clothing themselves. But with no avenues to buy imported American clothing, Kurosu and Hozumi's only option was to find local tailors willing to copy the styles. With assurances from Hozumi that the most quintessential Ivy League item was the "button-down" collar on a dress shirt, Kurosu took a few yards of black-and-white gingham check fabric to a local tailor and demanded, "Make me a button-down collar." The tailor, in response, made Kurosu a long-sleeve Hawaiian-style shirt, no front placket, with buttons at the end of the long collar points. This hybrid creation looked nothing like an Ivy League button-down, but Kurosu did not know any better and happily wore it around town.

Kurosu was now ready to make a suit. The tailor looked at the young man's sketch of an ideal Ivy League model jacket and sighed, "This is very peculiar." The results were again a failure. "At the time, Japanese tailors didn't know anything about Ivy style," explains Kurosu. "They couldn't do a natural shoulder, so you'd end up with these huge pads. I wanted a three-button Ivy suit, so they just put a third button on top of the normal two buttons. The silhouette wasn't Ivy or anything... it was just weird." While an American would have immediately seen the flaws, Kurosu, with no practical exposure to real Ivy clothing, thought himself the proud owner of an "Ivy" suit.

After Hozumi ordered himself a similar "Ivy" suit from the same shop, the two men founded the "Traditional Ivy Leaguers Club" with five other friends. The Traditional Ivy Leaguers held weekly seminars on Ivy style, looking up terms from American magazines in a yellowed prewar English clothing encyclopedia. They also invited an aging tailor to teach them about details associated with the American style, such as hooked vents (a key part of the stitching on the back of a blazer) and overlapped seams.

In their quest to recreate Ivy League style in Japan, Kurosu and Hozumi judged everything as either *honmono* —the "real thing"— or *nisemono*—"an imitation." Unfortunately, the more they learned, the more apparent it became that their early creations were pathetic nisemono. Kurosu recalls, "I proudly wore the black-and-white gingham shirt for about a year, but once I figured out what was wrong about it, I was so embarrassed that I threw it away." More broadly, their desire for "authentic" copies motivated Kurosu and Hozumi to master every detail of Ivy League style, and to drill down into more and more minor aspects of clothing design.

Perhaps they would never make a perfectly honmono item, but they strived for verisimilitude by replicating the minutiae of the original.

Kurosu and Hozumi liked Ivy in part because it was from the United States, which impoverished Japanese viewed as a beacon of civilization and prosperity. But Ivy League fashion was also a way to stand out in Japan without delving into casual delinquent styles: "Ivy was just the total opposite of Japanese fashion at the time. I couldn't even understand the look *as fashion*—it was too different. When I started wearing Ivy clothing, people would say, you look like a mayor of a small town in the countryside. But that's what made it fun. I didn't like it just because it was new, but because it was strange." And, with that, Japan had its very first "Ivy Leaguers."

IN 1959, KAZUO HOZUMI CONVINCED THE EDITORS OF *OTOKO no Fukushoku*—newly rebranded as *Men's Club*—to feature the Traditional Ivy Leaguers in a four-page story. All seven members appeared in dark Ivy suits for the group portrait, holding up a poster of a blond pinup girl to demonstrate their expertise in American culture. Hozumi secretly wrote the accompanying text, proclaiming the group to be "seven Ivy samurai."

Today, very little about the clothing in the photo would be identified as Ivy League style—certainly not Kurosu's porkpie hat, cuff links, silver-colored formal necktie, and pearl tiepin. Despite *Men's Club*'s position at the forefront of Ivy League fashion in Japan, nobody involved in the operation could accurately replicate the American East Coast collegiate look. Lacking firsthand experience with Ivy League students, the style in Japan was built on tiny scraps of information and *Men's Club* editors' educated guesses.

In March 1959, Kurosu finished up at Keiō University but faced a weak economy with few open positions. Unable to enter blue-chip firms, he tapped his fashion illustration skills to land a position at a kimono maker, and later, with a tailor in Ginza. His father was furious, "We didn't put you in Keiō so you could work at a clothing company!" The jobs were boring, but Kurosu had an

Traditional Ivy Leaguers in *Men's Club*, 1959 (Toshiyuki Kurosu on ladder in hat and glasses, Kazuo Hozumi in glasses at front). (©Akira Satō)

engaging side business writing articles about jazz and fashion for *Men's Club*.

At the magazine, Kurosu formed a friendship with a young editor named Shōsuke. One night over dinner, Shōsuke broke a troubling piece of news, "I have to quit *Men's Club* and go work for my father." Kurosu imagined his friend condemned to toil away at some mundane company out in the sticks, but Shōsuke quickly clarified, "My dad is Kensuke Ishizu from VAN." This was Shōsuke *Ishizu*, firstborn son of the man behind Japan's hippest clothing brand.

In 1961, Kensuke made Shōsuke the head of VAN's planning department and assigned him the important role of producing an Ivy League line for youth. Before this point, most of Kensuke's "Ivy" items relied on the fifty-year-old's imagination rather than

Toshiyuki Kurosu (left) and Shōsuke Ishizu (middle) in front of VAN's Nihonbashi office, 1961. (Courtesy of the Ishizu family)

popular styles from the East Coast campuses. Ishizu called shirts with a long vertical stripe "Ivy shirts," desert boots with a buckle on the back "Ivy boots," and pants with a buckle on the back "Ivy pants" with an "Ivy strap." Shōsuke's mission was to make more authentic Ivy League items, but he faced a dearth of accurate information and did not know where to start.

The obvious solution was to bring in Japan's foremost Ivy expert—Toshiyuki Kurosu. On May 2, 1961, Kensuke and Shōsuke Ishizu welcomed Kurosu to VAN's planning department. The two young employees then hunkered down to figure out how to mass manufacture Japan's first true copies of Ivy League clothing.

At the beginning, the two young employees struggled with even the core pieces—button-down collar shirts, no-pleat cotton twill pants, and crew-neck wool sweaters. With no connections to Ivy League colleges or university shops, Kurosu and Shōsuke had few concrete details on the latest campus fashions. They foraged

VAN Jacket logo.
(©VAN Jacket Inc.)

for hints in *GQ*, *Esquire*, *Men's Wear*, *Sports Illustrated*, the French magazine *Adam*, JC Penney and Sears Roebuck catalogs, and the ads in *The New Yorker*. These publications provided design ideas, but VAN's factories needed patterns and three-dimensional versions of the garments to make true copies. While traveling to the U.S. on business, Kensuke Ishizu bought up a few pieces at Brooks Brothers to use as guides, but these could not be extrapolated into an entire clothing line. Kurosu resorted to hitting the Ameyoko black markets where he could scrounge around in piles of discarded G.I. clothes for Ivy-like garments.

Shōsuke had his own challenges with Japanese factories: "No one could make the button-down collars. And no pattern cutter had ever made pants without pleats." He eventually tracked down an innovative factory in faraway Toyama that already made button-down shirts for export to the American market. Other items came down to trial and error—making and remaking shirts and pants until they finally resembled the American standard. Shōsuke found a strange joy in the process, "I was not into Ivy League clothing like Kurosu was. For me, the whole thing was like putting together a model airplane. It was like a challenge, let's see if we can go out and actually make this so-called 'Ivy fashion.'"

As the full Ivy line came together in 1962—chino pants, navy blazers, seersucker jackets, repp ties—VAN updated its logo to appeal to a younger audience. Kensuke Ishizu placed his original red-and-black stencil logo in a circle with the catchphrase "for the young and young at heart." With this final touch, VAN's brand image and merchandise were poised to fulfill Ishizu's vision of making ready-to-wear fashion popular for Japanese youth. Kurosu had spent the last decade in his bedroom and small tailoring shops trying to replicate Ivy style in Japan. Now at the wheel of Japan's hottest clothing brand, he and his colleagues at VAN were ready to unleash Ivy on a national scale.

"TAKE OFF ALL THESE GOLD BUTTONS, AND MAYBE WE'LL BE interested." Toshiyuki Kurosu heard this same complaint from department store buyers across Japan. These men, who snapped up VAN's high-quality jackets each season, balked at the new Ivy-inspired line. The buyers assumed all the Ivy details they had worked so hard to replicate were design errors: "This shirt pattern is fine, but these buttons on the collar get in the way." When Kurosu pointed out that American college students all wore navy blazers with gold buttons, they screamed back at him, "This is Japan—not America!"

The wider apparel industry refused to support the Ivy trend, but Kensuke Ishizu remained confident that Japanese youth would fall in love with the look if given a chance. Middlemen were simply getting in the way of their potential relationship with Ivy. Rather than waiting on curmudgeonly buyers to change their mind about button-down shirts, Ishizu decided that VAN would take the Ivy message directly to teens.

Men's Club was the obvious place to start, as younger, fashion-conscious men looked more to magazines than department stores for style guidance. From 1963 onward, VAN used its shadow editorial control to steer the magazine towards *Ivy über alles*. They filled each issue with minutiae of modern collegiate life. There were explorations of elbow patches, detailed looks into the "V-zone of an Ivy Leaguer," and essays from Kensuke Ishizu on critical matters such as "girls who understand Ivy and girls who don't." Desperate for visuals of Ivy style on real people, *Men's Club* reprinted any and all pictures of American college students they could get their hands on, from U.S. publications like *LIFE* to film stills of Ivy-inflected Hollywood stars such as Anthony Perkins and Paul Newman.

Despite these efforts, Ivy primarily existed in Japan inside the pages of *Men's Club*. Almost all youth still wore their gakuran uniforms or equally bland garments. Readers understood the magazine's imagery—a world where everyone lived surrounded by Ivy suits, Coca-Cola bottles, and jazz records—as a pleasant fantasy. Dressing like a *Men's Club* model in real life would certainly elicit ridicule from classmates and neighbors. VAN thus needed to prove to their readers that there actually were well-dressed youth roaming the cities of Japan.

In the spring of 1963, Kurosu started a column in *Men's Club* called "Ivy Leaguers on the Street" (*Machi no Aibii Riigaazu*), where he and a photographer took snaps of young passers-by in Ginza who dressed similar to East Coast preps. Kurosu picked the best images and wrote accompanying captions. Nicknamed *Machi-ai*, the photo page soon became readers' favorite part of the magazine. And with this, Kurosu may have invented "street snaps"—the distinct style of documentary fashion photography that now appears in nearly every single Japanese fashion magazine.

In truth, the column put the cart before the horse: Tokyo barely had adequate numbers of fashionable men to fill the pages of each issue. Kurosu recalls, "The first time I went with the cameraman to Ginza it was pretty terrible. It was only because the response from readers was really good that we went out and tried again." The strongest feedback came from outside of the capital, as the column allowed readers to keep tabs on the latest urban styles in real time. The work got easier once fashionable teens started to hang around the neighborhood's main avenues in contrived outfits with the hope of catching Kurosu's eye. Subsequent editions of the column showed a more pronounced Ivy League style, a trend which snowballed as teens tried to outdo the young men in the previous issue.

Illustration also became an important way for *Men's Club* to establish the Ivy worldview. Drawings from Kazuo Hozumi, as well as peers Ayumi Ōhashi and Yasuhiko Kobayashi, transported readers to a stylish American milieu. Perhaps the most famous illustration of the era is Hozumi's "Ivy Boy"—a gleeful cartoon youth dressed in various East Coast ensembles. Hozumi first drew the character in 1963 as a parody of Japanese woodblock prints, replacing the standard samurais with fourteen different Ivy Leaguers such as a Princeton cheerleader in all white, a football player geared up to hit the field, and a Harvard fan in a raccoon coat and long scarf. Kensuke Ishizu promptly turned Hozumi's work into a VAN poster. From then on, Ivy Boy appeared frequently in *Men's Club* as a means to illustrate the many facets of campus style. The character today stands as a universal symbol of "Ivy" in Japan, with nearly hieroglyphic resonance among the 1960s generation.

Since the content in *Men's Club* came directly from VAN employees and the brand's friends, the magazine quickly transformed into a cult of personality around Kensuke Ishizu, Toshiyuki Kurosu, Shōsuke Ishizu, and Kazuo Hozumi. This select team voiced their opinions on Ivy style in columns, interviews, round-table discussions, Q&A, advice columns, and transcripts from radio shows. *Men's Club* never hid the fact that these individuals worked for VAN, and outrageously, paid them for contributing texts. But the close relationship was mutually beneficial. VAN needed *Men's Club*'s authority to promote Ivy as the optimal style for Japanese youth. *Men's Club* needed VAN to provide cutting-edge content each month.

The Ivy push in *Men's Club* ended up reaching an important constituency beyond their young readers: small fashion retailers. As the ready-to-wear market grew in the late 1950s, gentleman's shops across the country came to rely on *Men's Club* as a weathervane for the latest trends. After seeing Ivy in *Men's Club*, these retailers flooded the VAN offices with orders. Ishizu was shrewd, however, picking just one store per city to be a franchisee. He updated their merchandising and store displays to better fit the Ivy aesthetic. VAN employee Yoshio Sadasue remembers the transformation of his own father's store in Hiroshima, "Ishizu personally re-designed the whole building. I was just floored—everything was rebuilt, the interior was incredibly nice, and everything was suddenly very fashionable." In this strategy, Ishizu built up a battalion of store owners whom fashion critic Shōzō Izuishi calls "Ivy believers in the VAN religion."

By early 1964, VAN enjoyed a national retail network and editorial control of the nation's top menswear magazine. The high price of VAN's clothing, however, limited the customer base to an elite few. Earlier in the decade, Prime Minister Hayato Ikeda had announced an "income-doubling plan," and, by 1964, Japan's GNP grew at a whopping 13.9 percent—an "Economic Miracle." But when compared to the United States, incomes were still low—just $1,150 in Japan versus $6,000 in the U.S. When incomes did increase, families first improved their households, buying the "three sacred treasures": black-and-white TVs, electric washing machines, and refrigerators. The new middle class then moved on to the "three Cs": cars, color TVs, and air conditioners (coolers).

Expensive clothing was an extravagance beyond the reach of most middle-class Japanese, especially for students. A single VAN button-down shirt cost one-tenth of the average monthly white-collar salary. And that was just the shirt: *Men's Club* demanded a full head-to-toe coordination of the Ivy look, including a navy blazer, khaki chinos, and leather loafers.

Due to these economic realities, VAN customers in the first half of the 1960s came exclusively from three groups: celebrities, creatives at top advertising firms, and the sons of very wealthy families. In the U.S., Ivy represented the casual style of elite university students, but the clothing itself was neither expensive nor exclusive. In fact, the Ivy style reached far beyond East Coast campuses because of its ease-of-fit, rugged materials, and reliance on basic styles.

Not so in Japan. By the beginning of 1964, VAN built the basic infrastructure to sell Ivy—the clothing, the media, and the retail network—but so far, they only found consumers at the very top of society. And even those customers caused headaches: rich youth had no idea how to properly style the VAN items they wore as status symbols. Kensuke Ishizu hated seeing these pampered teens wear his clothing in bad taste. Luckily, he was already working on a way to lay down the law in his Japanese Ivy Kingdom.

KENSUKE ISHIZU WAS ASKING THE IMPOSSIBLE OF JAPAN— the wholesale adoption of Ivy League style from scratch. No one had any experience with Ivy outside of *Men's Club*, and neither teens nor their big brothers and fathers owned any Ivy clothing. Youth fashion in the early Sixties was akin to young men rushing out to play a heretofore unknown sport like American football with only the vaguest understanding of a "touchdown" and no friends who owned a ball or helmets.

To make things easier on their pupils, Ishizu, Kurosu, and the others at VAN decided they needed to break Ivy down into a set of dos and don'ts. They summarized their mission thus:

> When you buy medicine, the instructions are always included. There is a proper way of taking the medicine, and if you do not take the medicine correctly, there may be adverse effects. Same goes for dressing up—there are rules you cannot ignore. Rules teach you style orthodoxy and help you follow the correct conventions for dress. Starting with Ivy is the fastest way to get you there.

In the pages of *Men's Club*, Kurosu became the unofficial head-master of the Ivy school. He ran an "Ivy Q&A" column in the back of the magazine, where he counseled teens on the minutiae of dressing up. He told readers, for example, not to wear ties with their sports shirts and to avoid tie tacks and cuff links with blazers. At the same time, he advocated for the mentality of Ivy: an easy

East Coast nonchalance. Kurosu warned a reader threatening to wear a button-down collar with the buttons undone, "It has to feel natural. It's the absolute worst if other people think you've left them intentionally unbuttoned."

There is a certain chutzpah in Kurosu, a twenty-something Japanese man who had never lived in the U.S., playing referee for what constituted proper Ivy League style. His confidence came from years of research—but also a good measure of bluffing. Kazuo Hozumi explains, "We started to just make up rules like, 'When you wear a button-down, you have to wear a plain knot, not a Windsor.' But then, everyone believed us."

VAN was so successful in using these definitive proclamations to get both readers and retailers on the same page that Japanese fashion today still retains this emphasis on rules. Kurosu remembers, "This is the era when people wanted us to take gold buttons *off* of blazers, so we had to tell them, it's a blazer *because* it has gold buttons. We had to frame it in rules, like 'Blazers shall always have gold buttons.' This sped up everyone's understanding of the style."

In the United States, Ivy League style was steeped in tradition, class privilege, and subtle social distinctions. No one read manuals on the style—they just imitated their fathers, brothers, and classmates. In Japan, VAN needed to break down Ivy into a distinct protocol so that a new convert could take up the style without having ever seen an actual American. The resulting pedantry, however, risked turning Ivy's youthful energy into sheer tedium. Back in the U.S., the best part of collegiate fashion was its unconscious cool. *Men's Club* often gave the same styles the fun of filing taxes.

Yet *Men's Club* readers ate it up, and their demand for instruction only resulted in an even greater tyranny of details. A true "Ivy shirt" had a small "locker loop" under the collar and a center box pleat. Ivy men wore a pocket square in the "Ivy fold," a necktie exactly 7 cm wide, and an "orthodox" pant length. A biblical dogma developed about the Ivy suit jacket's center hooked vent, even though its presence on the back of the jacket made it mostly

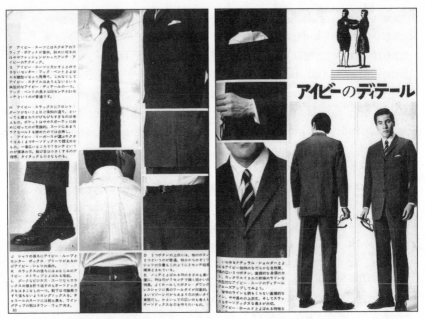

A look at "Ivy Details" in *Men's Club*. (Courtesy of Hearst Fujingahō)

invisible. *Men's Club*, meanwhile, warned against the danger of slanted jacket pockets—a nefarious "anti-Ivy technique." Beyond spreading knowledge about Ivy clothing, this homosocial one-upmanship brought fashion—previously belittled as a "feminine" pursuit—closer to technical "masculine" hobbies such as car repair and sports.

In 1963, Kensuke Ishizu laid down the master concept for Western dress in Japanese with just three letters: "TPO," an acronym for "time, place, occasion." Ishizu believed that men should choose outfits based on the time of the day and season, their destination, and the nature of the event. Ishizu was certainly not the first to think about fashion in terms of social context, but this simple phrase "TPO" (*tī pī ō*, in Japanese) set it as the central principle for how the Japanese adopted American style.

TPO made particularly good sense with Ivy, which represented a comprehensive fashion system rather than a single look. One could be Ivy in class, Ivy at church, Ivy playing football, Ivy watching football, Ivy as a wedding guest, and Ivy as the groom. TPO also resembled the rules on wearing kimono and other traditional Japanese garments, making Ivy not sound so alien after all.

Ishizu later formalized the TPO idea with a guidebook called *When, Where, What to Wear*. The pocket-sized volume offered lists of ideal outfits, coordination styles, and fabric types, as well as diagrams on how to get the perfect suit fit. Ishizu also wrote up short essays on proper looks for all occasions—long trips, short trips, European and Hawaiian vacations, U.S. business trips, PTA meetings, blind dates, ice skating excursions, and bowling nights. The book was an immediate best seller. Electronics maker Sony passed out copies to every male employee.

With these writings, Ishizu hoped to relay his conviction that Ivy fashion was not a fleeting industry trend but the path towards a noble way of life. Seeking to avoid the waxing and waning of so many previous fashion trends, he famously proclaimed, "I don't make trends—I want to create new customs."

By early 1964, the VAN crew and allies like Kazuo Hozumi had settled into their roles as the country's arbiters on "proper" Ivy. Over time, this campaign of style advocacy led not just to a more fashion-savvy public, but greater sales for Kensuke Ishizu's company. Perfect control over Ivy, however, would be fleeting: new customers meant new problems.

APRIL 28, 1964 MARKED A TURNING POINT FOR IVY IN JAPAN. A new magazine called *Heibon Punch* appeared on newsstands, offering a standard mix of politics, trends, sex, and cartoons. But compared to other cheap weekly magazines, *Punch* spoke to a much younger audience. The articles titillated college students and encouraged recently employed salarymen to keep up a lifestyle of leisure. And as part of this, *Punch* added a new topic to the content formula—fashion.

Ivy became the house style. They asked Kensuke Ishizu to write a column on menswear with illustrations from Kazuo Hozumi. For

The debut issue
of *Heibon Punch*,
May 1964, with
cover illustration
by Ayumi Ōhashi.
(©Magazine House)

the cover of the debut issue, young female *Men's Club* illustrator
Ayumi Ōhashi drew four boys in Ivy—blazers, short cotton pants,
loafers, sharply-parted Kennedy haircuts—chatting to a boy in a
red sports car.

Heibon Punch was an immediate success. The debut issue sold
six hundred twenty thousand copies, and within two years, circulation hit one million. The magazine benefited from demograph-
ics—the first wave of Japan's postwar baby boom entered college
right as it launched. Compared to the frugal youth coming of age
in the postwar, the baby boomers wanted to play in Japan's newly
emerging consumer society—and could afford to. *Heibon Punch*
became their guide. While hardcore clothing fans still preferred
Men's Club, *Heibon Punch* brought the Ivy fashion message to a
much broader audience—guys who liked to look at blazers, but

who also wanted to read about the newest Porsche, solicit advice on careers, and ogle topless girls.

Heibon Punch's momentum propelled the once small Ivy cult into the mainstream, introducing almost all Japanese men aged 15-30 to American collegiate style. More broadly, the magazine advanced the very idea of a fashion for young men. Writer Saburō Kawamoto recalled, in 1995, "With *Heibon Punch*, I first realized that it was okay to wear something other than my student uniform. The arrival of the magazine in 1964 heralded the very idea that men were allowed to dress up." And when they dressed up, Ivy was their look.

The excitement around *Punch* sent hundreds of young men directly to VAN's Ginza flagship Teijin Men's Shop to buy button-down shirts, blazers, cotton chino pants, and loafers. Soon these young men could be spotted everywhere, walking the neighborhood streets in their new fashions. During the quieter *Men's Club* era before 1964, Ivy fans were scattered and inconspicuous as a trend, and comprised almost exclusively of the rich. Now there were masses of upper-middle-class teens in Ginza wearing Ivy gear and pulling money from paper wallets made from *Heibon Punch* covers. In the humid Tokyo summer, their clothing matched the resort side of Ivy gear—white button-down shirts, bermuda shorts, and white chinos. Once these teenagers started to park themselves on Miyuki Street and stay all day, they became the notorious Miyuki Tribe (*miyuki-zoku*).

The term *zoku* means "tribe" in Japanese, but the postwar usage connoted "delinquent subculture." Before 1964, youth tribes picked clothing styles as an organic extension of their lifestyle. The Thunder Tribe (*kaminari-zoku*) bikers, for example, dressed in functional, durable leather that could withstand a daredevil motorcycle ride, while the Sun Tribe (*taiyō-zoku*) caused a ruckus on beaches in bright coastal clothing. The Miyuki Tribe, by contrast, learned to dress directly from the mass media—a youth brigade drafted straight from the models in *Heibon Punch*.

Parents did not approve of their sons wearing stylish clothing, so young men snuck out to Ginza in a student uniform with

VAN's iconic
shopping bag.
(©VAN Jacket Inc.)

their Ivy duds hidden in a rolled-up paper bag. They would change in café bathrooms and carry around the uniform all day. The paper shopping bag became a symbol of the Miyuki Tribe's weekend transformation—and also, a vehicle for VAN to promote its brand.

A few months prior to the emergence of the Miyuki Tribe, the company had started providing paper bags to retailers with a sleek modernist design featuring the logo in a red box at the bottom that stretched around the side. Former employee Hajime "Paul" Hasegawa explains, "We didn't have a big advertising budget, and we thought, how can we become ubiquitous? Coke was getting to be everywhere, and I thought we needed to come up with packaging of our own. When you are in a department store, everything gets wrapped in Seibu or Takashimaya paper, so we insisted that our products be wrapped in our own bags." These bags flooded the streets with VAN logos, and young shoppers came to fetishize the logo as much as the clothing it represented. Youth who could not afford to buy anything from an official retailer simply carried around an old rice bag with a VAN sticker on top.

While the Miyuki Tribe nominally dressed in VAN's version of Ivy, they made a few key adjustments to the formula. The Miyuki Tribe took the look to its casual extreme. The most striking change was high-water pants, with hems floating 10-15 centimeters above the shoe. Kurosu has long believed that teens wore their pants short in imitation of the top Teijin Men's Shop clerk who cuffed his pants high to show off his socks. Writer Kōsuke Mabuchi believed it instead to be a byproduct of teens' unfamiliarity with cotton trousers. When they saw their peers in slightly short cotton pants, they ran out to buy pants the same length—only to throw them in the wash and have them shrink. Then other teens saw those shorter pants and bought even shorter pants, and the cycle continued. Whatever the case, *Men's Club* editors wanted nothing to do with the short pants and urged "true" Ivy fans to maintain "orthodox" lengths.

Despite these minor rebellions in clothing, the Miyuki Tribe styled their hair much closer to actual Ivy League students than Kurosu and Hozumi ever did. The idea of a dapper youth haircut was as new to Japan as the concept of youth fashion. Before Ivy, mothers dragged their sons to the barber and chose between "short" and "long." The classic "Ivy look" was far more stylized—a straight part on the side of the head that split the hair into two blocks at a seven-three or eight-two ratio. Miyuki Tribe members brought copies of *Heibon Punch* to the barber for reference. At home, they used hair dryers to fluff the do and set it in place with a splash of Vitalis or MG5 hair liquid. Adults loathed the Miyuki Tribe's outfits, but they may have been most concerned about the "feminine" vanity of men caring for their coiffures.

As the summer of 1964 progressed and schools let out for vacation, high schoolers swelled the Miyuki Tribe's ranks, ballooning to two thousand members each weekend. With the Olympics approaching, the media demonized the Miyuki Tribe as a potential source of embarrassment for the nation. Paul

Hasegawa explains, "In this era, 80 percent of kids were in uni-forms all the time, so whoever wasn't in a uniform looked delin-quent, at least to the police." The Miyuki Tribe embodied a pivotal moment of the mid-1960s when parents misunderstood their sons' attempts at becoming wholesome media-savvy con-sumers as a form of deviancy.

VAN leadership viewed the Miyuki Tribe as a mixed blessing. On one hand, the teens proved that young people would adopt Ivy as their basic fashion, which led to an explosion in sales. On the other hand, the Miyuki-zoku brought Ivy down into the gutter, making it a target for the parental disapproval that accompanied all past youth subcultures. Even teens who liked Ivy style pleaded for distance from the Miyuki fad. A sixteen-year-old high school student in Ginza told reporters, "We hate being called members of the Miyuki Tribe—we're Ivy."

While newspaper editorials castigated the Miyuki Tribe as a social ill, the Ginza shop owners complained that these teens ob-scured window displays, blocked access to doors, and impeded trade. Once parents discovered the situation, they moved to ban anything resembling the "Ivy style" at schools. Administrators forced teens to pluck the buttons from the collars of VAN shirts. Parent-teacher associations sent formal requests to VAN retailers to stop selling clothes to students. And in many small towns, schools prohibited teens from carrying a VAN bag or even enter-ing shops that sold the brand.

Even those in the fashion industry saw something untoward in VAN's marketing to youth. Kurosu and Hozumi's former illus-tration teacher, Setsu Nagasawa, complained to *Heibon Punch*, "Right next to the salaryman who is worrying about whether to spend ¥2,000 on something, there's some kid who throws down ¥5,000. Adults are the ones who must be stylish. Kids can do with just one outfit."

The Tsukiji police raids against the Miyuki Tribe members in September 1964 eased the growing tensions around Ivy. But the media's handwringing about the problem made VAN seem even more attractive to teens. Young men defied PTA orders and lined up outside of menswear shops just to grab discarded cardboard boxes with the brand's logo. The word "Ivy" became synonymous with "cool." The home electronics company Sanyo worked with VAN to create a line of gadgets—the Sanyo Ivy Razor, the Sanyo Ivy Hair Dryer, and the Sanyo Ivy Junior Tape Recorder.

While the Miyuki Tribe spearheaded the embrace of American fashion among young men in Japan, the ensuing moral panic placed VAN on the radars of authorities and parents as an instigator of youth delinquency. Kensuke Ishizu was finally selling blazers and button-downs to teenagers but he alienated a lot of adults in the process. Kurosu and the other evangelists, meanwhile, worried that the Miyuki Tribe were debasing the Ivy style they had worked so hard to promote over a decade.

The former modern boy Kensuke Ishizu cared little about offending cranky conservatives, but he did worry that the clean-cut Ivy look would be forever misunderstood as a rebellious subculture. In 1964, his brand VAN manufactured Ivy, sold Ivy, promoted Ivy, and made youth lust after Ivy. Now he needed to legitimize American fashion—not just for youth, but for everyone.

THREE

Taking Ivy to the People

KENSUKE ISHIZU MAY HAVE ANTICIPATED BIRTH PANGS IN bringing American fashion to Japan, but he never imagined teenagers in Ivy League clothing arrested in mass raids on the streets of Ginza. Button-down shirts, which signified old money in the U.S., became linked with criminal behavior in Japan. Something got lost in the translation process, and VAN desperately needed to improve Ivy's image to win over a skeptical public.

The 1964 Summer Olympics would be Ishizu's first major opportunity to change opinions on a national scale. In August of that year, he moved the VAN offices to Aoyama, a quiet neighborhood in central Tokyo within walking distance of the athletic complex built for the Games. But Ishizu would not just be a spectator: as one of the few working menswear designers, he was invited by the Olympic Committee to plan the official Japanese uniform. The Japanese team would need to stand out as they made their dramatic appearance at the end of the Opening Ceremony. The world—and the Emperor—would be watching. The Japanese team had worn all-white suits at the 1960 Rome games, but Ishizu wanted something with more flash. He approached the problem through his TPO framework:

The VAN office in
Aoyama, 1964.

What would a national Olympic team wear in this particular
time, place, and occasion?

The answer, for Ishizu, was Ivy: bright red blazers with gold
buttons. The design ended up looking nearly identical to the red
jackets the Traditional Ivy Leaguers club made up for their final
party two years prior—jackets so flamboyant that Kurosu and Hozumi were embarrassed to wear them in public. Now Ishizu was
putting Japan's top athletes in the same dandy outfit on the most
important day of their lives.

The bright red color drew the most attention, but the blazer
itself was still a rare item in Japan. The most prestigious department stores refused to carry them. Ishizu was confident, however,
about his design choice: blazers were the classic jackets of sports
clubs in the West. On October 10, 1964, tens of millions of Japanese cheered at their TV sets as their national Olympic team entered the stadium—in white cotton pants/skirts, navy-and-red

The red suit jacket for the 1964 Japanese Olympic Team. (© Prince Chichibu Memorial Sports Museum)

striped ties, white hats and shoes, and three-button red jackets with gold buttons.

The uniforms drew immediate outrage from the old guard. Gruff journalists complained that the color was too feminine, while the head Olympic tailor was so enraged with the design that he ended up in the hospital. Watching footage of the 1964 Olympic Ceremony today, it is hard to understand what was so radical about the red-and-white ensemble. Almost all of the teams wore colored blazers based on their national flags, and the Nepal and Mexico teams wore very similar red jackets. Just as Ishizu believed, the blazer was completely appropriate for the occasion.

The wider Japanese public agreed, and the Olympic uniforms bestowed upon the blazer what the Japanese call *shiminken*—"citizenship." Toshiyuki Kurosu explains, "Right after the Opening Ceremony ended, the buyers at department stores suddenly changed their minds. They called up saying, 'That blazer you were trying to sell us was great, please send some over quickly.'" Ishizu's risky and very public ploy to legitimize the Ivy League blazer had worked.

The 1964 Olympics also provided VAN employees with an unprecedented chance to view the latest foreign fashions in real time. Years prior, Ishizu sent his team out to the affluent expatriate suburbs near Kōbe and the European-styled resort town of Karuizawa to observe clothing trends. Now, with tourists flooding Tokyo, VAN's designers and planners could just go up the street.

When the Olympic teams began to arrive, Kurosu took the monorail out to Haneda Airport with paper and pencil to sketch the outfits of athletes as they came into the lobby. For years, *Men's Club* assured their readers that passengers on international flights dressed to the nines. As someone who had never been on an airplane, Kurosu expected European athletes to emerge in sharp Continental-style suits and exquisite leather shoes.

Instead, a bevy of brawny men slouched through immigration in sweatshirts and sweaters, and, most shockingly, rubber-soled canvas shoes. Over the next few weeks, Kurosu spied this cheap athletic footwear on foreign visitors everywhere. Japanese children owned similar shoes called *zukku*, worn during recess and after-school sports, but wearing them in public was like hitting the town in toilet slippers. Like always, what others saw as taboo Ishizu saw as business opportunity. He decided that VAN would make these so-called "sneakers" for the Japanese market.

It took a few weeks for Kurosu to convince shoemaker Moonstar to copy this style of American footwear: "They kept telling us, 'There's no way these will sell well. These are just the shoes kids wear at school.' And we were going to sell them about double what normal athletic shoes cost. We had to finally just say, just trust us." VAN created two styles, a low-top similar to Keds and a high-top identical to Converse All-Stars but with the VAN logo in the circle on the ankle.

Master of branding Kensuke Ishizu knew the key to success was calling them something other than "athletic shoes" (*undōgutsu*). Kurosu says, "We used the more fashionable Western term 'sneakers'—just like they rebranded *hanagami* (literally 'nose paper') to 'tissue paper.' It was suddenly fine to wear athletic shoes in town

Advertisement for VAN's SNEEKER shoes, 1965. (©VAN Jacket Inc.)

as long as they were called 'sneakers.'" VAN used the English name, but they played with the spelling—"SNEEKERS"—partly for trademark purposes, partly for fun.

VAN's SNEEKERS went on sale in early 1965 and were a runaway hit. The once hesitant Moonstar offered VAN an upfront investment to make even more. SNEEKERS gave birth to the sneaker market in Japan, and from that point forward, the shoe became a staple of youth fashion. VAN employee Yoshio Sadasue remembers SNEEKERS taking the brand to an entirely larger scale, "Once the department stores wanted them, we had to rent an entire warehouse just for sneakers."

The Olympics served as a grand finale to VAN's breakout year of 1964. The company hit ¥1.2 billion in sales ($25 million in 2015 dollars)—a twenty-five-fold increase in just under a decade. The Miyuki Tribe may have brought infamy to Ivy League fashion among adults and parents, but the Olympics proved that the

Japanese public could understand the appeal of traditional American style once they saw the clothing in its appropriate context. All VAN needed to do was keep showing Ivy clothing on real-life Americans. But without the Olympics, there were no longer wealthy foreigners walking around Tokyo. If America did not come to VAN, VAN needed to go to America.

IN LATE 1964, TEENAGERS ACROSS THE COUNTRY WERE HANDing over their piggy banks for a chance to buy a button-down shirt, but few had ever heard of the "Ivy League," let alone could locate an Ivy League university on a map. While the first wave of Japanese Ivy fans had carefully read Toshiyuki Kurosu's long essays on the history and traditions of East Coast collegiate fashion in *Men's Club*, the new breed took their style cues straight from their peers or from the few paltry fashion pages of *Heibon Punch*.

Aibii was on its way to becoming a meaningless buzzword. A teen told *Asahi Newspaper* at the time, "I don't really know what 'Ivy' means—but it's cool, right?" Adults, meanwhile, learned the word from angry newspaper editorials and assumed it was pejorative for delinquent youth. The editorial writers themselves were not in any position to correct them: famed writer Shōtarō Yasuoka's heart sank when he saw a teenager in Ginza wearing a Princeton sweatshirt made by VAN, mistakenly lamenting that Japanese youth continued to wear hand-me-down clothes from postwar American charity drives in the midst of the Economic Miracle.

Faced with widespread misunderstanding, Shōsuke Ishizu and Toshiyuki Kurosu constantly discussed new ways to enlighten the masses on the true origins of Ivy style. One day Shōsuke threw out a wild idea, "Why don't we just go to the actual Ivy League and make a film of the students there?"

This idea was newly possible in 1964, thanks to Japan's recent liberalization of air travel. One snag: round-trip airfare to the U.S. cost ¥650,000 per person, approximately the price of a new car. Shōsuke and Kurosu calculated that they would need roughly ¥10 million ($200,000 in 2015 dollars) to make a film of the eight Ivy League campuses. This would be the most exorbitant promotional expenditure in the short history of the Japanese menswear industry. Fortunately, Kensuke Ishizu loved nothing more than big, audacious ideas. He promptly allocated the money for the project.

Now they needed someone who spoke English to help them on the ground. The obvious choice was the young Hajime "Paul" Hasegawa in VAN's promotion department. Son of Kensuke Ishizu's drinking buddy back in Tianjin, Hasegawa grew up in an English-speaking family. In the early 1960s, he studied at the University of California, Santa Barbara, and after graduation joined VAN. As the only person in the company who had actually attended university in the U.S., Hasegawa supplied most of the *Men's Club* articles about American college life. Once on board the film project, Hasegawa started sending formal letters to all the universities asking permission to shoot on campus.

For the film crew, Shōsuke and Kurosu chose a young, Sorbonne-trained director named Kyō Ozawa. He brought along a screenwriter, a cinematographer, and a lighting assistant. All of VAN's preparation focused on the 16mm film, but *Men's Club* editor Toyoho Nishida thought they also needed still photos to use in promotional materials. At the last minute, they decided to bring along *Men's Club* photographer Teruyoshi Hayashida, who happened to be the older brother of Ishizu's secretary. Kurosu told Hayashida he could shoot whatever he wanted as long as he stayed out of the way of the film.

On May 23, 1965, the eight-person team boarded a Northwest Orient Airlines flight to Boston. They were the only Japanese passengers on the plane. During the twenty-four-hour voyage, Shōsuke sweated over the contents of his luggage—stacks and stacks of yen notes required to fund the project. Japan's strict currency controls prevented tourists from taking more than $500 out of the country. The Ivy film would cost more than four-hundred-times more. With the Japanese yen artificially pegged to the extremely low ¥360 to the dollar, Shōsuke needed to illegally hand carry around ¥5 million into the U.S (around $105,000 in 2015 dollars).

Once they landed in Boston, the group had a night to recuperate at the hotel and get everything in order. Kurosu, finally in the land he obsessed over for decades, was unable to rest: "When I got to the hotel I just couldn't calm down. There was almost like a screeching sound inside my head." Kurosu spent the entire night pacing around the room.

Boston's balmy spring weather greeted the Japanese men as they headed over to Harvard University to begin filming. All eight universities answered Hasegawa's letters, but Harvard refused to lend them any support. To play it on the safe side, the crew pretended to be photo-happy Japanese tourists. Having slept little the night before, Kurosu was already a ball of nerves, and now he had to smuggle an entire film crew into Harvard Yard and pray that no one from the university caught on.

All of this anxiety melted away as he entered the gates to Harvard. Kurosu looked up at the Georgian red brick majesty of the dormitories and thought, *This is it, I'm here!* Ozawa and Hayashida set up their cameras as Kurosu waited for the students to drag themselves out of bed. The campus looked exactly like he had always imagined—and now he expected the students to appear in three-button jackets, Ivy-strap pants, white oxford button-down collar shirts, regimental ties, and wingtips.

Yet the first students to exit their dorms that hot Monday morning slumped into view wearing frayed cut-off shorts and decaying flip-flop sandals. Maybe these were the class derelicts, Kurosu thought. But then the next group appeared, and they looked just as sloppy. Kurosu remembers, "I was shocked at how dressed-down they were—actually, it was absolute despair."

Japanese "Ivy" meant suits, attaché cases, and narrow umbrellas—the complete opposite of what they were seeing. As Hayashida and Ozawa burned through rolls of film trying to capture usable images of students, Kurosu panicked: *This was all worthless!* Footage of students in T-shirts and cut-off pants would not convince anyone in Japan to rethink Ivy. Before they left Japan, Hase-gawa had warned Kurosu, "Jacket and ties were for Sunday chapel, the occasional date, or when you wanted to impress someone," but Kurosu refused to believe him. Now he deeply regretted not listen-ing. He had almost certainly squandered VAN's war chest on a fundamental misunderstanding of American campus style.

The crew had another problem: many of the students did not want their photos taken. Kurosu recalls, "They'd ask, 'What are you making this film for?' And we'd say, for a Japanese brand, VAN, and they'd say, 'That's a commercial, and I don't want to be in a commercial.' So we'd take most of the images secretly. We'd set up quickly, shoot the photos, and run."

As the day progressed, however, things looked up. The crew found students in madras blazers and khaki pants filing out of Memorial Church. Ozawa and Hayashida used up all the film they brought on the first day. Yet the team could not locate any students wearing the three-button worsted wool suits that everyone in Ja-pan believed was *the* standard uniform on East Coast campuses. The professors looked more like the Japanese ideal than the stu-dents. The crew was also depressed to notice that the few students who dared wear dark suits and ties on campus were Japanese ex-change students. They looked hopelessly uncool next to their non-chalant American peers.

After a tense day at Harvard, the team drove up to the quiet, woody streets of Hanover, New Hampshire to film at Dartmouth. The college attached a public relations person and helped find pro-fessors and students to act out scripted scenes.

Kensuke Ishizu requested the team return with footage of American football—what he believed was the quintessential Ivy League sport. Dartmouth rebuffed these requests, noting that training in the summer was a violation of league rules. Sensing the Japanese team's disappointment, the PR man took them out to the boathouse to shoot the crew team. The coach was coopera-tive, putting a few teams in the water so Ozawa could film a row-ing sequence.

Taking advantage of the support, the team spent three days in Hanover—shooting intramural baseball games, students riding around town on bicycles, and the interiors of laboratories, libraries, and cafeterias. But the extra time there forced them to cut Cornell University and the University of Pennsylvania from their trip.

After brief explorations of Brown and Columbia, they arrived at Yale. Students from a fashion study group acted as their hosts— but could not understand why these Japanese men were asking so many questions about clothing. Kurosu recalls, "Most students acted like they were completely disinterested in fashion, even if they looked like they cared. They didn't seem proud of being stylish. They would just say to us dismissively, 'I just came here to study. I don't care what I wear.'" Others were incredulous that Japanese employees came all the way to America to ask them about classic Ivy League style in 1965, a year when the Vietnam War and the hippie counterculture were pushing traditional clothing towards complete extinction. After returning to Japan, Shōsuke rationalized this disconnect to *Men's Club*, "We just have a different sense of fashion. They do everything unconsciously, so when we suddenly asked them about their clothing, they didn't know how to answer." When Kurosu saw a Yale student with high-water cotton pants, he inquired, "Are really short pants in style?" only to be told defensively, "I've never thought about it. They just shrunk when I washed them."

The final destination on the trip was Princeton. They arrived to find an intramural softball tournament and a wild party hosted at Nassau Hall, sponsored by a beer company, where groups of drunken students sang fight songs in good spirits. Once they committed these events to celluloid, the campus production was officially over. The team then headed back to New York to shoot additional footage for "a day in the life" segment about the Big Apple—including the shop windows of traditional clothiers like Brooks Brothers as well as graying former Ivy Leaguers out on the streets.

After returning to Japan, *Men's Club* ran round-table discussions with Kurosu, Shōsuke, and Hasegawa about their trip. Kurosu re-

Take Ivy authors in Hawaii coming back from Ivy League campuses (from top left, clockwise: Teruyoshi Hayashida, Paul Hasegawa, Shōsuke Ishizu, and Toshiyuki Kurosu). (Courtesy of the Ishizu family)

assured readers, "Young people in America are wearing exactly the same things you see in *Men's Club*'s 'Machi no Ivy Leaguers' column." The group regaled readers with tales of uniquely American phenomena, such as the university cafeteria system, where young men queued up to dine on piles of hot dogs and hamburgers.

Perhaps most of all, the team was surprised to see how much the country reverently protected the architectural styles of its universities, even in an era of rapid economic growth. The Japanese postwar obsession with America stemmed from the idea that the U.S. was a land of unbelievable riches and modern technology. But in New England, they saw families routinely modernize the insides of their houses while keeping the exterior design intact. This felt poignant at a time when Tokyo developers summarily leveled old wooden structures to build bland, concrete apartment complexes. Kurosu told *Men's Club*, "Japan is much older than America, but no one thinks about protecting the classic feel of a place. They just build everything modern, not thinking at all about whether there is a balance to the buildings around it. It's really sad." During the trip, Kurosu awoke to something that Kensuke Ishizu always said: Ivy represented veneration for tradition, not just chasing the latest modern trend.

Nevertheless, the VAN team faced the challenge of explaining why Ivy League students did not wear suits to class. Shōsuke told *Men's Club*, "Japanese Ivy is not actually very student-like—Ivy fans in Japan are more stylish. Japanese Ivy fans wear Ivy suits while they are students, like they are adults." They compared the dressed-down Americans to *bankara*, the early twentieth century Japanese university students' stylish look of disheveled uniforms. American Ivy League students demonstrated status through their nonchalance. After seeing this firsthand, Kurosu believed that Japanese Ivy could learn to relax from the Americans. "After seven years of Ivy getting bigger and bigger in Japan," he wrote in a *Men's Club* column in late 1965, "I feel that we're approaching a time to start moving forward without all the hyperconsciousness."

But with just two months to prepare the film for VAN's Autumn/Winter campaign kickoff, the team did not have enough time to give these concerns full editorial consideration. Ozawa went off to edit, hiring famed jazz musician Hachidai Nakamura to score the movie in an improvised session. Hayashida, meanwhile, developed the photos, and, to everyone's surprise, they were just as illustrative as the moving imagery. *Men's Club*'s editor Nishida asked if Fujingahō could publish the photos as a book. VAN agreed, and the team, mostly Hasegawa, hunkered down to write up blurbs for each photo as well as essays at the back explaining the tenets of campus fashion. ("The American bankara style is about having a bit of fun and it is not a consequence of genuine poverty that is typical amongst students in Japan.") VAN's production team meanwhile looked at Hayashida and Ozawa's visuals to grab ideas for items in the fall collection.

Upon completion, the project needed a name. Kurosu proposed *Take Ivy*—a joke on the Dave Brubeck Quartet's famed jazz piece "Take Five." In Japanese, "Ivy" (*aibii*) and "Five" (*faibu*) sound

Take Ivy jacket and cover. (Courtesy of Hearst Fujingahō)

vaguely similar, but the fluent English speaker Hasegawa countered that "Take Ivy" would make no sense to Americans. Like always, VAN employees ignored Hasegawa's proper English corrections when they got in the way of artistic ambitions. To this day, Kurosu still proudly claims, "Someone who knows English never would have thought of that name!"

On August 20, 1965, VAN premiered the *Take Ivy* film at an all-day party in Tokyo. The company rented out the entire Akasaka Prince Hotel and invited two thousand distributors, retailers, and young fans to celebrate the debut. Franchisees distributed tickets providing a full day of access to the hotel to their top customers. At 10:30 a.m., Kensuke Ishizu waved the green flag on a seven-hour stock car rally around the city for VAN-clad drivers in vintage cars. Hundreds of teens came dressed in their madras, seersucker, and off-white jackets.

At the end of the day's festivities, VAN screened the *Take Ivy* film—an energetic montage of footage from the campuses set to

Japanese youth at *Take Ivy* launch party, August 1965, in November 1965 issue of *Men's Club*. (Courtesy of Hearst Fujingahō)

an upbeat jazz soundtrack. Beyond the basic documentary photography, there are a few scripted scenes—a student arriving late for his Asian Art class and a groovy nighttime party around a record player in a dorm. After its auspicious debut at the Akasaka Prince Hotel, the VAN crew took the film on tour across the brand's franchises to screen the film and put on a fashion show. But after the tour, the film dropped permanently out of circulation. The book came out in late 1965, priced at a hefty ¥500—ten times the cost of *Heibon Punch*. It was far from a success. Fujingahō published twenty thousand copies, and just like the very first issues of *Otoko no Fukushoku*, VAN bought up about half the print run to sell through its retailers. The other copies languished on shelves.

The lackluster response to *Take Ivy* belies the influence the work had on Japan. Retailers and fashion insiders changed their mind about Ivy after seeing real images of healthy, elite Americans wearing madras blazers and chino pants among the majestic brick and stone buildings of old New England campuses. And from 1965 onward, Ivy fans treated the *Take Ivy* photos as canonical representations of Sixties East Coast prep style. From the perspective of sales impact, the campaign was an unbridled success. Teens snapped up VAN's campus-inspired fashion in late 1965 unlike in any previous year.

This growth was likely organic—1965 was already a boom time for Ivy—but as Hasegawa recalls, "Kensuke Ishizu was not the kind of businessman who cared about return on investment. He thought, as long as the company doesn't go into the red, we're okay." The film was not just a master stroke of promotion, but an additional tool VAN could use to convince skeptics and authorities that Ivy was an age-old American tradition. This included teens, department stores, and parents—and soon, the police.

DESPITE THE POLICE CRACKDOWN OF THE PREVIOUS YEAR, A wave of teenagers in Ivy clothing returned to Ginza in the summer of 1965. Unlike their peers from the year before, they moved beyond Miyuki Street and roamed the entire neighborhood. After a year of media saturation around the Ivy clothing trend, newspapers and tabloids more accurately dubbed 1965's youth congregation the Ivy Tribe (*aibii-zoku*).

The Olympics and ongoing popularity of *Heibon Punch* had fostered more sympathy for Ivy fashion, but 1965's Ivy Tribe members were not cut from the VAN cloth. Kurosu recalls, "It started to get a little more hippie-like and more extreme. It brought back the image of Ivy as clothes for delinquents." Thanks in part to the VAN's SNEAKERS on their feet, the Ivy teenagers of 1965 were much more dressed down compared to their predecessors. They carried around clothing and toiletries for overnight stays inside pitiful hemp sacks called *fūten* bags. There was also a rival faction who dressed up their Ivy to a ridiculous degree. The so-called Umbrella Tribe (*kōmori-zoku*) wore dark suits while clutching attachè cases in one hand and ultra-slim umbrellas in the other.

Newspapers continued their editorial campaigns against teenagers' presence in Ginza as fervently as before. (Even the *New York Times* covered the controversy, calling them "a weird bunch of wealthy teen-agers who dress in black... and roam Miyuki Street in search of one-time bedmates.") In April 1965, the police launched another round of street sweeps. This time the youth did not go quietly. An apprehended Ivy Tribe member complained to the *Asahi Newspaper*, "What's wrong with wearing cool clothing and walking through Ginza? We're not like those country bumpkins around Ikebukuro or Shinjuku." As schools let out for summer vacation in July, the numbers ballooned again. Youth came in from the nearby prefectures Saitama, Kanagawa, and Chiba to join in the Ginza fun.

Unlike the previous year, the media knew exactly whom to blame for this youth revolt: Kensuke Ishizu. His secretary Takeyoshi Hayashida remembers, "We got a lot of phone calls from parents complaining that their children were spending too much of their allowance on VAN." Once Ginza shop owners identified Ishizu as the central figure of Japanese Ivy, they begged the police to neutralize him as a decapitating blow to the entire youth movement.

The police already had Ishizu in their sights. Kurosu says, "The Tsukiji police noticed that the kids were all wearing this logo that said VAN and thought that it must be VAN causing all the trouble." One day in September 1965, Kurosu and Kensuke Ishizu visited Tsukiji Police Station to clarify that they never told teenagers to hang around in Ginza nor encouraged youth deviance. During their initial discussions with the officers, it was quickly apparent the ill will stemmed from a familiar problem: the police did not understand what the word "Ivy" actually meant. Based on the disgraceful behavior of the teens, the officers assumed it was the latest slang for the word "beggar." They could not understand how Ishizu and his team so shamelessly sold "beggar fashion."

At this point, the *Take Ivy* film was complete, so Ishizu and Kurosu decided the quickest way to explain Ivy fashion would be to show the style in its original American context. They put together a screening at the Tsukiji Police Station for dozens of grizzled and graying cops. Upon seeing Ivy in its natural environment, the top officer turned to Ishizu and said, "Hey, this Ivy thing in the U.S. isn't so bad!"

From the minute the film ended, the cops stopped grilling Ishizu as a co-conspirator in the Ginza predicament and tapped him as an ally. The Tsukiji detectives realized that Ishizu alone had the power to stop the Ivy Tribe once and for all. They pleaded with Kurosu, "Whatever we say to the Ivy Tribe, they won't listen. We need you to tell them to leave Ginza, because you are like gods to them." Ishizu, who also hoped to clean up Ivy's reputation, agreed to step in.

The Tsukiji Police immediately organized a "Big Ivy Meet Up" in Ginza, where the Ivy Tribe would hear a speech from Kensuke Ishizu on why they should not loiter around the neighborhood. The police booked the sixth floor of the expansive Ginza Gas Hall and plastered the surrounding streets with two hundred posters for the event. Officially, the August 30, 1965 event was a meeting for the Chūō Ward Committee on Juvenile Problems—and for the first time in committee history, the problematic juveniles willingly attended. Just ten days after the official film launch for the brand's most loyal fans at the Akasaka Prince Hotel, VAN held an exclusive screening of *Take Ivy* for its least obedient devotees.

Nearly two thousand teens packed into Gas Hall for what was possibly the most exciting meeting of any "committee on juvenile problems" ever. After the screening, the fifty-four-year-old Kensuke Ishizu took the stage and imparted his wisdom: "Ivy is not a momentary trend that you follow, but a tradition to be honored, passed down from your father and grandfather. It's not just clothing, but a way of life." Then he got to the point: "So you can't just hang around town like this. And if you understand what I am saying, you'll tell your friends as well." With that, the Godfather of Japanese Ivy did a Q&A with the Tsukiji Police Chief, followed by a rock set from musical act Mickey Curtis and His Vanguards. At 4 p.m., the program ended, and the attendees walked away with free VAN shopping bags.

A few days later, the Ivy Tribe disappeared from Ginza. Kensuke Ishizu took full credit for bringing closure to the crisis, and the police came to see him as a powerful fashion icon who held tremendous sway over the baby boomer generation. Kurosu thinks that they simply lucked out on timing: "The event was at the end of summer, so the teens went back to school and stopped showing up anyway. But the police thought they left because we showed the film, so we looked really good." From that point forward, Japanese law enforcement worried less about the menace of clean-cut American youth fashion. In fact, they were so impressed with Ivy style that they asked Ishizu to redesign their uniforms.

IN THE SECOND HALF OF THE 1960S, JAPAN'S ECONOMY CON-tinued to grow over 10 percent a year. With exports booming, the Japanese government began to encourage more domestic consumption. Graying finance ministers expected salaried workers and their wives to lead the charge, but the older generation—condi-tioned for frugality or simply too busy to shop—instead passed the extra cash to their offspring. Japanese teens were thrilled. Uncon-ditioned by prewar austerity or postwar poverty, they wanted to participate in the ever-expanding consumer market and happily took their parents' yen.

VAN was a direct beneficiary of this influx of cash into young people's pockets. As a small company targeting wealthy capitalists in 1954, VAN pulled in revenues of ¥48 million ($1.17 million in 2015 dollars). By 1967, VAN saw that amount hit ¥3.6 billion ($71 million in 2015 dollars), and, at the end of the decade, revenues would hit ¥6.9 billion ($111 million in 2015 dollars). During the peak of the Ivy trend, around 1966 and 1967, VAN production could not keep up with demand. Goods that arrived in the morn-ing were gone by late afternoon. Ishizu's secretary Takeyoshi Ha-yashida remembers, "We employees could never buy anything from VAN, because there wasn't anything left. We got things de-livered from Ōsaka, the sales guys would sell it all to stores within a week, and then they'd just play around for the rest of the month."

As VAN racked up revenues, the brand also won over more Ivy fashion fans at the top of society. The Emperor's nephew, His Im-perial Highness Prince Tomohito of Mikasa, loved Ivy League

Yoshio Sadasue as a VAN employee, 1968. (Courtesy of Kamakura Shirts)

clothing and made public appearances in high-cut three-button suits. The May 1965 issue of *Men's Club* showed Mikasa in his best dress with the cheeky caption, "Imperial Ivy."

VAN eventually surpassed a one-thousand-person staff across Tokyo and Ōsaka. A key employee during this Golden Age of VAN was Yoshio Sadasue—now the founder and chairman of successful Japanese apparel company Kamakura Shirts. Sadasue's father ran a VAN shop in Hiroshima, and this connection landed him a job at VAN proper. The twenty-six-year-old former electrical engineer Sadasue entered the Ōsaka office on April 1, 1966 wearing pointy-tipped shoes with a high shine, to which the VAN salesmen proclaimed, "Hey everyone, it's the boy with the magical shoes!" On day two, they hid Sadasue away in a warehouse, where he worked for the next six years.

But once he started wearing his company-provided Ivy wardrobe, Sadasue learned the appeal of the VAN product firsthand. "I would go out in a VAN outfit—madras blazer and bermuda shorts—and people would turn their heads when I walked by. I could suddenly get into clubs for rich people and exclusive hotel pools even though I didn't even have ¥100 to my name. When I wore VAN, I looked rich. I think that's why Ishizu's strategy worked."

Sadasue's experiences in Ōsaka also demonstrated the degree to which Ivy became a true nationwide trend—not just something exclusive to urban dandies. In fact, most of Japan's hardcore Ivy obsessives, both at the time and today, lived outside of the capital. Ishizu's franchises across Japan created local Ivy indoctrination centers for young men who would have otherwise been disconnected from big city trends. Ivy represented a brand new paradigm for mass media and fashion brands, where *Men's Club* could serve as a media proxy to explain the latest in Tokyo fashion.

Another sign of VAN's success in the late 1960s was the rash of clone brands. The nearest rival, JUN, offered copies of VAN's Ivy items at slightly lower prices. Other so-called "three-letter brands" appeared, including ACE, TAC, JAX, JOI—and even YAN. Textile maker Toray used a primitive computer to register trademarks for every other possible three-letter variant. Shōsuke Ishizu told *Heibon Punch* at the time, "We are like guinea pigs. I just wish that these brands who copy us would copy us more closely. It's just terrible when they change the color and shape and flood the streets with just awful stuff." Despite the competition, none of the other brands ever rivaled VAN in terms of broader social impact. Paul Hasegawa says, "JUN and the other brands were making *clothes* but nothing else. We were trying to promote a total lifestyle."

VAN's unrivaled authority in the fashion world allowed the brand to keep popularizing new and more risqué American styles—including the T-shirt. Until the mid-1960s, the Japanese saw the T-shirt as nothing more than an undergarment. During the Occupation, the Japanese giggled at G.I.s walking around town in nothing but underwear on top. VAN had first tried to sell T-shirts in 1962, but customers balked. When VAN put its stenciled logo on T-shirts as promotional giveaways, no one dared wear the shirts outside. A passionate debate raged inside the company over whether they should be making them at all.

Attitudes changed with *Take Ivy*. Kurosu remembers, "T-shirts really started to sell after we put out the book. In the pictures you can see students all wearing T-shirts with the logos of their schools, so we made identical shirts in the school colors. White T-shirts looked too much like underwear, so we had an orange shirt for Princeton, blue for Yale. We called them 'color tees.' We were able to demonstrate the fact that 'All American students wear these!' and then everyone suddenly started to buy them. They sold like crazy through the summer of 1966."

With the success of *Take Ivy*, VAN ran an integrated sales campaign each season. The most iconic installment came in Spring/Summer 1967—"Cape Cod Spirit"—in which VAN hoped to channel the timeless charm of John F. Kennedy on a yacht. (Although no one at VAN could find Cape Cod on a map.) Next came the Southwestern ranch-chic "Discover America"—a phrase that later inspired Japan National Railways' hit 1970 domestic travel campaign, "Discover Japan."

The campaigns were just one example of Kensuke Ishizu's pioneering cross-media promotional tactics. VAN sponsored a radio show called "Ivy Club" with Kurosu, Shōsuke, and Hasegawa chatting about men's fashion. Ishizu then moved into TV with a half-hour Sunday night show called "VAN Music Break," featuring famed jazz and pop musicians performing their hit songs while wearing the latest Ivy duds. VAN was also the first Japanese fashion brand to endorse athletes and race car drivers. Kensuke Ishizu organized an amateur football team called the Vanguards. And, in 1966, he opened a restaurant, VAN Snack, in Ginza, which offered hamburgers three years before McDonald's opened its doors down the street.

VAN taught the Japanese business world how to sell Americana to the Japanese—and he succeeded so well that even the expatriates running Japanese subsidiaries of multinational companies

VAN's campaigns in the late 1960s: "Sports American" and "Cape Cod Spirit." (©VAN Jacket Inc.)

took note. Pepsi Japan CEO Alan Pottasch, a legend in the advertising world for creating the "Pepsi Generation" ad campaign in 1963, headhunted Paul Hasegawa away from VAN in 1968. Hasegawa recalls, "Alan liked what we were doing at VAN. Until I met him, I hadn't taken a professional point of view towards the things we were up to." Later, Coca-Cola became a strategic ally of VAN, working together on promotional goods through the 1970s and at one point borrowing the exact look of a VAN commercial for its own TV campaign.

As much as Kensuke Ishizu wanted Ivy League style to become Japan's permanent template for basic fashion, East Coast style eventually lost its monopoly on youth fashion. Beginning in 1966, elegant European suits—known as Continental or *konchi* in Japanese—hit the mainstream, fueled by VAN's rival, JUN, who found their own lucrative niche with the look. For as much as he was "Mr. Ivy," Kensuke Ishizu personally preferred British fashion, and he started a sub-label called Mister VAN to make flamboyant items pulled right off Carnaby Street. The Beatles played two historic concerts at the Nippon Budokan in flashy mod suits during June 1966, so Ishizu's move looked like a smart bet on the era's trends. But the style was perhaps too garish: mod fashion never took off in Japan, and Mister VAN was a failure. Regardless, VAN continued to diversify into separate lines for different constituencies, including VAN Brothers, VAN Mini, and VAN Boys for younger teens.

VAN's attempts to chase the vagaries of teenage style, however, had the unintended effect of isolating the brand's original cohort of loyal customers. Hardcore Ivy fans first panicked in 1964 when they saw Ginza teenagers in button-down shirts, and their sense of dissociation only grew as middle-school students started to regularly wear "Ivy shirts" as their play clothes. Twenty-something shoppers at Teijin Men's Shop asked for their purchases not to be put in a VAN-logo bag, lest they be mistaken for an Ivy Tribe member.

In 1966, Ishizu asked Toshiyuki Kurosu to win back former customers by revamping VAN's adult-oriented line, Kent (slogan: "for the exclusive man"). The older clientele still loved American style but found the word "Ivy" increasingly toxic. Kurosu smartly recast the Kent style under a new term—"Trad" (*traddo*). Kurosu told American blog "The Trad" in 2010, "The word 'traditional' existed but it was difficult to pronounce and rarely used in Japan. I was looking for a short word that was easy to remember and I found the expression 'Trad Jazz' in a jazz book."

The Trad moniker would prove crucial for the future of American style in Japan. Trad offered an obvious contrast to Ivy's trendy ephemerality, and encompassed heritage brands beyond the United States. Trad men could wear a classic Burberry jacket or Irish fisherman's sweater and not worry about breaking the strict "America-only" rules of Ivy. Kent never had the lasting impact of VAN, but Kurosu's invention of trad kept the door open for the next forty years of Japanese Anglo-American obsession.

Despite VAN's outsized influence among the baby boomer generation, many adults continued to hold a grudge against Ivy. Tabloids constantly bashed Ishizu. Weekly *Shūkan Gendai*, for example, ran an unsigned piece in 1966 called "The Reputation of Mr. Kensuke Ishizu—a Designer Who Will Lead to National Ruin." The anonymous author accused VAN of encouraging young men to become lecherous, and included this quote from sportswriter Daikichi Terauchi:

> Prewar youth contributed to our statist system, but twenty years after the war, youth do nothing. It's only their bodies that are big—they're wimpy on the inside. One manifestation of this is their clothing. They dress like a second-fiddle actor in a theater production—it's not what the main character would ever proudly wear. Even if you think women are instinctively attracted to fashion, VAN's version of Ivy isn't even fashion. It's just guys who want to pick up girls.

This smear not only demonstrates how much middle-aged males disliked Ishizu, but also how intensely the older cohort stuck to prewar ideals of an austere Japanese machismo. They could only see stylish menswear like VAN as a symptom of sexual perversion—the need to look feminine in a mad drive for lust. But such grumbles were the final cries of a lost cause: VAN gave youth a new set of attitudes for fashion better set for a consumer age.

Today, most baby boomers remember VAN fondly as their introduction to both personal style and an Americanized lifestyle. In teaching the entire "Ivy" milieu, VAN employees imbued youth with aspirations and dreams that reached beyond clothing into music, hobbies, automobiles, and food. With traditional Japanese culture discredited by their defeat in WWII, youth were desperate for a new set of values. And at just the right time, VAN offered up an idealized version of American life. Ishizu was a gifted designer and marketer, but he made his fortune in a form of cultural arbitrage. Kurosu says, "All VAN would do is create things that they had in America but not in Japan. We'd just copy, but no one realized what we were doing."

VAN also benefited from the fact that real Americans were gradually disappearing from the Tokyo landscape. By the mid-1960s, G.I.s were few in number and generally confined to their bases in remote areas. Youth in Tokyo instead learned about the American people from VAN, *Men's Club*, and Hollywood films. They came to see the United States as not a wartime enemy or postwar occupier, but as the home of jazz, fancy colleges, button-down collars, and blond bombshells.

In the history of Japanese fashion, Ivy marked a critical moment in the 1960s when men started dressing up, but more importantly, the look set the pattern on how the country would import, consume, and modify American fashion for the next fifty years. After Ivy, Japan had an infrastructure to create and disseminate the latest in American styles—not just the clothes of clean-cut New England youth, but even the wilder looks of the counterculture.

FOUR

The Jeans Revolution

KOJIMA, POPULATION SEVENTY-FIVE THOUSAND, SITS ON THE Seto Inland Sea at the very bottom of Okayama Prefecture. The salty soil and low rainfall discouraged attempts at rice agriculture, but the land was well-suited for growing cotton. Robust harvests of the white fiber attracted auxiliary businesses, such as textile weaving and indigo dyeing. By the twentieth century, Kojima was known for its production of Japan's sturdiest fabrics, including sailcloth and the cotton drill used on the soles of traditional *tabi* socks. In 1921, a Kojima businessman donated twenty sewing machines to spearhead an entire new sector—school uniform manufacture. This snowballed into a large-scale industry, and, by 1937, 90 percent of Japanese students wore uniforms made in Okayama Prefecture.

Kojima's dominance of the uniform business continued after the war, but with most cotton textiles shipped overseas in the export drive, local companies began to produce uniforms made of vinylon, a lightweight, weatherproof synthetic. That performed well until 1958, when a vastly superior polyester called Tetoron hit the market. Its makers, Toray and Teijin, launched expansive marketing campaigns for this new wonder fiber, and schools nationwide soon demanded uniforms made from Tetoron. But Toray and Teijin refused to supply the fiber to anyone outside their closed manufacturing group, cutting out the top companies in Kojima.

Workers at the city's top uniform maker, Maruo Clothing, watched in sorrow as stacks of unwanted vinylon garments piled up in its warehouse. Founder Kotarō Ozaki needed to act. In the fall of 1964, he summoned his two lead salesmen, Shizuo Kashino and Toshio Ōshima, back to headquarters for a meeting on the fate of the company. After strange dreams each night about ninth century scholar-poet Sugawara no Michizane, he decided to take the two men on an impromptu overnight pilgrimage to Dazaifu Tenman-gū, the Kyūshū shrine where Michizane was deified. After paying religious tribute, the Maruo team received their divine inspiration at a nearby hot springs resort. Ozaki asked what kind of clothing Maruo needed to make to rescue the business. Without hesitation, Kashino and Ōshima both answered *jiipan*, or "G.I. pants." Americans knew them as "blue jeans."

Kashino first learned about jiipan from the store Maruseru in Tokyo's Ameyoko district. While no longer a black market, the area was still chaotic in the late 1950s; packed crowds roamed hundreds of stalls selling pickles and fish, pilfered hotel supplies, smuggled contraband, semi-legal parallel imports, and luxury items illicitly procured from PXs. Maruseru's proprietor, Ken'ichi Hiyama, found his own lucrative niche reselling surplus American military garments, as well as new American-style work coats and pants from makers like Maruo.

During the Occupation, American soldiers often paid Pan Pan girls in old clothing rather than cash, and the streetwalkers went straight to Ameyoko stores like Maruseru to sell it off. Hiyama noticed that many of the women came in with faded, indigo-blue work pants, which rumors identified as the bottom half of American prison uniforms. Anyone who had visited U.S. military bases knew that soldiers often wore pants like that while off-duty. Lacking a better descriptor, Hiyama nicknamed them "G.I. pants," and the shortened term jiipan (or "G-pan") became common parlance around the neighborhood.

By 1950, jiipan made up more than half of Maruseru's sales. Hiyama's wife Chiyono told *Shūkan Asahi,* in 1970, "We would buy them at ¥300–¥500 a pair and then sell at ¥3,200. Jeans were so scarce that when you put them in the store, they would sell out before you even put on the price tag." At the time, most men's pants came in wool, and the cotton jiipan was much better suited to Japan's temperate climate. The blue color also stood out in the khaki sea of wartime *kokuminfuku* ("citizen clothing") and American soldiers' uniforms. In the words of writer Masatake Kitamoto, jeans glowed with the "blue of victory."

In the hunt for more jiipan, the Hiyamas noticed that boxes sent from America to family members stationed in Japan often contained torn-up jeans as packaging material. They bought up these scraps and hired companies to patch the holes. The results were Frankenstein-like creations that stitched together disparate elements of mangled pairs, but even these sold out immediately.

By the early 1950s, Ameyoko stores had developed a brisk trade in used jiipan, but no one in Japan was able to buy a new pair. There was one notable exception—elite bureaucrat Jirō Shirasu. The handsome, Cambridge-educated businessman and diplomat first discovered jeans while living in San Francisco in the late 1930s. After the war, he played a critical role in facilitating relations between the Japanese and American governments, and it was this intimacy with General Douglas MacArthur's GHQ that allowed him to purchase a crisp new pair of Levi's 501s from a PX. Shirasu nominally wanted the denim to wear when tinkering with his car, but he ended up living in them. When he boarded a flight to San Francisco in 1951 to sign the peace treaty with the U.S., he immediately shed his suit and spent the rest of the flight in his Levi's. In 1951, the entire country learned about his love of jeans when a photographer captured the graying gentleman lounging in his favorite outfit.

Shirasu's crisp new jeans contrasted starkly with the ragged, stitched-up pairs sold at Maruseru. Thus began the dual identity of blue jeans in Japan—an exclusive, rare garment simultaneously marred with the seedy connotation of black markets. This duality continued in the early 1950s when Tokyo saw a new influx of American soldiers on R&R from the Korean War. No longer confined to their uniforms, soldiers wandered around Tokyo in worn-in jeans, CPO shirts, lambswool v-neck sweaters in primary colors, white socks, and loafers. They looked stylish, but the foreign soldiers' tendency to hang around dubious parts of town only further complicated blue jeans' reputation.

Between these Americans in Tokyo and Marlon Brando and James Dean films at the box office, blue jeans took on a new cultural cachet among attentive Japanese youth in the mid-1950s. New stores popped up in Ameyoko, with names like Amerika-ya and London, dedicated exclusively to jeans and military surplus items. American jeans, unfortunately, did not fit the Japanese body particularly well. The pants were made for thickly-built, long-legged Americans. An interested customer at Maruseru could only pray that an identically-sized American decided to part with an old pair. To solve the sizing issue, the Ameyoko stores started shipping their used jeans off to companies such as Kojima's Maruo Clothing to recut them for the Japanese body.

In 1957, the Japanese government relaxed its protectionist regulations on apparel imports, opening the door to formal trade in used clothing from overseas. When the news broke, Shigetoshi Takahashi of Tokyo surplus retailer Eikō Shōji immediately hopped on a plane across the Pacific and purchased twenty thousand used jeans at a washing operation in Seattle's suburbs. This stockpile of denim was the first large-scale importation of American jeans into Japan. Soon after Takahashi returned with his bounty, bureaucrats eased regulations even further to allow the importation of new clothing. He got right back on a plane to the U.S. and came home with a contract to distribute eighty thousand pairs of new Lee jeans. At the same time, rival Ōishi Trading signed a deal to import thirty thousand pairs of Levi's each month.

These two contracts flooded Japan with real American denim, and surplus clothing stores expected their customers to snap up the authentic American jeans. But Japanese shoppers were not impressed. They liked washed-out denim with a soft touch and complex fade. The new jeans' starchy fabric was rigid, dark, and uncomfortable. They wondered whether Americans really subjugated themselves to the torture of wearing these terrible, stiff pants.

Men's Club illustrator Yasuhiko Kobayashi was one of Japan's first customers for this early batch of new jeans. He came to lust after denim after seeing them in Hollywood Westerns, but it took him years to discover they could be purchased in Ameyoko. After happening upon a pair of Levi's, he used his entire monthly art supply allowance to pay the ¥3,800 price. Thinking the color too dark, Kobayashi begged the rich housewife next door to give the pants multiple soaks in her washing machine set on the longest mode. The washes lightened the color, and to replicate the wear-and-tear, he took a scouring pad to the jeans' fabric under cover of night. It was all worth it when Kobayashi became one of the few Japanese youth in the late 1950s strolling around Shinjuku in blue jeans that looked straight out of a movie.

In these early days, jeans' high sticker price limited them to young actors, dedicated art students, and rebellious teens from wealthy families. Levi Strauss first made jeans to withstand the rough work of gold mining in the 1870s, but in postwar Japan, they were too expensive for blue-collar workers. And yet, blue jeans' status as a foreign import could not counterbalance the pants' association with "incorrigible people." Fashion critic Shōzō Izuishi wore jeans as a middle-school student in the 1950s and remembers, "Everyone wanted to wear them because they made you look like an outlaw. I wouldn't do anything bad, but everyone would look at me and say, there goes a bad kid."

Pairs of imported American jeans in *Men's Club*, Spring 1963. (Courtesy of Hearst Fujingahō)

In Ameyoko, the Hiyamas at Maruseru felt their trade in jeans was hampered by high prices and low supply. Many street-side shops offered cheap imitations—indigo-dyed, lightweight blended-cotton pants in a five-pocket style—but Hiyama wanted someone to make an affordable domestic version that felt like the American originals. Each time Kashino of Maruo Clothing came in to drop off shipments of the re-stitched used jeans, the couple begged him to try and make Japan's first true blue jeans. At that hot spring hotel in late 1964, the Maruo team presented this request again to President Ozaki, but this time the boss did not need further convincing: Maruo Clothing would learn to make Japan's best jeans. That was the only way to save the company.

AFTER THE DECISION TO GO INTO JEANS MANUFACTURE IN late 1964, Maruo Clothing's Shizuo Kashino returned to Maruseru to procure a pair of American jeans for dissection and analysis.

During the autopsy, Kashino puzzled over a strange detail in the fabric: the blue cotton threads were not dyed all the way through. Compared to other dyestuffs, indigo does not easily permeate to the core of cotton. So industrial indigo dyeing tends to create a blue ring around the thread's surface and leave the center white. But it is precisely this defect that gives jeans their unique beauty: when heavy wear scuffs away the indigo, the undyed cotton pops out to create expressive and subtle layers of fading.

Japanese craftsmen had been expertly dyeing with indigo since the seventh century, but their traditional method—repeatedly dipping yarn in tubs of fermented organic dye, then twisting the yarn to oxidize the color—fully permeates the cotton fibers with blue coloring. No Japanese dyers at the time could make indigo yarns with the distinct white center of American denim. Kashino resigned himself to use a lightweight, chambray-like material for Maruo's jeans, but Hiyama barked at him, "No, no, you have to think more carefully and figure out how to make pants exactly like American-made jeans." Maruo had no other choice—the company would have to import fabric from the United States.

Through back channel connections to bureaucrats, Kashino heard that one-time Levi's importer Ōishi Trading had just received an exclusive right to import bolts of American denim. President Tetsuo Ōishi failed to get denim from Levi's North Carolina fabric supplier Cone Mills, but eventually found a willing trading partner in Georgia's Canton Mills. In 1964, Ōishi set up sewing factories in Tokyo to make jeans for the Japanese market under the Canton brand, and, luckily for Maruo, had denim left over. Maruo Clothing signed a contract with Ōishi that allowed the manufacture and sales of Canton jeans in Western Japan. After inking the deal and handing over a wad of cash, three thousand yards of sturdy 14.5-oz denim arrived in Maruo Clothing's Kojima factory in February 1965.

But as Maruo's eager female seamstresses dug into the denim, their Mitsubishi and Juki sewing machines failed to lay a single stitch into the stiff material. The Maruo bosses changed the needles and tried alternative sewing methods, but nothing could pierce the starched Canton cloth. After much research, Ozaki ordered a batch of used Union Special sewing machines from the United States. The workers then realized that they needed another specialized set of materials—orange-colored thread used in stitching the jeans, copper rivets critical to the jeans' durability, and steel zippers to close the fly. They went back to Canton Mills for more thread, ordered zippers from the American company Talon, and procured the rivets from the American company Scovill. To make American-style jeans in Japan, Maruo Clothing ultimately had to import all the materials—and the sewing machines—from the U.S.

In mid-1965, Maruo produced its very first pair of jeans under the Canton brand. Kashino and Ōshima made the rounds to their retailers, but met with the same resistance as had the previous generation of importers: Japanese consumers hated the feel of raw denim. Despite the fact that new jeans sold for ¥800 compared to the exorbitantly high ¥1,400 for pre-worn American imports, used jeans outsold new jeans 10-to-1.

The obvious solution was to give the jeans a single wash to soften the material and fade the color. After a week of heavy use, however, the factory washing machines all broke down. Kashino tried to outsource the task to a nearby laundry service in Kojima, paying them double the usual rate, but the indigo ended up ruining most of the machinery. To placate the angry owner, Maruo Clothing bought up all his washing machines and placed them in every free corner of their building. Their sewing factory now doubled as a washing operation. When the machines could not handle the increasing loads, the employees dropped jeans into backyard trenches filled with water and hung them to dry from ledges and beams.

The brand's "one-wash" denim saw better sales, but to completely replace their struggling uniform business, the company needed to turn the passionate niche for jiipan into a mass consumer trend. The success of fellow Okayama native Kensuke Ishizu inspired Maruo Clothing to target youth directly, much like VAN had done. Moreover, Maruo's Toshio Ōshima believed that Ivy left an important market opening: "Americans wore jeans more than chinos on campus, but VAN only carried chinos." During a friendly chat, Ishizu told Kashino that they should first try to win over Isetan—the Shinjuku department store that acted as Tokyo's arbiter of style.

The subsequent meeting at Isetan was disastrous. The department store buyers gasped at Maruo's one-wash denim, "You already washed these pants? We only sell new products! What in the world are you thinking?" At the end of the meeting, the buyer threw the pair on the ground in disgust. After being chased out of Isetan, Kashino tried rival department store Seibu, but the buyers there voiced similar concerns about selling prewashed pants. And they balked at offering a product normally distributed through dingy G.I. surplus shops.

At the same time that Maruo Clothing was being shot down by traditional retailers, they also faced new competition in Tokyo from a denim brand called Edwin. The brand's founder, Yonehachi Tsunemi, ran an American surplus business that imported used jeans from the U.S. While Maruo worked on Canton, Tsunemi ramped up his own Japan-made jeans line under the brand name Edwin (*Edo-uin*). Tsunemi claimed Edwin to be a jumble of the letters for "denim" with the "M" turned upside down (or perhaps a reference to U.S. Ambassador Edwin Reischauer), but Maruo Clothing saw the title as an aggressive boast—"Edo," the old name for Tokyo, was going to "win" against companies in Western Japan.

To please the Japanese department stores and maintain their lead against Edwin, Maruo Clothing set out to create an original jeans brand. They convinced Cone Mills in North Carolina to send them any and all scraps, short yards, and factory seconds. Once supply was secure, they hunkered down to think up a catchy name. At the time, Kashino espoused the belief that all good brand names—like Nissan, Bridgestone, and Kirin—ended in an "n" sound. Japanese brands also created foreign-sounding brands by

An early advertisement (left) and sales tag (right) for Big John jeans 1968. (© Big John)

playing with the founder's name: whiskey brand Suntory came from the "Torii-san" of founder Shinjirō Torii. Using this technique, Ōshima and Kashino tinkered with variations on Ozaki's first name, Kotarō. Since the "ko" sound used the Japanese character for "small," and the American equivalent of Tarō would be "John," they came up with "Little John" jeans. But they did not want to mock their boss's diminutive 4'11" stature, so they decided to go with "Big John" instead. The name sounded like an authentic American brand, reminding them of "Big John" Kennedy (JFK).

In 1967, Maruo Clothing debuted its straight-leg, preshrunk Big John M1002 jeans. The attached paper sales tag promised "Authentic Western Jeans" and showed a man being thrown off a rodeo bull. At least in its iconography, Big John jeans appeared to most young Japanese to be smuggled from the Western frontier of the United States. Sales were immediately strong. By picking up the line, Seibu became the first department store in Japan to offer denim. The once patronizing Isetan called a few months later to sheepishly ask for a chance to also carry the prewashed Big John line.

Thanks to an affordable price point, youth snapped up Big John jeans. But, in 1967, the majority of fashionable Tokyo teens stuck to the two proper looks of the era—American Ivy and European Continental. For jeans to take off with the same force as VAN, Maruo Clothing needed more than a new brand name—it needed a revolution.

JUST A FEW MONTHS AFTER VAN DOCUMENTED EAST COAST campuses in *Take Ivy*, those very campuses transformed into radical hotbeds of cultural experimentation and antiwar demonstrations. The students' clean-cut look of button-down collars, flat front khakis, and smooth Vitalis hair unraveled into T-shirts festooned with political slogans, frayed jeans, and unkempt locks. A handful of isolated campus troublemakers dominoed into a full-scale, nationwide counterculture—a merger of left-wing, pacifist activism with bohemians advocating for psychedelic consciousness and a return to less materialistic living.

Japanese youth were going through similar but much less profound psychic shifts at the time. The constitutional ban on war prevented Japanese men from being conscripted to assist the U.S. effort in Vietnam. Very few people had access to recreational drugs, and the country's consumer society was too nascent to warrant an anti-materialist backlash. Yet disobedience was in the air. Radical youth turned their back on the work-obsessed Japanese lifestyle and challenged the right-wing status quo. Different subcultures pursued different goals, but they all agreed on a favorite article of rebellious clothing—blue jeans.

The largest countercultural force at the time in Japan was the Marxist student movement. Youth activism first erupted on a mass scale in 1960, when hundreds of thousands gathered in front of the National Diet Building to protest against the *Ampo* Japan-U.S. Security Treaty. As the decade progressed, dozens of leftist student cells formed on elite college campuses to chart a course further

Student demonstration on the train tracks of Shinjuku Station, October 1968.
(©Jiji Photo)

leftward than the Japanese Communist Party. Marxist sects poured
into the streets for battle with the police, armed with long wooden
sticks called *gebabō* and the occasional Molotov cocktail. After a
few initial skirmishes, the student revolution began in full on October 8, 1967, when young protesters demonstrated at Haneda
Airport against Prime Minister Satō's trip to the U.S., to promise
further support of the Vietnam War. As political action combined
with protests against tuition increases, the student movement began to occupy university buildings across Japan, with the Zenkyōtō
"Joint Struggle" famously barricading Yasuda Auditorium inside
the University of Tokyo for an entire year.

Marxist students also took their armed struggle to the city
streets. Shinjuku became the scene of political demonstrations on
Saturday nights, which inevitably descended into fights with riot
police. These tear gas-soaked clashes only added to the neighbor-

hood's reputation for decadence. Shinjuku had long rivaled Ginza as a nightlife destination, but where Ginza was Western European and stunningly illuminated, Shinjuku lurked in the shadows with a vaguely Russian flavor. In the 1950s, Shinjuku bars became home to Japan's beats and existentialists, and by the mid-1960s, the back alleys filled up with modern jazz and go-go clubs. As word came from overseas about the psychedelic movement, dozens of underground bars appeared with names like LSD and Underground Pop.

By 1967, a new breed of rebellious teens took over the east side of Shinjuku train station—homeless youth known as the Vagabond Tribe (*fūten-zoku*). Unlike their Marxist peers, the Vagabonds did not involve themselves in political struggle; they simply dropped out. They sat around a cluster of shrubs called the "Green House," bumming cigarettes from friends and having afternoon trysts in the bushes. When they needed pocket money, they took the occasional day job. With no LSD in the country and a pitiful supply of marijuana, most Vagabonds took a cocktail of prescription drugs—sleeping pills, tranquilizers, and menstrual cramp relievers. They also partook in the nasty habit of huffing paint thinner in clear plastic bags. The *New York Times* also noted, "All of the fūten-zoku, it is said, are expert go-go dancers."

It would be easy to cast the Vagabonds as "Japan's answer to the hippies" if not for a separate youth tribe called the *hippie-zoku*. Unlike the bedraggled, alienated, jazz-loving fūten-zoku, Japanese hippies borrowed their bohemian identity directly from the United States. They listened to American rock and dreamed of moving to communal farms in the countryside. The Vagabonds, by comparison, did not plan on going anywhere beyond Shinjuku.

At both groups' peak, two thousand hairy teens crowded Shinjuku station each night. Hardcore hippies only made up 20 percent of the area's youth crowd, but they were joined each weekend by the *tsūten* (a pun on the word for commuting)—fūten-zoku who would transform into their ragged state only once they reached the train station. Illustrator and youth culture chronicler Yasuhiko

Japanese hippies at a rock festival, 1971. (©Kyodo)

Kobayashi explains, "Most Japanese hippies still had to conform to social conventions. A lot of kids would only be hippies limited to a specific area. They were hippies with their friends, but they looked normal until they got there."

Despite being on the fringe of society, Shinjuku's counterculture greatly influenced the street styles of the era. Blue jeans were the unifying factor between these disaffected tribes, and received the most attention. Fashion critic Makoto Urabe wrote retrospectively, "Jeans were the optimal thing to wear in the violent expression of youth power." The fūten-zoku and hippie-zoku both borrowed their basic wardrobe from their American counterparts—T-shirts, dirty jeans, and sandals. The leftist radicals built upon that with more battle-friendly accessories—sturdy shoes, towels to shield their faces from cameras and tear gas, and colored hard hats with logos identifying their sect.

The Japanese counterculture never grew to the numbers seen in the United States, but in their role as the cultural vanguard, the Shinjuku movement shifted youth away from neatly-pressed cotton chinos to rough-and-ready clothing. Trendy consumers who would have been VAN shoppers in 1965 now bought blue jeans from local surplus stores. The political and cultural revolt expanded the jeans market, which grew from two million pairs sold in 1966 to seven million in 1969.

Counterculture's growing influence came at the expense of Ivy, which came under ideological attack from Japanese radicals. Agitated Marxist revolutionaries saw the United States as the great enemy and pointed out that the elite planners of the war in Vietnam wore button-down shirts. Underground theater castigated VAN as a meaningless "non-political" entity in a politically-charged era. A character in countercultural dramatist Shūji Terayama's play *Throw Away Your Books, Run into the Streets!* proclaimed, "We hate the spoiled sons of good families, with their VAN jacket thrown over the seat of their sports car, with Kensuke Ishizu's *Practical Guide to Style for Men* hidden in their pocket."

On a more basic level, Ivy looked staid set against the era's turmoil. After years of symbolizing teenage delinquency, Ivy had come to represent conventional fashion. As Yoshio Sadasue explains, "Ivy ultimately became 'PTA fashion' because it was the clothes that your father and mother would be most relieved to see you wearing." Even the men who brought Ivy to Japan rethought their affiliation with the style. Toshiyuki Kurosu once said, "When I started wearing Ivy, it was the clothes of the antiestablishment. But then America—the model for Ivy—went bad, and I could no longer hide my disappointment."

Maruo Clothing originally hoped that teens would buy blue jeans along with cotton chinos in their embrace of America, but by the end of the 1960s, teens looked to jeans as the most powerful antidote to Ivy style. Ironically, Japanese youth's act of rebellion against American hegemony involved wearing the most iconic piece of American clothing ever. Despite this obvious hypocrisy, no one dared return to traditional Japanese clothing, and the industry had positioned European clothing as even more elegant and bourgeois than East Coast fashion. By the late 1960s, Japanese society

Big John advertisements from late 1960s featuring real American hippies.
(©Big John)

offered only two extreme poles of youth fashion—from but-toned-up Ivy to shaggy hippie—and classic American items fleshed out the style on both sides.

At first, Japanese denim brands Big John, Canton, Edwin, and Big Stone played up their association with cowboys and the American West. But at the end of the 1960s, Maruo Clothing adapted its advertising to conjure up the fun and sun of counter-cultural California. The ads started with a fresh-faced surfer vibe—folky types with colored jeans frolicking on a West Coast campus. The next wave of advertisements went further with real hippie models, pulling visuals deep from the bowels of San Fran-cisco counterculture.

These hippies would have looked completely alien in the small town of Kojima, but, despite this cultural distance, Big John found a winning business strategy in embracing the youthquake. In 1970, Japanese domestic brands sold four times the amount of American imports, and Ozaki's once failing uniform company held the top spot. The counterculture saved Maruo Clothing, but the company started to worry, could jeans grow beyond the radicals?

HIPPIES AND LEFTISTS CREATED THE FIRST SIGNIFICANT market for Japanese jeans, but to achieve true mainstream success, the denim pants needed to establish an identity independent of fanatical groups. Fortunately for Big John and the other brands, Japan's youth rebellion flamed out spectacularly in the early 1970s.

Some of this came from increased police suppression. In a highly symbolic act, law enforcement arrested the entire Japanese cast of the rock musical *Hair* for possession of marijuana in February 1970. Cops then cleaned out Shinjuku's Green House, and the remaining hardcore hippies fled Tokyo to form communes on abandoned islands.

Next went the student movement. On March 31, 1970, members of the Red Army Faction—a militant, underground offshoot of the Japanese New Left—hijacked a Japan Airlines flight en route from Tokyo to Fukuoka with samurai swords, handguns, and dynamite, and hitched a ride to their Marxist "ally" North Korea.

The incident marked a violent new era for the student movement, with the majority of the casualties arising from skirmishes between rival leftist factions. These internal rifts steadily chipped away at the student movement's already damaged legitimacy. Public support of the New Left fully collapsed in February 1972 when a group called the United Red Army holed up in a mountain lodge called Asama-sansō and engaged with police forces. In a saga that unfolded live in front of a nationwide television audience, the radicals killed two officers and one civilian. The deaths shocked the public, but even more horrifying news was yet to come: in custody, sect leaders admitted to executing fourteen of their own group members weeks earlier in an ideological training gone awry. After the wanton murder at Asama-sansō and then the Japanese Red Army's attack on Israel's Lod Airport in May 1972 that left twenty-six dead, student groups appeared to be a greater evil than the conservative forces they opposed. Political fervor evaporated from Japanese youth culture overnight.

This dissipation of extreme cultural and political elements allowed the more moderate Sixties aesthetic—dressed-down, down-to-earth, back-to-basics—to win over a mass audience. Jeans benefitted the most: the industry sold an extraordinary fifteen million pairs in 1971, which tripled to forty-five million in 1973. This was enough denim material to go to the moon and back ninety times. The key to success was the bell-bottom. The straight-leg and slim cuts looked best on men, but the flared leg spoke equally to both sexes, thus doubling the market.

Maruo Clothing's massive success with Big John spread to Kojima's other manufacturers. By the early 1970s, Maruo's sales impressed Cone Mills enough to warrant a stable supply of high-quality denim. In 1971, Maruo president Kōtaro Ozaki recruited his younger brother at Yamao Clothing Industry to launch a lower-priced denim line called Bobson. Kanewa Clothing sewed pairs for Edwin, and after two years, started its own jeans brand, John Bull. The city once known for manufacturing the country's school uniforms now produced almost all of its blue jeans. But even with such competition, the brands made a nearly identical product. Former John Bull employee and Capital founder Toshikiyo Hirata complains, "The only way the brands would distinguish themselves was through the stitch design on the back pocket."

Just as Kojima ramped up production of Japanese-sewn jeans, however, the American supply route for denim cloth started to run dry. Labor strikes at factories in the U.S. South resulted in late or inadequate shipments, causing Japanese jeans makers to miss orders. The many textile mills and indigo dyeing plants in Okayama and the nearby Fukuyama area of Hiroshima seemed like an obvious alternative source of fabric, but no Japanese company had yet mastered the art of making the heavy denim used in jeans.

Japanese mills and dyeing plants had spent the 1960s selling inexpensive, high-quality cloth to global markets, but this system came to an abrupt end in 1970 when the Nixon Administration asked Japan to slow down its textile exports to heal the "injury" to struggling Southern mills. Nixon then decoupled the dollar from gold, which took the yen up from its artificially weak rate of ¥360 to the dollar to ¥308. Between the closing of America and a more expensive product, Japanese textile mills could no longer rely on exports—previously 95 percent of their business. With Kojima nearby, denim became an obvious domestic market to explore.

Around the time of the "Nixon shock," Big John started working together with nearby textile mill Kurabō (Kurashiki Bōseki) on an attempt to make the first true domestic denim. They wanted something that could compete against Cone Mills's "686," a 14.5-oz preshrunk denim used in Levi's straight-leg zipper-fly 505s. Kurabō first needed to retool its machinery to spin heavy cotton yarns previously unknown in Japan. Next the company searched for a partner who could dye indigo in a way that produced the "white-center" of American denim.

Kurabō eventually called upon Kaihara in Fukuyama, Hiroshima, an imperially-recognized dyer and weaver of *kasuri* cloth used in traditional kimonos since 1893. Kaihara found its niche in the postwar exporting indigo-dyed sarongs to the Islamic world, but, in 1967, relations with their importer in Aden broke down after the British fled the Yemeni city. With Kaihara months away from bankruptcy, the company bet its entire future on denim. After hearing offhand that Cone Mills used something called "rope dyeing," the president's son, Yoshiharu Kaihara, worked with master craftsmen to design a mechanical system that would continuously move yarn in and out of indigo baths.

Kaihara's resulting color looked authentic to the American original, and Kurabō's new denim KD-8 was on par with that of Cone Mills. Eight years after making Canton jeans exclusively from imported parts, Maruo could now produce "pure Japanese jeans" for Big John with everything sourced locally. Japan's YKK provided the zippers, while Mitsubishi and Jūki regauged their sewing machines to handle thick denim. Kurabō put KD-8 in front of Bob Haas, Jr. of Levi's, who praised their handiwork and purchased five hundred thousand yards for use in the company's Far East operations.

While jeans originator Levi Strauss & Co. maintained only a small presence in Japan to monitor imports, its American rivals were moving in. Long-time denim importer Horikoshi established Lee Japan in 1972, and VAN partnered with textile maker Tōyōbō and trading company Mitsubishi to form Wrangler Japan in 1972. By the mid-1970s, Japanese consumers had access to an enormous variety of jeans—from pseudo-American domestic lines like Big John, Bobson, Betty Smith, Bison, John Bull, and Edwin to real American heritage brands Levi's, Lee, and Wrangler. In the twenty-five years between 1950 to 1975, the Japanese denim market went from a rubbish pile of soldiers' dirty jeans to a ubiquitous and competitive retail network. Toshiyuki Kurosu wrote in early 1973, "Jeans have gone beyond 'being in style' or 'widely worn.' They've fully rooted as part of our contemporary culture to the degree that people are calling this the 'Jeans Generation.'" Big John parlayed its first-mover advantage into a long-held leadership position—selling nearly ¥15 billion worth of jeans in 1976 ($210 million in 2015 dollars) compared to Edwin's ¥6.5 billion ($90 million in 2015 dollars) and Levi's Japan's ¥5.6 billion ($78 million in 2015 dollars).

In the overabundance of the 1970s, Japanese youth no longer needed to pour their life savings into a single pair. Most teens could afford to own five or six. Shops popped up in small towns across Japan specializing in blue jeans and denim repair. The constant demand for denim provided significant economic benefits in both Okayama and Hiroshima prefectures, breathing new life into indigo dyeing factories, cotton mills, and sewing operations. Everyone under the age of twenty-two needed jeans, and the Japanese were now self-sufficient in their own supply. The diversifying jeans market also saw increased demand for pre-worn looks, which in turn created a new industry in Kojima around washing, bleaching, and stressing raw denim.

The final barrier to the full acceptance of jeans in Japanese society was, ironically, an American. In May 1977, fifty-six-year-old Osaka University Adjunct Professor Philip Karl Pehda chastised a denim-clad coed in his classroom for being improperly dressed: "The woman wearing jeans needs to get out!" After leaving the room, the student lodged a formal complaint against her ornery professor, asking administrators why men could wear jeans on campus but women could not. The so-called "Jeans Controversy" dominated media around the country for several weeks. Pehda would not budge from his dogmatic anti-jeans stance, giving *The Japan Times* pointed quotes such as "Women should be first-class women. Women who come to classes in jeans are second-class women." The American stood alone in these sentiments. Most educators sided with the young female in jeans, and schools nationwide amended their official dress codes to allow women to wear denim. Twenty years after the first importation of new jeans and ten after the debut of Big John, the famed American blue denim pants were officially written into the national wardrobe.

FIVE

Cataloging America

IN AUGUST 1969, JUST DAYS AFTER THE WOODSTOCK MUSIC festival, illustrator Yasuhiko Kobayashi and *Heibon Punch* editor Jirō Ishikawa walked into a Doubleday bookstore in New York City, where they came upon an entire wall covered with a single magazine. Its cover photograph showed a "blue marble" Earth floating above the moon in the blackest of outer space. The title read: "*Whole Earth Catalog*, access to tools." Unbeknownst to the two men upon their first encounter, this magazine would not just shape Japanese fashion for the 1970s, but forever change the look of all Japanese magazines.

The *Whole Earth Catalog* was American artist-activist Stewart Brand's hypersaturated guide to tools necessary for self-sustainable communities. Brand hoped the catalog's pages would develop the "power of the individual to conduct his own education, find his own inspiration, shape his own environment, and share his adventure with whoever is interested." Kobayashi and Ishikawa pulled the magazine down and skimmed its pages. Neither could make any sense of it. Why was it printed on such low-quality paper? Why was it in black-and-white like cheap Japanese comic

Yasuhiko Kobayashi on his first trip to the U.S. in 1967. (Courtesy of Yasuhiko Kobayashi)

books? Why did it include full reprints of other catalogs? Kobayashi put it back on the shelves.

This was perhaps the most confusing thing the two men had ever encountered on their travels for Kobayashi's column "Illustrated Reportage," the Japanese media's first attempt to cover overseas culture and fashion in real time. Instead of taking photos of foreign lands, Kobayashi sketched vignettes of his travels paired with short essays. The two men kicked off the column in September 1967, penetrating into a countercultural America that had yet to make a mark on Japan. They met hippies in San Francisco's Haight-Ashbury district, experienced the psychedelic revolution in Manhattan's East Village, and dined with black nationalists in Harlem. These dispatches helped move Japanese youth—as well as the authors—towards the far-out tastes of their foreign peers. By the end of 1967, both Kobayashi and Ishikawa shed their Ivy button-down dress shirts and grew out their hair.

The next year Kobayashi and Ishikawa traveled to Europe for the column, feeding the increased interest in Continental style among Japanese youth. In London, they observed ghost-like hippie men with long hair, pale skin, dark sunglasses, and musty antique clothing. In Paris, they introduced readers to the preppy look of students in double-breasted navy blazers hanging around Saint-Germain-des-Prés.

For 1969's installment, Kobayashi and Ishikawa debated whether it would be appropriate to return to the United States. Japan's Marxist student movement was in full bloom, and the war in Vietnam was tarnishing America's image even among non-political types. In a 1968 public opinion poll from national broadcaster NHK, only 31 percent of Japanese answered "I like America," tumbling from a postwar high of 49 percent in 1964. In the same survey, 30 percent of Japanese respondents wanted to travel to Europe compared with only 13 percent for the United States.

Kobayashi understood this hostility towards the U.S. He loved American culture—especially jazz and Hawaiian music—and spent many weekends drinking beers with American soldiers near the Navy base in Yokosuka. But he despised the United States' military presence across Asia: "During the day, we screamed, 'Go home, American bastards!' and at night we would party with soldiers. We were leading completely contradictory lives."

Kobayashi's first journey to the United States in 1967, however, had revealed thousands of young Americans calling for political and cultural change he agreed with. He and Ishikawa eventually decided to return for a few weeks in the summer of 1969, where they found an even stronger push towards radicalism in New York. Looking to bring back proof of this transformation, Kobayashi's mind kept returning to the mysterious *Whole Earth Catalog*. He did not understand what it was but he assumed it held a blueprint for the new America. He returned to Doubleday at the end of the trip and picked up a copy.

If the format of *Whole Earth Catalog* was confusing to Kobayashi, its message made even less sense. The pioneers of Japan's nascent pop culture celebrated consumerism—jazz, rock 'n' roll, Ivy clothing, diner food, sports cars, and electronic appliances. By

Drawing of America's eco-friendly cultural movement in 1972 edition of "Illustrated Reportage." (©Yasuhiko Kobayashi)

contrast, Stewart Brand asked American youth to forget meaning-less, fleeting trends of mass culture and go back to building civilization with their own hands. The Japanese could understand hippies as the latest trend in American music and fashion, but the *Whole Earth Catalog* moved along a completely different vector. It encouraged a revolutionary set of values, ideas, and practices intended to change the very essence of society. Back in Japan, Kobayashi shared his copy among friends, but no one could make heads or tails of it.

In 1970, Kobayashi and Ishikawa returned to New York for another round of "Illustrated Reportage." This time around, Brand's vision looked prescient. "Being back in New York after a year," Kobayashi wrote in his column, "the thing I feel most strongly is young Americans' attitudes about going 'back to nature.'" Kobayashi had long considered the United States the "Kingdom of the Automobile," yet he found men and women intentionally *running* around Central Park—a new form of exercise called "jogging." In the Park's open green spaces, he saw teenagers throw around strange plastic disks known as "frisbees." On country roads, young bearded men hitchhiked across the nation while carrying all of their possessions on their back in large daypacks. And America was no longer a land of hamburgers and hot dogs: co-ops offered long-haired patrons in New York and San Francisco endless choices of organic and health food. For the column, Kobayashi examined the do-it-yourself agriculture of *Mother Earth News*, and stripped off his clothes in Hawaii with fellow *Punch* staff to interview members of a nudist colony.

Compared to drugs and radical politics, a return to simplicity made sense to Kobayashi. He says, "I very much welcomed the new American lifestyle because I was already interested in outdoor sports. This whole movement was very close to my life. I found it much easier to cover than the hippies." In the early 1970s, Kobayashi dropped any Ivy remnants for an outdoor-friendly fashion look—jeans, T-shirts, and loose sweaters. He traveled to Alaska and the Himalayas as a devotee of ecotourism, shaping himself into the closest thing Japan had to an unofficial ambassador for the *Whole Earth Catalog* movement.

His peers at *Heibon Punch*, on the other hand, were skeptical about his reports of a reformed America. Magazine editors still harbored anti-American feelings and looked instead to England as culture's guiding light. Japanese select shop UNITED ARROWS co-founder Hirofumi Kurino remembers, "In the early 1970s, everything was about London pop and glam rock. People in conservative clothes started wearing really pop clothes or slightly loud, feminine outfits." French elegance was another major influence. Japanese mass apparel maker Renown took the business suit market by storm in 1971 with seductive commercials for its new D'urban line starring French actor Alain Delon.

Even manufacturers of blue jeans looked to Europe to reposition their brands. Big John framed its pants with a European angle in an advertisement from the era: "British and French people's were don't like to mimic the American. But you will find the COCA COLA and BIG-JOHN (indigo jeans) were very popular amang European [sic]." Meanwhile, Wrangler Japan searched for new product ideas on the Riviera. President Yūsuke Ishizu (second son of VAN's Kensuke Ishizu) visited Saint-Tropez during the summer of 1973 and discovered legions of French women wearing completely bleached jeans. Within months, Wrangler Japan debuted its own tight "ice wash" denim.

On the surface, Japanese pop culture engaged more and more with European trends, but, on a deeper level, the country was going through a similar soul-searching about modern life that fueled America's "back-to-nature" drive. Years of economic growth, industrial expansion, and urban development had taken a toll on the archipelago's natural environment. Tokyo's air was thick with photochemical smog that stung eyes and induced fits of coughing. On July 18, 1970, the polluted air caused four girls in the suburbs to collapse on their school grounds. An anti-pollution movement mobilized middle-class voters to action. As Japan surpassed Western Germany as the second largest economy in the free world, citizens demanded that the government pause its singular pursuit of industrial production in order to clean up the air and water. Socialist Tokyo Governor Ryōkichi Minobe ran his successful 1971 reelection campaign on the slogan: "Give Tokyo back its blue sky!"

Then the 1973 OPEC oil embargo, known in Japan as the "Oil Shock," caused the first major economic slump of the postwar period. Consumers cut back on spending and focused their expenditures on essentials. Panicked about possible shortages, middle-aged women raided grocery stores and hoarded toilet paper. Ginza turned off its famous neon lights. Apparel sales plummeted.

The Japanese economy ultimately weathered the Oil Crisis much faster than expected, but for the years that followed, frugality took over the consumer mindset and influenced the arts. The anti-materialist allegory *Jonathan Livingston Seagull* was a bestseller in 1974. Urban modernity became passé. The *Annon-zoku—*

Yasuhiko Kobayashi in front of L.L. Bean headquarters in Maine. (Courtesy of Yasuhiko Kobayashi)

young readers of women's fashion magazines *An•An* and *Non•no*—dressed in folklore-inspired garb and fled to the countryside on the weekends by train to "discover Japan."

As Japanese youth turned their backs on Tokyo, once dismissive editors came around to Kobayashi's previously heretical idea that Japan had something new to learn from America. Yasuhiko Kobayashi was ready to preach his gospel, but now he needed the right media outlet to spread the word.

JAPAN'S COLLECTIVE STEP AWAY FROM MATERIALISM IN THE 1970s only added to the problems at *Heibon Punch*. After banner years in the 1960s, obscure avant-garde content and increased competition from salacious rivals like *Weekly Playboy* caused sales to plummet from nearly one million to three hundred thousand copies per issue. In response, Heibon Publishing dumbed down the content and purged everyone responsible for the editorial misdirection. This included Jirō Ishikawa of "Illustrated Reportage." *Punch*'s former editor-in-chief, Yoshihisa Kinameri, quit the company at the same time on an unrelated issue, and moved to a small

Debut issue of *Ski Life*. (©The Yomiuri Shimbun)

subsidiary called Heibon Planning Center. Kinameri convinced the departing Ishikawa to join him there.

Heibon Planning Center's core business was printing novelty playing cards, but when Kinameri arrived, card sales were grinding to a halt. In need of additional revenue sources, he looked for freelance editorial assignments. Newspaper publisher Yomiuri asked Kinameri to help revive its struggling skiing guide *Ski Tokushū*. The magazine was a cynical vehicle for collecting advertising from ski gear manufacturers, filled with dry technical diagrams and useless wisdom from graying ski masters. To provide a new editorial focus, the Heibon Planning Center chief assembled a crack team, including Ishikawa, Yasuhiko Kobayashi, and "the best freelance editor of all time," Hisashi Terasaki.

None of them knew the first thing about skiing, but Kobayashi recognized the magazine as the perfect outlet to report on the

Photos of skiers on the Alaska ski slopes from *Ski Life*. (©The Yomiuri Shimbun)

American outdoor boom. Up until this point, the Japanese ski world had found its inspiration in Europe; the best gear came from France or Germany, and people dreamed of skiing in the Alps. Under Kobayashi's guidance, the Heibon Planning Center crew chose to cover the Alaskan slopes instead. While in Anchorage, Kobayashi sketched his usual brand of illustrated reportage, and a photographer shot street snap-like portraits of groovy, bearded Americans on the snowy slopes zipped up in down jackets. Completely enthralled, the editors concentrated much more on the freewheeling ski lifestyle than on the sport itself.

The magazine hit stands in October 1974 as "*Ski Life: A Book that Rethinks Skiing.*" Yomiuri asked for a basic guide to skiing in

Japan, but instead received a winter fashion magazine made by non-skiers. This was, evidently, what teens wanted: the issue sold out in record time.

Emboldened by the success of *Ski Life*, Kinameri asked Yomiuri for another assignment. This time the publisher wanted a *mook* ("magazine-book") of high-end goods for men. Yasuhiko Kobayashi immediately thought of the *Whole Earth Catalog* and proposed to make a "Japanese version." But instead of a philosophical manifesto like Brand's publication, he wanted to make a mock mail-order catalog of American-made products: clothing, shoes, outdoor supplies, electronics, musical instruments, tools, and furniture.

The Heibon Planning Center team all grew up devouring discarded American mail-order catalogs—a medium they believed was the ultimate representation of life in the U.S. As Kobayashi explains it, "You could understand the entirety of American life from the Sears-Roebuck catalog." They imagined American families snuggled around the fireplace, flipping through the pages and dreaming of a better life. Since Japan lacked a culture of mail order, making such a catalog felt magical and foreign—like Americans producing a book of *ukiyo-e* woodblock prints.

The team set off to Colorado, New York, Los Angeles, and San Francisco to take photos of three thousand different objects from every walk of American life: Madison Avenue repp ties, cowboys' Pendleton knockabout cardigans, Jeff Ho's Zephyr Production surfboards, and the generic shovels, rakes, plows, screwdrivers, and pliers that sat in suburban garages. The resulting 274-page catalog drowned the reader in product shots, including sixteen pairs of Indian moccasins, twenty-three styles of Keds, twenty-four cowboy boots, forty tchotchkes from Columbia University, eighteen NFL helmets, twenty-nine acoustic guitars, thirteen pieces of Abercrombie & Fitch safari-print luggage, and three hundred pieces of turquoise jewelry. The back of the publication also included a fifty-six-page reprint of the 1974-1975 Hudson's Camping Headquarters mailer, with pages upon pages of tents, charcoal braziers, and sleeping bags. Ishikawa came up with the perfect publication name—*Made in U.S.A.*—after noticing a small tag printed with the slogan inside his jacket.

Made in U.S.A. arrived in bookstores in June 1975 with its cover displaying a pair of button-fly Levi's 501s, a hammer, a wood burning stove, an acoustic guitar, a Red Wing work boot, and a colonial-style chest of drawers. The introduction made it clear that this was not simply a mook of high-end goods—but a pictorial manifesto for a new era:

> Americans use the terms "catalog joy" and "catalog freak" for people who like to look at and collect well-known catalogs. The mook you are currently reading compiles American youth's favorite American-made lifestyle gear. We discovered a new way of living among American youth, who express their culture through these "tools." We thought that the catalog format could introduce this "new lifestyle" to Japanese youth. Additionally, this mook also works as a time capsule that captures Seventies youth culture, which can be a valuable resource for understanding the entire Earth in the late 1970s.

"Catalog joy" may not be an actual English expression, but in this opening blurb, the editors established their own *Whole Earth Catalog*-inspired mission to leave a record of material culture for future generations. *Made in U.S.A.* included a signed blessing from John R. Malott, Economic/Commercial Officer at the U.S. Embassy in Japan, "I believe that this *Made in U.S.A. Catalog* will introduce America's present life style, in all its various aspects, to Japan's young people."

Just like *Ski Life* before it, *Made in U.S.A.* was an immediate hit, selling over a hundred fifty thousand copies. While nominally a catalog of everything American, the first dozen pages focused on clothing brands: Levi's, Red Wing, J. Press, Pendleton, Eddie Bauer, The North Face, and Hunting World. The publication's success catapulted American fashion back into the limelight, and an entirely new generation of youth came to lust after American style. Since 1968, Japanese aesthetes had rejected the United States' monopoly control of global culture—but now classic, quintessential Americana was back. Instead of East Coast collegiate clothing, however, this new American trend focused on rough-and-ready outdoor gear, classic regular fit Levi's 501s, work boots, and sturdy backpacks slung over shoulders.

Beyond introducing many of these brands to the Japanese market for the very first time, *Made in U.S.A* also established the "catalog magazine" format—one that still provides the basic form for Japanese fashion media to this day. Never before had a magazine featured such a vast array of material objects. While *Men's Club* and *Heibon Punch* gave readers a wide menu of content such as inspirational photo shoots, essays, and panel discussions on current trends, *Made in U.S.A.* was simply a dump of raw information. Teens loved browsing its endless list of American goods.

Kobayashi and the other editors may have intended the format to help introduce the "tools" needed for an American lifestyle, but readers simply used the catalog as a detailed map right back to pre-Oil Shock materialism. Editor Hisashi Terasaki wrote many years later, "We got the initial idea from the *Whole Earth Catalog*, but we intentionally eschewed the philosophical part and focused on the goods. Youth who aspired towards a new lifestyle mostly cared about gear and material objects." Yasuhiko Kobayashi thought that the influence of outdoorsman catalogs would emphasize functionality in the fashion world—a more rational and socially-conscious justification for wearing clothing than mindless industry trends and planned obsolescence. This quickly descended, however, into an obsession over the technical specifications for items—"specs." Youth no longer wanted "American jeans" and "rain jackets"—they wanted "14-oz denim" and "60% cotton / 40% nylon parkas."

Made in U.S.A. re-excited young men about American clothing, but the garments featured inside were nearly unobtainable. The catalog mockingly listed prices in dollars, as if to say, "This is how much it costs, but you can't buy it." The only possible place to purchase the goods was Tokyo's notorious shopping district Ameyoko. Perusing the crowded and unkempt stalls required both bravery and patience. Vintage expert and apparel industry veteran Yōsuke Ōtsubo recalls, "Ameyoko only had a few small stores that sold American fashion goods, and the clothing was all piled up. The staff was scary, and you had to be accepted by them to really be a customer." Teens outside of Tokyo, meanwhile, begged the American military for part-time jobs so they could shop for imported goods in the base shops.

Taken as a style guide, *Made in U.S.A.* advocated a wardrobe of rugged, traditional American clothing and functional outdoor gear. This look, however, did not have a name until later in the year. In the fall of 1975, Yasuhiko Kobayashi started a new *Men's Club* column called *"Honmono sagashi tabi"* ("A journey in search of real things") that chronicled visits to traditional Japanese craftsmen making rubber-soled construction shoes, aprons, and knives. The article's sub-headline promised that the series would be a survey of "heavy-duty" things. Kobayashi thought Japan was too "delicate" and fashion-focused, and he wanted to introduce more of a "gruff, redneck" L.L. Bean feeling into the culture. He explains, "I started noticing the word 'heavy-duty' in catalogs. Everything was described as 'heavy-duty' something or other." Just as intended, Kobayashi's prominent use of "heavy-duty" resonated with readers, and within months, the term became the de facto name of the new American-inspired outdoor look.

While the rustic Americana of Heavy Duty looked very different from the polished Americana of Japan's 1960s Ivy boom, Kobayashi believed that Heavy Duty and Ivy were two sides of the same coin. Both were "systems" of clothing—a wide set of traditional garments worn according to the time, place, and occasion. Inside the Ivy system, students wore blazers to class, duffle coats in winter, three-button suits to weddings, tuxedos to parties, and school scarfs to football games. Inside the Heavy Duty system, men wore L.L. Bean duck boots in bad weather, mountain boots when hiking, flannel shirts when canoeing, collegiate nylon wind-breakers in spring, rugby shirts in fall, and cargo shorts when on the trail. In the introduction to his standalone *Heavy Duty Book*, Kobayashi wrote, "I call Heavy Duty 'traditional' because it's the outdoor or country part of the trad clothing system. You could even say that it's the outdoor version of Ivy."

Kobayashi later formalized the connection between Ivy and Heavy Duty in a September 1976 *Men's Club* piece titled "Heavy Duty Ivy Party Manifesto." He called for a new hybrid look called "Heavy Duty Ivy" (*hebi-ai*). The opening illustration showed a young man in mountain parka, Levi's 501s, and climbing boots. Readers used the article as a guide to wearing Heavy Duty cloth-ing in a more fashionable way than simply as outdoor gear. Despite Kobayashi inventing the style as a joke, his hypothesis was funda-mentally accurate: American university students, especially in rural locales like Dartmouth and the University of Colorado, dressed in a seamless combination of outdoor gear and classic Ivy style. They no longer wore blazers and repp ties but layered button-down shirts with down jackets, jeans, and sneakers.

Made in U.S.A. kicked off the Heavy Duty trend, but the "Heavy Duty Ivy Party Manifesto" widely popularized the style as town wear. By late 1976, kids appeared across Japan in perfect imitations of Kobayashi's illustrated characters from the "Heavy Duty Ivy Party Manifesto"—goose down vests, hiking boots, and 60/40 parkas. The down vest was previously completely unknown in Japan. When the Heibon Planning Center editors returned from Alaska in 1974 wearing them, passersby asked them if they had forgotten to take off their life jackets after yachting. By the Heavy Duty boom, Ginza looked like a weekly convention of res-cue-and-recovery workers.

Japanese brands also stepped in to capitalize on the Heavy Duty boom. The jeans market moved away from bell-bottoms, ice wash, and nautical trousers and back to copies of straight-leg Levi's 501s. Big John launched a new line of sturdy denim pants, jackets, and overalls called World Workers through faux-vintage

Big John World
Workers advertisement
from mid-1970s.
(©Big John)

ads of grizzled, middle-aged Caucasian men standing beside cars rusting out in the countryside. VAN Jacket ran campaigns "Good Old American Jacket" and "Ride On! Tweed Jacket," and, in Fall 1975, gave three thousand lucky customers a full carpenter's kit as part of "My Woody Country." In 1976, VAN opened its own Heavy Duty brand called SCENE.

Heavy Duty continued to dominate the menswear market in Japan for the second half of the 1970s. Yasuhiko Kobayashi's "back-to-nature" vision became a reality—at least in appearances. Inspired by *Whole Earth Catalog*, Kobayashi and his compatriots at the Heibon Planning Center brought Japan's nascent youth culture from its deepest anti-American moment back to its American origins. Styles may have shifted from East Coast to West Coast, but America was back on the map.

Unlike the 1960s, however, the cultural pioneers were not the founders of clothing brands, but a small clique of rogue freelance magazine editors. Youth looked to the glossy pages of monthly publications to discover new styles, and the editors pushed their own idiosyncratic tastes on this captive audience. So when the Heibon Planning Center group themselves grew bored of Heavy Duty, they prepared to take readers to a new place—one with sunnier climes.

Buoyed by the success of the *Made in U.S.A.* catalog, Yoshihisa Kinameri and Jirō Ishikawa returned to Heibon Publishing in 1976 on the condition that they would be allowed to launch a new magazine of their choosing. The two editors knew that whatever they made would follow their tried-and-true catalog format, but they struggled to find a new style concept distinct from Heavy Duty. Desperate for ideas, Kinameri and Ishikawa drove out to Yasuhiko Kobayashi's house for a brainstorming session. Kobayashi gave them two words to define the new magazine's cultural milieu—"polo shirts." This sounded insane: in Japan, only middle-aged golfers wore polo shirts. Kobayashi countered that they were the favorite of UCLA and USC students. This convinced Kinameri and Ishikawa, who, right then and there, agreed to focus their new magazines on the athletic lifestyle of West Coast teens. Ishikawa boarded a plane to Los Angeles with six others for a fifty-day junket to collect material for the first issue.

Ishikawa wanted to call the new magazine "City Boys," but rival subcultural magazine *Takarajima* already called itself "The Manual for Cityboys." Weeks prior, Kinameri saw the cartoon character Popeye's name written out in English for the first time, and realized that it split into "pop eye." This would make the perfect magazine name—keeping an "eye" on "pop." Popeye had been a popular figure among Japanese youth in the late 1950s, and the cartoon sailor vividly brought back childhood memories for Kinameri's generation. The much younger Ishikawa hated it, imagining the phone calls he would have to make in Los Angeles that started with, "Hi, I'm calling from *Popeye* magazine… no, it's not a comic book." Kinameri ignored his junior's naysaying and

Debut issue
of *Popeye*,
Summer 1976.
(©Magazine
House)

negotiated for weeks with the Japanese representative of King
Features Syndicate to secure the rights.

Popeye debuted in June 1976 with the subtitle "Magazine for
City Boys" and an airbrushed cartoon of Popeye smoking his corn
pipe. The cover story "From California" looked at hang-gliding
("Natural High"), skateboarding, jogging, and sneakers. Yasuhiko
Kobayashi's illustrated reportage provided a detailed shopping
map of the UCLA campus.

While most of the *Popeye* staff came directly from the *Made in
U.S.A.* editorial team, the magazine's aesthetic was distinct from
the Heavy Duty trend. The outdoor boom's flannel shirts and
hiking boots conjured up rocky mountains obscured in autumnal
grays. The style was also inherently nostalgic—going "back" to
nature and older forms of living. By contrast, the 1976 *Popeye*
world was a sunny take on life in California, where youth were
carving out the future for the rest of civilization. West Coast teens

invented new sports, wore new kinds of clothing, and took up new healthy values. Los Angeles youth culture felt like a bright light in a dark America still recovering from Vietnam and Watergate.

In his opening editor's note, Kinameri wrote that Japan was in a "state of drift," and he wanted to introduce youth to a more health-conscious lifestyle. The editors proposed sports as the anchor for Japan's future: "We think that a life of athletics will be very important for your personal health as well as the survival of contemporary man. The idea of having fun while playing sports is a wonderful message from our American peers. We should use all of our free time on sports, no matter how trivial the activity."

Japanese people of all ages loved watching sports like baseball and sumo, but few did anything athletic after high school. The dense sprawl of Tokyo severely limits space for public parks and fields. Golf was exclusive to white-collar executives charging exorbitant green fees to the company card. The *Popeye* editors thus found inspiration in UCLA students exercising and playing outdoors, right in the middle of an urban setting. Frisbee, skateboarding, and roller-skating, in particular, would work well in Japan since they required no specialized recreational facilities or organized teams.

For the debut issue, *Popeye* editors focused on the accessible sport of skateboarding as a way to turn young readers on to athletics. The magazine's coverage of the California-based skate movement was not just new to Japan but timely even by American standards. Just a year before *Popeye*'s debut issue, *Skateboarder* magazine re-opened, the legendary Zephyr Productions' "Z-Boys" team formed in Santa Monica, and the Del Mar Fairgrounds hosted the first major skateboarding tournament since the 1960s. *Popeye* covered Jeff Ho's Zephyr shop in the first issue, and, in good catalog fashion, laid out thirty-one different skateboards on two pages. As a publicity stunt, the forty-six-year-old editor-in-chief, Yoshihisa Kinameri, skateboarded around Tokyo's Roppongi neighborhood late at night in California-style short-shorts. The sport caught on with incredible speed. *Popeye* helped establish a true skate culture in Japan. Today, the All Japan Skateboard Association recognizes the magazine's debut as a key moment in the sport's local history.

Popeye's focus on California also bolstered the Japanese surfing scene. Japan has dozens of decent beaches, but no one thought to ride the waves until Americans brought the sport to the Chiba and Shōnan beach areas after the war. In 1971, there were fifty thousand official members of Japan's surfing clubs, but after *Popeye* turned its attention to surfing, Japan's surfer population became the third largest in the world. Then, in 1977, surfer fashion left the beaches and went urban. Thousands of teens in fake tans, tank tops, short shorts, bead belts, and rainbow flip-flops amassed on the streets of Tokyo's Shibuya and Roppongi neighborhoods. Young women sported a long floppy Farrah Fawcett-like hairstyle called the "surfer cut." Even though hardcore beach bums derided city dwellers as *oka* surfers ("hill surfers"), the merger of sport with fashion made surfing a permanent part of pop culture for urban and coastal teens alike.

The *Popeye* editors succeeded in bringing a "sports boom" to Japan, at least with skateboarding and surfing. Like *Made in U.S.A.*, however, the magazine still focused most of their young readers' attention towards the fashion aspects of outdoor activities. The first issue of *Popeye* did not introduce sneakers in the context of arch support and a proper jogging stride, but as a trendy fashion item. *Made in U.S.A.* may have originated the catalog-cum-magazine format, but, by becoming a regularly publishing title, *Popeye* became the definitive "catalog magazine" that forever changed how fashion media communicated with readers. In each issue of *Popeye*, editors picked up hundreds of goods, laid them out in different categories, and then provided accurate prices, store addresses, and telephone numbers in order to connect readers with sponsoring retailers in Japan. This let teens shop before even setting foot in a store.

The format was widely successful, but came with a backlash. California in the late 1970s was rife with New Age spirituality, meditation, conspiracy theory, recreational drugs, and body tattoos, but critics noted that *Popeye* was interested only in "things that had a price tag." There was a saying in Japan that men's magazines needed the three Ss: sex, suits, and socialism. *Popeye* had none of these, and instead focused on material trappings. Many assumed *Popeye*'s wholesomeness was a part of the licensing deal for the Popeye name or a reflection of the "healthy" lifestyle. In reality, the editors liked commercial goods more than members of the opposite sex.

This materialist streak was also a direct reflection of Heibon Publishing's business strategy. Sponsors loved the catalog format for blurring the lines between editorial and advertising; Heibon loved making more money from big-brand advertising than from newsstand sales. Critics complained that *Made in U.S.A.* and *Popeye* bred a generation of "monomaniacs"—a bilingual portmanteau from the Japanese word *mono* meaning "goods." Compared to the Ivy boom of the Sixties, Japanese youth in the Seventies were not interested in wearing their new fashions as much as they were in owning clothing as a collection of material possessions. Youth no longer bought things as an avenue towards new experiences—record players to listen to jazz LPs, suits to impress girls, mountain parkas for hiking. Youth fetishized goods *as* goods.

While *Popeye* launched many new trends—UCLA T-shirts, skateboarding, surfing, and sneakers—the actual magazine sold poorly for the first few years. Heibon Publishing printed a hundred sixty thousand copies of the debut issue, but retailers returned half. *Popeye* did find, however, devoted readers among affluent teens who could afford to travel overseas. After the first issue, Japanese youth constantly invaded the UCLA student union, buying up all the small and medium sized T-shirts in bulk. Tour buses unloaded in front of sports stores across the U.S. where young Japanese men pointed to goods in *Popeye* for the staff to procure in their sizes.

At a higher level, *Popeye* proved that the renewed interest in America after *Made in U.S.A.* was not a fluke. Teens loved American goods again. This reversal seemed inexplicable to the lingering remnants of the Japanese counterculture, who suspected that dark forces were conspiring behind the scenes to manipulate the popular consciousness. The most damning piece of evidence was right on the credits page of *Popeye*'s debut issue: "With the support of the American Embassy of Tokyo United States Travel Service." This single sentence bred years of speculation—even from members of the *Popeye* staff—about whether the magazine received funding from the C.I.A. or other organs of the American government. The conspiracy theory postulated that the fervent revolutionary Marxist agenda of Japanese students in the late 1960s had convinced the C.I.A. to put together an operation to win over Japanese youth through "psy-op" techniques. Covert operatives funded publishers who filled their magazines with Nike sneakers and Patagonia rugby shirts.

Both Ishikawa and Kinameri have long denied American government funding, but it is widely known that the writers at Heibon Publishing did receive logistical assistance from the U.S. Embassy of Japan starting with "Illustrated Reportage." Japanese editors travelling to the United States needed guidance on where to stay and what to do, and until the 1980s, the American embassy was the best place in Tokyo to obtain that information. *Popeye*'s primary funding came from commercial entities with a clear business interest: airlines and trading companies underwrote *Popeye*'s overseas reporting in hopes that the stories would encourage Japanese youth to travel and buy imported goods.

Whether there was a conspiracy or not, the C.I.A. certainly must have been happy with *Popeye*'s results. America was cool again in Japan—seen as a bright, shiny place of hopes, dreams, and desirable fashion goods. Yasuhiko Kobayashi once quipped, "The U.S. government should erect a memorial in front of the American embassy in Japan thanking *Heibon Punch* and *Popeye*." From a nadir of only 18 percent "liking America" in 1974, NHK poll numbers went up to 27 percent in 1976, and then rose yearly until hitting 39 percent in 1980.

Many of the *Popeye* editors, however, remained skeptical of the United States. Staff writer Takashi Matsuyama admitted, "I was not especially interested in America. It's probably the country I hate most." Members of this generation often explain that they love "American culture," but hate "the American state." VAN's Paul Hasegawa elaborates on this feeling, "All of us maintained at the time that the 'United States' and 'America' were two different things. Coke, Major League Baseball, and Hollywood are all American, and we thought that you could separate those from the government."

But in the late 1970s, the Vietnam war was over, and the Occupation felt like ancient history. The latest generation of Japanese youth did not understand the roots of anti-Americanism. Kinameri and Ishikawa both loved the U.S. and believed that the new, healthy California lifestyle could fill the existential hole that existed in Japan after the collapse of the student movement. Kinameri explained, "There was something lacking in Japan. Ishikawa used to say, 'Let's just all become Americans!' Japan just wasn't cool or interesting."

Despite lackluster sales, the *Popeye* team kept pushing forward with their mission. The editors repeatedly flew to America, opened up the yellow pages in the hotel to discover new places to visit, and reported on their travels to their readership back home. On each trip, they would take oversized duffel bags to fill with items for review. Through this system, *Popeye*'s small team of editors, writers, and photographers took VAN Jacket's original information link between American and Japanese culture and updated it to operate in nearly real time.

JUST AS *POPEYE* USHERED IN THE WEST COAST CRAZE, THINGS were looking grim for the originators of the 1960s East Coast craze. On April 6, 1978, Kensuke Ishizu and other members of the VAN Jacket board announced the company's bankruptcy. At the time, this was the largest bankruptcy ever for an apparel company, and the fifth largest of any Japanese company in the postwar period. Police officers worried that Ishizu would try to take his own life, like so many Japanese executives before him, and personally escorted him home from the press conference.

What went wrong? Ishizu was a creative thinker, marketer, and salesman but as Paul Hasegawa explains, "He didn't really know how to balance his books. All of the top guys were skilled merchants, but it was far too much for them to manage a company of VAN's size." Influenced by their trading company partner Marubeni, VAN scrounged for higher revenues by expanding into every possible area. Beyond its two-dozen clothing labels, the company licensed overseas lines like Spalding Golf and Gant. It opened an interior goods shop, Orange House, a flower shop, Green House, and a theater called VAN 99 Hall.

As VAN diversified, revenue swelled. Compared to just ¥9.8 billion in 1971 ($159 million in 2015 dollars), VAN reached a peak of ¥45.2 billion in 1975 ($662 million in 2015 dollars). This pursuit of profit, however, drained the brand of any cachet. The company that teenagers once saved up for years to buy was now sold to suburban mothers in supermarkets looking for a bargain on tube socks. With piles of clothing sitting in warehouses, VAN started to run large-scale bargain sales, which further devalued the brand. And in the era of *Made in U.S.A.* and *Popeye* actively promoting the purchase of imported *honmono* (genuine) items rather than copies, VAN just could not compete. Paul Hasegawa says, "Levi's and Red Wings are real, authentic things. VAN could never be Levi's. VAN was a very innovative imitative creator but not 'the real thing.'"

Around 1976, sales plummeted beyond any repairable margin, and, by 1978, bankruptcy was the only option. Kensuke Ishizu volunteered to personally pay back ¥100,000 each month until the debts were settled, but his accountant noted that this would take four hundred years. After the bankruptcy, Ishizu retired from the apparel business; he told magazine *Studio Voice*, in 1980, "I have absolutely no interest in clothing right now."

June 10, 1978 issue of *Popeye* on VAN's legacy, with cover art by Kazuo Hozumi. (©Magazine House)

The bankruptcy came as a major shock to *Popeye* writer Tsuneo Uchisaka, who had worked as VAN's public relations officer in the mid-1970s. In response to the bad news, Uchisaka pitched editor-in-chief Kinameri on a cover story about VAN's legacy. Kinameri initially thought it untoward to run a hagiographic issue all about a company in the midst of a tragic bankruptcy. But after sleeping on it, he gave Uchisaka the green light. *Popeye* asked quintessential Ivy artist Kazuo Hozumi to draw the cover and interviewed the brand's former employees and friends. Uchisaka wrote the story like an alumni report from a university, believing "VAN wasn't a company, it was a school." From here he came up with a legendary piece of copy—"VAN was our teacher."

The opening paragraph of the main feature read, "We now know a lot about America, but the first people to teach us about America were Coke and VAN. We learned about the student life of Americans through VAN clothing and became aware of American sports through VAN ad campaigns. It's time to finally say, thank you, VAN." For its first two years, *Popeye* failed to achieve sales figures that matched its cultural leadership. But the June 10, 1978 issue on VAN was a runaway success—the most popular issue until that point, with 217,000 copies selling out on the spot.

Those who grew up on Ivy in the 1960s and 1970s picked up the issue out of nostalgia, but the VAN feature turned young readers on to classic East Coast fashion as well. Two years before, Yasuhiko Kobayashi pitched Heavy Duty as an alternative to Ivy, but now *Popeye* readers clamored for more information on Ivy itself. In just ten years, Japan made a cyclical pilgrimage through American looks—from Ivy to hippie to outdoor Heavy Duty to Heavy Duty Ivy to California campus clothes, and now back to East Coast style. On the solemn occasion of VAN's demise, Ivy style was rising from the ashes.

But this litany of American looks only applied to the wealthiest, most educated youth in Japan. Working class youth of the 1970s were also flocking to American style—but instead of hippies and surfers, they wanted something with a little more machismo.

SIX

Damn Yankees

In 1982, thirty-seven-year-old bar proprietor and fashion impresario Masayuki Yamazaki completed work on a five-story, pastel art deco retail space called Pink Dragon right between the youth shopping districts Harajuku and Shibuya. The first floor and basement sold clothing and accessories from Yamazaki's Fifties-inspired brand Cream Soda. Upstairs was an American-style diner called Dragon Cafe, complete with vinyl leopard-skin couches and a vintage jukebox. Yamazaki lived in a luxurious apartment on the top floor, and he carved off the second basement level as a rehearsal space for Black Cats, a rockabilly band under his patronage. The swimming pool on the roof was a truly gratuitous luxury, seeing that Yamazaki could not swim.

This extravagant compound stood as a monument to Yamazaki's successful business selling rock 'n' roll clothing to teens. After pocketing ¥2.8 billion ($33 million in 2015 dollars), he often compared Harajuku to an untapped "gold mine." But Yamazaki's riches came not just from creating a new fashion trend in the late 1970s to follow Ivy and Heavy Duty. He forged his own unique path to success by creating styles that appealed to a

Pink Dragon in Harajuku, circa 1995. (©Pink Dragon)

previously ignored group of youth: high school dropouts and juvenile delinquents.

Until the late 1970s, the vast majority of fashionable Japanese teens—whether pseudo-Ivy Leaguers, weekend hippies, chic backpackers, or UCLA groupies—came from privileged backgrounds. Brands and magazines assumed their audiences would enjoy white-collar careers with ever-climbing salaries and growing piles of disposable income. *Heibon Punch* prepped office drones for climbing up the corporate ladder, while *Popeye* lectured its "city boys" on which imported goods most impressed girls in collegiate tennis clubs.

In reality, very few Japanese youth had any experience with those affluent lifestyles. Less than 20 percent of men went to university in the 1970s, and even fewer women. Most teens, especially those living outside of the big cities, abandoned education after middle or high school and took blue-collar jobs. But by the 1970s, the economy was so strong that even teens in manual labor could buy clothes, drink with friends, and maintain their own vehicles.

When these working-class teens emerged as consumers, they did not follow the leads of their socioeconomic betters, but instead gravitated towards a new set of styles. As anthropologist Ikuya Satō discovered, blue-collar teenagers thought college kids were "effeminate and affected" and wanted clothing that manifested "outright showmanship tinged with deliberate vulgarity." Through Yamazaki and other media influences, these teens found their greatest inspiration in fearless rebels of the past—specifically, Japanese postwar ruffians and archetypal hard-ass juvenile delinquents from 1950s America. These two fashion streams eventually merged into a subculture known as *yankii*—a word which originally referenced roughneck "yankee" G.I.s, but later evolved into an original Japanese expression.

From his castle, Pink Dragon, Masayuki Yamazaki cavorted with the country's top fashion designers, models, stylists, and celebrities. But his sympathies long lay with small-town delinquents. At the height of his fame in 1977, Yamazaki wrote, "I want to be an outlaw—even a little snotty punk is fine." After being shunned for his iconoclastic style as a youth, Yamazaki hoped to make the silent majority of working-class teens proud of their outsider status. He wanted Japan to be a little more rock 'n' roll, and that is exactly what he got.

BORN IN 1945, MASAYUKI YAMAZAKI GREW UP IN THE HOK-kaidō coal-mining town Akabira. Yamazaki's father worked in the mine, while his mother worked part-time as a cleaner in executives' mansions. Living in a flimsy row house, Yamazaki searched for glamour where he could find it. He studied photos of Japan's top stars in celebrity magazines, but the best dressed in Akabira were always the neighborhood gangsters. From a young age, Yamazaki came to understand that "all cool fashion is delinquent fashion."

This statement was especially true in the first decade after the war. While the impoverished masses wore tattered rags, strong-armed youth gangs called *gurentai* ("band of thugs") cruised down-towns areas in three-piece suits. They not only had money to spend on clothing, but knew how to bribe American servicemen through Pan Pan Girls to procure fabric from military PXs.

Next came the *apure* (*après-guerre*) delinquents who epitomized a casual chic in un-tucked Hawaiian aloha shirts, nylon belts, rub-ber-soled shoes, and General MacArthur-style aviator sunglasses. The apure were most notorious for their "regent" (*riizento*) hair-style—the front up in a pompadour, sides slicked back with grease. Postwar youth revived this 1930s look in a calculated rebellion against the ubiquitous military cut. Parents hated the regent for its insult to austerity as well as its co-option of family funds to pay for black market pomade. Jazz musicians' and low-level mobsters' love of the look made it synonymous with the demimonde.

In middle school, Yamazaki took his first step into delinquent fashion with "mambo pants"—black, tapered, high-waisted trou-sers held up by suspenders. The garment took its name from a 1955 fad for mambo music, when young couples spent nights in sweaty clubs dancing to Latin rhythms. Mambo men wore one-button jackets with enormous shoulders, paired with loud shirts, skinny ties, and the aforementioned bottoms. Although the mambo boom quickly faded away, the distinct fashion and the clubs' dubious clientele turned the word "mambo" into a slang term for "young punk." Mambo pants then lived on as the favorite trou-ser style of rebellious teens.

The regent hairstyle got a further boost in 1958 when the me-dia went crazy for rockabilly singers Mickey Curtis, Masaaki Hi-rao, and Keijirō Yamashita. These Japanese Elvis Presley clones wore greasy curled pompadours, mambo trousers, and country-and-western-style jackets. They put on wild performances at the Nichigeki Theater's "Western Carnival," which attracted forty-five thousand in a week and had women flinging their underwear onto the stage. The rockabilly moment was brief, but lasted long enough to make the regent hairstyle popular with bad boys across the country. Thirteen-year-old Masayuki Yamazaki saw the spectacle on TV in Akabira and remembered it as "hugely influential—an intense shock."

Teenagers out in the sticks loved regents, mambo, and rockabilly, but wealthy Tokyo teens scoffed at the looks. Illustrator Yasuhiko Kobayashi explains, "Anyone who was a student really hated the look of Hawaiian shirts, regents, and mambo. They all looked like bad kids." The pompadour, in particular, signified a distinctly plebeian glamour. Wealthy beach bums of the Sun Tribe (*taiyō-zoku*) preferred a shorter, athletic hairstyle, and, by the early 1960s, the popular clean-cut Ivy League fashion buried the regent further as an old-fashioned relic.

Masayuki Yamazaki followed his girlfriend to Tokyo after high school, but within months, she left him for an interior designer. Yamazaki vowed to find a stylish job to win over a new belle. To update his personal style to match Tokyo's reigning Miyuki Tribe look, he bought himself a VAN suit with short-cropped pants, wore his hair in a Kennedy cut, and sported clunky dress shoes. The wardrobe landed him a job at the traditional menswear shop Mitsumine, in Shinjuku, where he learned the secrets of retail and even modeled for *Heibon Punch* as an exemplar of the Ivy look.

Everything changed one day when a fellow sales clerk rolled up wearing a black leather jacket, black shirt, slim black jeans, and a greasy regent. The boy hailed from the coastal city of Yokosuka, an hour outside of Tokyo and home to a working-class fashion movement called *sukaman* ("Yokosuka Mambo"). Hanging around the U.S. military base in Yokosuka, sukaman teens picked up style tips from the roughest enlisted men as well as debonair African-American soldiers. They ordered one-button "contemporary model" suits in lustrous materials from tailors near the base, in an intentional rejection of the slim, three-button Ivy model. Some of the sukaman teens imitated the closely cropped hair of American G.I.s, but the regent was more common.

Two *sukajan* (Yokosuka jumper) satin souvenir jackets. (Courtesy of fake alpha/Berberjin)

Sukaman teens loved the "souvenir jacket"—a rayon satin version of the classic American letterman baseball jacket, embroidered with Oriental eagles, tigers, and dragons on the back. Local Japanese teens called them *sukajan* ("Yokosuka jumpers") and snapped them up at stores targeting American sailors on shore leave. Yokosuka teens were the first to embrace the jackets as "colonial chic," but the garment went national after appearing on the main character of the 1961 film *Buta to Gunkan* ("Pigs and Battleships").

Illustrator Yasuhiko Kobayashi haunted the same bars as the Yokosuka Mambo and remembers, "Yokohama had a lot of nice restaurants and luxury bars for foreigners, but Yokosuka and Yokota were full of young navy guys—lots of American derelicts. They would wear delinquent-like clothing like jeans, and they'd whistle and curse." In Kobayashi's illustrated reportage of Yokosuka trends for *Heibon Punch Deluxe*, he used a very specific term to describe their look: "Yankee style." He explains, "We started to call American delinquent fashion 'Yankee.' Most kids lacked the money to imitate the older Americans who wore proper suits, but it was easy to dress like American delinquents."

The day after seeing his Yokosuka friend in the sukaman look, Masayuki Yamazaki ditched Ivy and slicked his hair up in a regent. In the summer of 1966, he quit Mitsumine and found a job at an unpopular resort in the beach town of Hayama to be closer to the sukaman action. While Yamazaki presided over an empty hotel, he watched elite college kids in Ivy style take over nicer establishments and strum folk songs on their guitars. He wrote later in life, "I got so pissed off every time I saw those guys serenading girls." Yamazaki came to see Ivy as a mark of the enemy. He read *Men's Club* each month just to "do the exact opposite of what was written."

By 1967, the sukaman style had spread to Tokyo, mixing with similar youth movements emerging in downtown working-class neighborhoods. The sukaman loved African-American soul singers like James Brown, whose curly and fluffy pompadour gave them further guidance for their regents. These teens dreamed of dancing with their girlfriends to soul records in Shinjuku clubs, but Tokyo go-go bars explicitly banned anyone with a regent or sunglasses.

With the action moving back into Tokyo, Yamazaki begged his former employer to help him open two small bars in Shinjuku. Unfortunately, neither establishment attracted many customers, and, after a year, the owner asked him to sell them off. Yamazaki scraped together the money to buy the inferior of the two, and, in 1969, he re-opened the decaying, fourth-floor walk-up as a rhythm-and-blues bar called Kaijin 20 Mensō ("The Fiend With Twenty Faces"). He painted the walls black, on top of which an amateur artist friend drew crude portraits of Elvis Presley and Marilyn Monroe. Kaijin 20 Mensō played soul records at maximum volume all night long, and the staff dressed in matching leather jackets, jeans, and pompadours. In this dark corner of Shinjuku—a neighborhood otherwise known for radical student

Masayuki Yamazaki
(far right) with
coworkers at
Kaijin 20 Mensō.
(©Pink Dragon)

protesters and long-hair hippies—Yamazaki gave the country's
greased-up delinquents a place to call their own.

IN THE EARLY 1970S, YAMAZAKI ASSUMED THAT HE AND HIS
bar staff were the only adults in all of Tokyo to dress like yankee
greasers. But while skimming through *Weekly Playboy* one day, he
found four soulmates in the rock band Carol. Bassist and singer
Eikichi Yazawa grew up in the ruins of post-atomic Hiroshima,
abandoned by his mother and left an orphan when his father died
from a radiation-related illness. His only joy each day was listening
to American music on the radio. After graduating from high
school, he settled in a ragged part of Yokohama, working odd jobs
and recording a slew of rejected demos.

On August 15, 1972—the twenty-seventh anniversary of
World War II's end—Yazawa formed the band Carol. The idea was

Rock band Carol (Eikichi Yazawa, second from right). (©Universal Music)

to recreate the rock 'n' roll of the Beatles during their pre-Fab Four days in Hamburg playing marathon gigs in slummy Reeperbahn clubs. Carol's guitarist Johnny Ōkura decided that they needed a uniform, and gravitated toward the retro 1950s "Roxy" style popular at the time in London. They put their hair up in pompadours, wore menacing black leather jackets and leather pants, and posed astride heavy motorcycles. *Weekly Playboy* called this look "yankee style," recognizing it as a caricature of American hoodlums from the past.

National broadcaster NHK banned Carol from its airwaves for several years, believing their biker look was a hallmark of "poor education." Venues in big cities refused to host Carol concerts due to concerns about fights, riots, and destruction to property. But once the group got its big break on the national TV show "Ginza Now," their yankee look spread to teens in the countryside. Writer Kenrō Hayamizu explains the group's appeal, "Eikichi Yazawa, with his sunglasses, leather jacket, defiant feeling, and motorcycle, looked like a hero in an era where youth battled with school administrators. Yazawa spread American rocker style into juvenile delinquent culture."

Tokyo's fashion scene, meanwhile, saw Carol's regents and classic rock 'n' roll as a Japanese analog to the Fifties revival happening inside the British glam rock movement. As part of the trend, fashion magazine *an•an* wrote a small blurb on Kaijin 20 Mensō, which attracted a more elect set to the bar. Fashion designer Kansai Yamamoto and members of Carol became regulars. At its peak, more than a hundred people would pack into Kaijin 20 Mensō each night, with a line snaking all the way down the staircase to the front of the building.

Kaijin 20 Mensō appealed not just to fashion elite imitating American teenage delinquents, but also to actual teenage delinquents. These ruffians dressed in loud Hawaiian shirts, leather jackets, and regent hairstyles. Fights broke out nightly, so Yamazaki and his lieutenants trained in self-defense techniques on the roof. Martial arts, however, could not keep up with a dangerous new kind of juvenile delinquent who occasionally appeared at the bar— the *bōsōzoku* (the word *bōsō* meaning "out of control"). These were teenage outlaw biker gangs notorious for group riding, warfare over territory, and extreme styles of dress.

In the mid-1970s, bōsōzoku bikers came to notoriety throughout provincial cities across Japan. They rolled through main streets on Saturday nights with heavily modified and mufflerless vehicles. They huffed paint thinner out of empty juice cans, and, in the early years, brawled with rival groups to the death. But the bōsōzoku were perhaps most infamous for their fashion sense, influenced primarily by Carol's "yankee style" of regents and leather. Based on appearances alone, these bikers resembled American "greasers" as closely as VAN fans resembled Ivy League students. But in the bōsōzoku's case, the teens had little idea about the American origin of the style; they simply copied singer Eikichi Yazawa. For them, style legitimacy came from a domestic rather than a foreign authority.

Bōsōzoku bikers driving the streets of Tokyo on a group run, November 1978.
(©The Yomiuri Shimbun/Aflo)

On top of Carol's influence, the bōsōzoku added anything that would frighten straight-edged society. School-aged members wore surgical masks to hide their identities. Instead of safety helmets, they wore headbands to push back their hair. Shaved heads were common, but most bōsōzoku got permanents—sometimes in the tight "punch perm" or the pseudo-afro "negro." They then put it up high on their heads with a little grease pushing back the sides. Bōsōzoku continued to call this the "regent" even though it looked more mutant James Brown than Elvis.

Masayuki Yamazaki often preferred real youth gangs to the trendy fashionistas who appropriated his beloved regent hairstyle in imitation of faraway Brits. His sympathy for Shinjuku's wild ones came to an abrupt end, however, when a gang mugged him after work. The criminals held knives to his neck and came close to cleaving off a finger when he could not slip off his ring. Between this incident and the growing number of fights inside the bar, Yamazaki decided it was time to relocate.

Yamazaki's personal exasperation with the underbelly of Shinjuku mirrored wider changes in the counterculture during the early 1970s. The student movement collapsed, and the police managed to flush the remaining hippies out of the bushes. From August 1970 onward, police closed off roads to create a "pedestrian paradise" (*hokoten*) each Sunday, which prevented bikers from drag racing on the streets. With Shinjuku sanitized, the remnants of the youth underground went looking for a new place to congregate. The strongest candidate was a quiet residential area a few train stops away by the name of Harajuku.

HARAJUKU IS A SHORT WALK FROM THE BUSY COMMUTER HUB Shibuya, bordering the green of Yoyogi Park and the Meiji Jingu shrine. American Army officers lived there during the Occupation, and, in 1964, the neighborhood housed the main Olympic stadium. But after that brief heyday, Harajuku went dormant. In the words of writer Hiroshi Morinaga, "Harajuku was as insignificant as a tiny island in the South Pacific, quiet both day and night."

The only action focused around a building called Central Apartments, at the intersection of Meiji Street and the tree-lined Omotesandō Avenue. Inside, up-and-coming fashion designers rented single rooms (called "mansions" in Japanese-English) to sew small batches of arty clothing. These "mansion makers" formed a nascent creative class, and during their downtime, they held court in first-floor café Leon with other long-haired, bearded friends.

Since most of Kaijin 20 Mensō's stylish customers worked in and around Central Apartments, Yamazaki decided that Harajuku would be the perfect location for his next bar. In 1974, he asked his father to take out a ¥2.5 million advance loan on his company pension, which Yamazaki used to pay the security deposit on a primitive basement drinking hole. He named it King Kong, covering the walls in leopard print and an enormous mural of a

Caribbean woman looking out over a tropical beach. Patrons sat on empty beer cases.

The pitiful space attracted few customers for its first few months, but one customer would forever change Yamazaki's life—the British-born, half-Japanese model Vivienne Lynn. After a few hours of conversation in limited Japanese, Yamazaki and Lynn hit it off. A few weeks later, the nineteen-year-old Shiseido campaign model and the twenty-nine-year-old coal miner's son were a couple. In the ensuing months, Yamazaki completely drained his businesses' bank accounts to keep up with Lynn's jet-setting lifestyle. But her role as creative muse ultimately proved lucrative: after a memorable rendezvous with Lynn in Southeast Asia, Yamazaki opened a kitschy 1950s tropical-themed bar in May 1975 called Singapore Night. The establishment was an instant hit with both celebrities and bikers.

Lynn also helped Yamazaki refine and define his own tastes. Yamazaki became obsessed with George Lucas' film *American Graffiti*, which he saw in Paris during a visit to Kansai Yamamoto's fashion show. He wrote in his autobiography, "Watching the film made me remember my hometown Akabira. When I was in high school, I would ride aimlessly around town with friends at night on bicycles. Pop music would play from speakers in the shopping area, we'd hit on girls, go to dance parties, get in fights." During that trip to Europe, Yamazaki had taken the ferry to the U.K. and visited Malcolm McLaren and Vivienne Westwood's rockabilly boutique, Let it Rock. During this trip, he saw images of his beloved American juvenile delinquents floating around pop culture, but continued to dismiss his own retro interests as little more than a personal quirk.

Finally, in late 1975, Lynn dragged Yamazaki back to London to see the neo-Teddy Boy scene firsthand. At Brighton Market, Yamazaki found stalls selling vintage clothing, and he picked up a crate of bowling and Hawaiian shirts, rubber-soled brothel creepers, boxy suits, pleated pants, and jackets with shoulder pads. Lynn's mother commented, "Yama-chan, you sure like the Fifties."

The exterior of Cream Soda in Harajuku in its early years. (©Pink Dragon)

Yamazaki had never heard this word before, but it put everything into context: He liked "the Fifties"!

Looking to sell the vintage clothing he brought back from London, Yamazaki opened his first pure retail space in Harajuku—Cream Soda. This would be the neighborhood's first vintage clothing store. Yamazaki wrote on the façade, "Too fast to live, too young to die," a slogan cribbed from McClaren's new name for Let it Rock. Within weeks, Cream Soda was Yamazaki's biggest success to date. Charging six times what he paid for the clothing in London, the yen rolled in, and the once impoverished bar proprietor enjoyed a robust cash flow. But within weeks, apparel industry insiders quickly snapped up all the original vintage pieces, which forced Yamazaki to produce a line of low-priced Cream Soda originals. Teens loved these even more and lined up to buy the brand's loud shirts and skirts in garish leopard-print and sherbet tones.

Yamazaki soon needed more stock to keep up with demand. After hearing a rumor about cheap secondhand items in California, he headed to San Francisco in 1976. None of the used clothing shops, however, had anything resembling his Fifties style. Just as he was about to give up, a mysterious British hippie approached him, claiming to have piles of garments tucked away in his house. Yamazaki followed him back to the Haight-Ashbury area and spent the day poring through an enormous vintage collection. He shipped ¥2 million worth of the merchandise back to Harajuku, and once that sold out, he forked over another ¥10 million for an additional 30-foot shipping container of musty garments. This investment retailed for ¥100 million ($1.4 million in 2015 dollars) on the streets of Tokyo.

Cream Soda was practically printing money selling retro American clothing to Japanese youth. Inspired by Yamazaki's success, clone brands Peppermint and Chopper popped up nearby to get a piece of the action. Less scrupulous buyers bought stock at Cream Soda and sold it for double the price up the street. Japan's top apparel conglomerates and department stores all knocked on Yamazaki's door, but he refused to go "major." He kept the growing business centered around his own small firm, 1950 Company, and shuttered his bars to focus solely on the retail business.

By 1977, Yamazaki's one-time fantasy of a Fifties revival in Japan had come true on the streets of Harajuku. Teens wore a mix of Teddy Boy favorites—brothel creeper shoes (called "rubber soles") and long, colorful jackets—as well as classic American teenybopper items—red letterman cardigans, baseball jackets, saddle shoes, and tight 501s. The tipping point came when a print advertisement for Sony's portable radio-cassette player ZILBA'P

Two examples of G.I. style in *Men's Club* during the mid-1970s. (Courtesy of Hearst Fujingahō)

featured Caucasian youths leaning against vintage autos, dressed as if they had just walked off the set of *American Graffiti*. (Their clothing, of course, came from Cream Soda.) Each weekend, boys in ducktails and girls in ponytails descended upon Harajuku from all over the country, eager to participate in Japan's cutting-edge present by inhabiting the styles of America's past.

During the Fifties' fashion craze, some teens even started dressing like U.S. Army privates—the classic khaki or olive uniforms with short-sleeves, military-tucked neckties, MacArthur-like Aviator sunglasses, and a pointy garrison hat. The teenagers in these outfits did not necessarily intend to glorify the American military, but they certainly cared very little about the antiwar protests of the previous decade. Army uniforms became chic fragments of nostalgia rather than symbols of occupation and imperialism.

In 1978, the hit musical film *Grease* added even more momentum to the rock 'n' roll boom, and Cream Soda's original goods sold ¥300,000 ($5,000 in 2015 dollars) per day. Teens across Japan dreamed of trips to Tokyo just to buy Yamazaki's pink and neon yellow leopard-print wallets. Five years prior, barely anyone in Japan had ever heard the term "rock 'n' roll"; now Cream Soda was the best-selling rock clothing shop on the planet.

Needing additional stock of cheap American gear for his new store, Garage Paradise, Yamazaki took his entire staff to Korea on a scouting trip. At a grungy market outside the U.S. military base, they discovered leather bomber jackets piled up for just ¥5,000 ($87 in 2015 dollars)—a fraction of what Japanese rockers paid in Ameyoko for similar items. Yamazaki bought two hundred and requested more be sent over to Japan. The item was an overnight hit, adding to Yamazaki's fortune and outfitting the youth population in leather.

Cream Soda and Garage Paradise built up Harajuku from a serene residential neighborhood to the national center of youth fashion. Throughout the 1970s, Japanese pop culture had looked beyond Tokyo for its inspiration—the Annon-zoku went to small country towns, Heavy Duty kids looked to the great outdoors, and surfers spent their summers at Shōnan beach. The Fifties boom put Tokyo firmly back in the spotlight. At the end of the decade, teens from 100 km away would wake up early on Sunday to take the train into Tokyo, and spend their days strolling up and down Omotesandō Avenue and Takeshita Street.

And just like in the Ivy era, youth fashion meant American fashion. But Yamazaki's Fifties style played so heavily with delinquent motifs and impulses that the fashion market could never perfectly control the consumers. Delinquents would certainly want to decide their styles themselves.

IN THE MID-1970S, BŌSŌZOKU GROUPS FROM RURAL LOCALES drove into Tokyo each weekend and slowly rode their bikes up and down the streets of Harajuku. Just like in Shinjuku, the town council

The Roller Tribe dancing on Sunday in Harajuku, 1982 (©The Mainichi Newspapers)

endeavored to deter these gangs by closing off the tree-lined Omotesandō Avenue every Sunday to become a pedestrian paradise. This attempt to squash one form of delinquency, however, created another. Groups of ex-bōsōzoku, dressed in rock 'n' roll outfits bought from Cream Soda, gathered in Harajuku to dance to American hits from the 1950s around a ZILBA'P stereo. The men wore black leather jackets, white pocket T-shirts with the sleeves rolled up, worn-in straight leg jeans, motorcycle boots, and topped off the look with tall, greasy pompadours. Their female companions twirled around in poodle skirts with their hair tied back in ponytails with gigantic bows, feet in saddle shoes with short frilly white socks and white lace cocktail gloves on their hands.

The boys and girls danced highly choreographed variations of the twist and jitterbug. But not together in this highly homosocial world: the boys huddled together in the middle while the girls shimmied together on the perimeter. The teens eventually organized into official groups that met up each Sunday to dance the day away. The media called them "Rollers," as in "rock 'n' rollers."

The police soon booted the Rollers off Omotesandō Avenue, forcing them to regroup on a similar pedestrian paradise in nearby Yoyogi Park. This small patch of asphalt right outside Harajuku station would become their new promised land, every Sunday from 10 a.m. until dark. In the otherwise straight-laced Japanese society, Harajuku promised a weekly "festival," letting teenagers dress up and dance merrily without the overbearing supervision of parents or teachers. The popularity of the Rollers in Yoyogi attracted a similar subculture called the Bamboo Shoot Tribe (*takenoko-zoku*), who discoed in brightly colored kung fu outfits.

Most of the teenagers who joined the Rollers and takeno-ko-zoku were listless youth working blue-collar jobs. A June 1980 documentary from national broadcaster NHK, *Young Plaza: 24 Hours in Harajuku* followed a fifteen-year-old takenoko-zoku member, "Yayoi," who complained about living like a "doll," always having to say yes to parents and authorities. Sunday was the one day she could express her true opinions and be her true self. NHK's documentary also profiled "Ken," leader of the popular Rollers group, Midnight Angels. Ken came to Tokyo from rural Akita Prefecture after dropping out of middle-school. He spent his weekdays working part-time and living in a cramped, windowless apartment decorated with posters of James Dean, biker gangs, and Carol's Eikichi Yazawa. On the day NHK filmed the group, Ken announced that he had to move back to Akita to work on the family farm.

As the documentary showed, most Rollers were *tsuppari*—the era's term for delinquent teens. The choreographed dances may have seemed square, but the groups were mainly comprised of tough and troubled dropouts. Group leaders often had to adver-tise that they did not want members who engaged in reckless motorcycle riding or thinner-huffing. By 1980, eight hundred dancers in forty different Rollers and takenoko-zoku groups came out each Sunday. A year later, the Rollers ballooned to a hundred twenty groups nationwide. The police, who did not distinguish between the Rollers and the bōsōzoku, apprehended a dozen dancers each weekend for underage smoking, drinking, and other minor transgressions.

By tapping into a retro toughness, Cream Soda had forged a shaky alliance in Harajuku between provincial delinquents and fashion people—but tensions were inevitable. The February 1978 issue of *an•an* quoted two sixteen-year-old girls in matching long white-and-red-tipped collegiate cardigans on the streets saying, "We hate tsuppari boys. We like the cute ones." Yamazaki also had mixed feelings about his style becoming a staple of tsuppari youth. He was offended that teachers confiscated Cream Soda goods in schools as "bōsōzoku paraphernalia." Yamazaki preached in his own publications, "I don't think delinquency and the Fifties have anything to do with each other. Fifties is different than tsuppari fashion." Ultimately, however, the Fifties movement became much bigger than Cream Soda and Yamazaki—it was the central pillar of delinquent style nationwide.

IF MIDDLE-CLASS TEENS HATED SHARING THE FIFTIES CRAZE with working-class teens, the working-class teens really hated that the fashion complex sucked all the toughness out of leather jackets, Hawaiian shirts, and jeans. Biker gangs needed a more frightening look. From the mid-1970s, they gradually shifted aesthetic allegiance to Mob-affiliated, right-wing groups known as *uyoku*. These ultra-nationalists appeared at protests in makeshift paramilitary gear made from zip-up, navy-blue cleaning uniforms. The bōsōzoku copied these blue jumpsuits and rebranded them "kamikaze clothing" (*tokkōfuku*). Teenage bikers festooned the suits with gold embroidery making out right-wing slogans. Likewise, the bōsōzoku hoped to channel the Imperial era by writing out their English-language gang names in old-timey Chinese characters in-

Kensuke Ishizu's photos of Princeton students in *Men's Club* #18, April 1960. (Courtesy of the Ishizu family)

Kazuo Hozumi's first drawing of his famous "Ivy Boy" cartoon for a poster, 1963. (©Kazuo Hozumi)

Photos of Miyuki Tribe members in *Men's Club*'s "Ivy Leaguers on the Street,"
Summer 1964. (Courtesy of Hearst Fujingahō)

The Ivy Tribe
in Ginza, 1965.
(©Tōru Nogami)

Jirō Shirasu wearing
Levi's jeans, 1951.
(©Keisuke Katano
for Hiroshi
Hamaya Archive)

Japanese hippies in Shinjuku, 1969. (©The Mainichi Newspapers)

Cover of *Made in U.S.A.* catalog. (©The Yomiuri Shimbun)

A page of Red Wing boots in *Made in U.S.A.* catalog. (©The Yomiuri Shimbun)

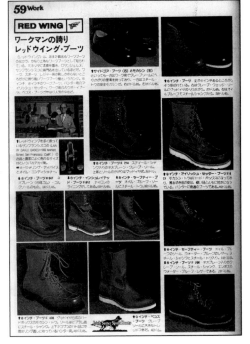

HEAVY-DUTY IVY

ヘビアイ党宣言

いまここに確立された新しい世代の風俗体系──ヘビーデューティー・アイビー・ルックの全貌を発表！

構成／イラストレーション＝小林泰彦

ヘビアイ・ナンバーワンと自他ともにみとめるのがこれ　マウンテン・パーカなり　生地は言わずと知れた誇り高き60／40すなわちヘビーデューティーのシンボル　機能的にもこれ以上は改めようのない決定版であるからしてすなわち古典＝アイビーたるゆえんだ　ならばこそフードのドローコードエンドのレザーやデルリンジッパーのつけ方まで気になってあたりまえ　501ジーンズにクライミングブーツ　いやなんといってもヘビアイ青年は読書家です　デイパックの中にヘミングウエイやフォークナーは欠かせません

151

"The Heavy Duty Ivy Party Manifesto" from *Men's Club* #183, September 1976.
(©Yasuhiko Kobayashi)

Young man in Yokosuka
Mambo style, Yokosuka 1967.
(©Shōmei Tōmatsu)

Tsuppari teens on the
Omotesandō pedestrian
paradise, June 1977.
(©The Mainichi
Newspapers)

May 1980 issue of *Hot Dog Press* shows a comparison between 1960s and 1980s Ivy League looks. (Courtesy of Kōdansha)

Popeye editor-in-chief Takahiro Kinoshita photographed on The Sartorialist. (Photograph by Scott Schuman)

stead of the normal *katakana* syllabary or roman script. They also flew the Japanese Imperial battle flag in group runs and placed swastikas on their headbands. Two biker gangs took the names Nazi and Hitler.

Despite this fascist pageantry, the bōsōzoku had little interest in right-wing ideas. During his fieldwork with bikers in Kyoto, anthropologist Ikuya Satō found them "indifferent to nationalist ideology" with generally negative views towards right-wing organizations. The bikers mostly enjoyed the power to shock that came from embracing the taboo of wartime imagery.

By 1980, bōsōzoku style was equally influenced by the Axis as by the Allies, creating a hybrid of right-wing kamikazes and American greasers. Bōsōzoku numbers exploded in the early 1980s, peaking in 1982 with over forty-three thousand members and 712 recognized groups. The bōsōzoku look eventually crystallized into a single form: a floppy regent haircut held back by a headband emblazoned with the group's name, a blue jumpsuit, a thin moustache, shaved eyebrows, and sunglasses bent at a 45° angle. At school, rebellious teens altered their traditional black wool uniforms—ballooning the legs or extending the gakuran's collar to ridiculous heights.

With bōsōzoku terrorizing the entire archipelago, tsuppari style broke out of its fashion ghetto and merged with mainstream pop culture. The popular band Yokohama Ginbae made it big in 1980 by dressing up like bōsōzoku—dirty moustaches, shaggy regents, sharp sunglasses, leather jackets, and baggy white pants—and explicitly referencing delinquent culture in songs like "Tsuppari High School Rock 'n' Roll" and "Yokosuka Baby." Then came the Nameneko, kittens photographed to look like tsuppari high schoolers. The official Nameneko photo album sold five hundred thousand copies. A fake Nameneko driver's license, which bōsōzoku often pulled out when stopped by police, shifted fifteen million units. In total, the business of selling kittens dressed up as tsuppari brought in sales of a cool ¥1 billion ($12 million in 2015 dollars).

Cover of Yokohama Ginbae's 1982 single "Omae sara sara sāfā gāru, oira tekateka rokkunrōrā" ("You're a silky surfer girl, we're slick-backed rock'n'rollers"). (©King Record Co., Ltd.)

As the style spread, the word tsuppari morphed to denote teens who altered their school uniforms. Japan would need a new term for this overall milieu of delinquent youth. The Osaka term for bad boy teens—*yankii*, with an accent on the *ii*—became the accepted jargon. The term's roots clearly went back to the "yankee style" of Yokosuka Mambo and Carol, but the direct derivation came from barbers in Osaka calling the regent hairstyle "the yankee." By the early 1980s, however, no one could imagine that these extreme Japanese teens in right-wing costumes had anything to do with Americans. Many assumed that

Nameneko cats dressed up as yankii. (©Group S)

the word yankii came from Osaka teens' regional dialect of ending sentences with the sound *yan ké*. The yankii themselves certainly knew nothing of the term's history; they were imitating their older brothers and famed Japanese outlaws, not G.I.s in grungy Yokosuka bars.

By 1982, both the yankee greaser and yankii biker movements in pop culture had hit their peak and started to fade out. Increased criminal penalties on group riding decimated the bōsōzoku. The standard tsuppari look began to fade in the mid-1980s and had gone nearly extinct by the end of the decade, save for in a few tiny rural villages in the furthest reaches of the country. And just as Pink Dragon opened its doors in Harajuku in 1982, the rock 'n' roll craze had all but evaporated. The fervor around the Fifties, however, did give rock 'n' roll a permanent place in the Japanese fashion canon. In 1985, Yamazaki's house band Black Cats appeared in a Coca-Cola commercial—wearing tight black T-shirts and extreme pompadours. American delinquent style, once banned from Shinjuku clubs, became a marketing tool for American companies.

Looking back today, the diffusion of American styles among Japanese delinquents reveals an important and often overlooked fact about Japan's interaction with clothing from the United States. Yankii fashion challenges the widely held assumption that Japanese youth always respectfully imitated American originals. VAN may have offered perfect copies of Ivy, and the hippies looked like a costume drama about the East Village. But, in comparison, delinquents cared little about perfect imitation. They used American influences to terrorize the public—regent haircuts, Hawaiian shirts, dirty jeans—but abandoned them when right-wing garb offered greater potency. Cream Soda may have channeled delinquency but followed the VAN model: taking a past subcultural look and converting it into a stable set of style principles. Broadly speaking, the American styles that are subsumed into the Japanese media-consumer complex tend to become static—like exhibits in a museum—because brands and magazines needed to build explicit rules about what is and what is not part of the style. Much of the Japanese "reverence" for America came not just from bookish obsessives like Toshiyuki Kurosu preaching the look as part of an evangelist mission, but from the fashion industry's functional needs to sell it.

By turning Harajuku into a fashion neighborhood and kicking off an entire clothing craze around the 1950s, Masayuki Yamazaki is arguably one of the most important fashion entrepreneurs of the twentieth century. Today, however, historians and nostalgics give his rock 'n' roll revolution less attention than other fashion movements. Critics argue that the Japanese Fifties boom added few new ideas to the vintage rock canon. Like Kensuke Ishizu, Yamazaki made his money introducing an unknown set of American historical references to Japan, but he never provided teens with new influences beyond Elvis, James Dean, and Marlon Brando. Yamazaki fans defend this lack of creativity as a meta-statement on Japan's Americanized postwar culture. A Cream Soda fan once explained, "My regent, hat, and clothing are all imitations of people and films. More broadly speaking, Japan is just an imitation of America. It all started as an imitation, so you can't think about whether that imitation is bad or good." In other words, why moralize on copying inside Japan culture when society as a whole was a copy?

While John Lennon and Aerosmith loved shopping at Cream Soda, other Westerners found it ludicrous that Japanese teens were borrowing styles from past delinquents with such precision. The opening segment of Jim Jarmusch's 1989 film *Mystery Train* mocks a Carl Perkins-loving Japanese Roller named Jun, in a green Teddy Boy jacket and ducktail, on a disappointing trip to Memphis. Miami humorist Dave Barry encountered a few remaining Rollers during his trip to Japan in the early 1990s, and wrote:

> The first thing we saw was the Bad Ass Greasers. These were young men, maybe a dozen of them, deeply into the 1950s American-juvenile-delinquent look, all dressed identically in tight black T-shirts, black pants, black socks, and pointy black shoes. Each one had a lovingly constructed, carefully maintained, major-league caliber 1950s-style duck's-ass haircut, held in place by the annual petroleum output of Kuwait. They did not seem to sense that they might look a little silly, like a gang of Hell's Angels that tries to terrorize a small town while wearing tutus.

This was a slightly unfair critique against the final remnants of a moribund subculture, but Barry's quips demonstrate the degree to which Americans did not like their iconic delinquent look being turned into a standard-issue uniform. Everyone looked like identical rebels without causes.

Japanese delinquents of the 1980s were damned on both sides—belittled for copying yankees and hated for being yankiis.

Not that they cared; the perpetual outlaw Masayuki Yamazaki kept his rockabilly empire going strong even when mainstream trends moved in alternate directions. But perhaps the best measure for the success of yankii fashion in Japan in the early 1980s was the strength of the backlash. When yankii style fell out of fashion, Tokyo teens moved on to classy, Old Money American clothing with a vengeance, as if they wanted to rinse the taste of pomade out of their mouths for good.

SEVEN

Nouveau Riche

OSAMU SHIGEMATSU STOOD OUT FROM OTHER TEENAGERS in the early 1970s: he wore real American clothing. Growing up in the beach town of Zushi, he often asked Navy brats in nearby Yokosuka to buy him items from shops inside the base. At nineteen, his flight attendant sister put him on a plane to Hawaii, where he stocked up on clothing unavailable at home. In the early 1970s, Japanese companies started making licensed goods under foreign brand names, but Shigematsu dismissed them as inauthentic: "They used local sizing, so the balance of the garment was off."

After college, Shigematsu suspected his peers were starting to feel the same way about faux foreign clothing—especially surfers in Shōnan who wanted to dress like their heroes in California. But those teens would never sacrifice beach time to rummage through piles of imported garments all the way out in Ameyoko. There was a clear business opportunity in bringing genuine American casual wear right into the heart of Tokyo's trendy shopping districts. Shigematsu just needed financial backing to open a store.

In 1975, a friend introduced him to a "guy from a cardboard box company"—Etsuzō Shitara, president of packaging manufacturer

Shinkō Inc. After twenty years of growth in tandem with Japan's export boom, Shinkō hit a wall during the Oil Crisis of 1973; paper prices went up, and fewer product shipments meant lower demand for boxes. To revive his company, Shitara needed to diversify into new businesses with potential for higher profit margins. Shigematsu pitched Shitara on a sure-fire new venture: selling real American clothing to youth in Harajuku. Shitara loved the idea. The employees of Shinkō and his family, however, had serious doubts. What did this fifty-six-year-old box company president know about the fashion business? Shitara ignored their concerns and sold off unused factory land to pay the lease on a 210-square-foot space in the Harajuku neighborhood.

Finding a location was easy: sourcing imported goods was the hard part. Rival store Miura & Sons—the first retailer to take imports out of Ameyoko and into the chic side of Tokyo—appeared to rely on the *Made in U.S.A.* catalog as its merchandising guide. Miura worked with Japanese importers to stock Heavy Duty items such as Levi's jeans, flannel shirts, and Red Wing boots. In search of even more exotic products, Shigematsu would need to go right to the source. He procured cheap plane tickets from his sister and traveled to California with enormous empty bags. He loaded up on clothing at ordinary retailers, pleading for a discount on his bulk purchases at the cash register.

On February 1, 1976, Shitara and Shigematsu opened the doors to their new store, American Life Shop Beams. They set up the shop interior to resemble the dorm room of a UCLA student, complete with sneakers, skateboards, collegiate T-shirts, painter pants, and baggy chinos. Beams sold a wide variety of American goods no one in Japan had ever seen before. This included a pair of *ni-kay* running shoes featured in *Made in U.S.A.*—otherwise known as the Beaverton, Oregon brand, Nike.

At first, Beams' clientele was limited to fashion industry insiders. *Popeye* stylist Katsuhiko Kitamura recalled in 1998, "In the mid-1970s, America felt very far away from us. We couldn't touch real American clothing or shoes on a daily basis. And yet,

Beams lined up all these American goods. Before Beams, you had to search around Ameyoko like crazy while drenched in sweat to find these things, and now you could just find them in Harajuku." Within months, others caught on to Beams' magic, and the expanding customer base and steady sales allowed Shitara and Shigematsu to open a second store in Shibuya. The same year, rival Miura & Sons set up its next shop in Ginza with a similar name—Ships.

By the end of 1977, stores like Beams and Ships allowed wealthy teens to forego Japanese copies of American items in favor of authentic foreign goods. Youth were perhaps adopting their parents' preferences, who were going overseas in record numbers and buying up luxury goods by the cartload. From 1976 to 1979, the yen rose strongly in value against the dollar, up from 300:1 to 200:1. And, in 1977, the government loosened regulations on currency exchange, allowing travelers to take up to $3,000 out of Japan. This currency adjustment bred the *endaka narikin*—a new class of Japanese nouveau riche who felt a sense of affluence while visiting foreign countries. Older Japanese women snapped up French and Italian luxury brands on trips through Europe, with Louis Vuitton handbags and key holders becoming the go-to souvenirs for friends and family. The allure of luxury goods at cheap prices in turn encouraged more overseas travel. From 1971 to 1976, the number of Japanese travelling overseas hovered steadily around two million a year, but, in 1977, it shot up to 3.15 million. Louis Vuitton, Céline, and Gucci handbags began to overrun the posh areas of Tokyo, Ōsaka, Kōbe, and Yokohama.

Luxury goods first trickled down from adults to young women. In the glamorous port city of Kōbe, college coeds shopped at boutiques that normally catered to the city's Old Money matriarchs in a style called *nyūtora* (New Traditional). A few years later, a similar style, *hamatora* (Yokohama Traditional), developed in Eastern Japan's port city of Yokohama. Hamatora merged the class-conscious elements of nyūtora with the youthful energy of the city's private schools—frilly tops, mid-length skirts, knee-high socks, and sporty ensembles. The quintessential hamatora item was the crew-neck logo sweatshirt from Harajuku trad shop Crew's. Ships and Beams both made their own logo sweatshirts for the hamatora trend, with Beams' version accounting for 40 percent of total sales in the early years.

After *Popeye*'s "VAN was our teacher" issue in April 1978, Ivy emerged as menswear's answer to nyūtora and hamatora. Beams capitalized on the Ivy revival with a new store in Harajuku called Beams F. Inspired in part by the look of affluent teens in California's Newport Beach, Shigematsu stocked brands popular with American college students such as Brooks Brothers, L.L. Bean, and Lacoste. He also discovered a high-end, Massachusetts-based shoe brand called Alden and brought their merchandise to Japan for the first time. Shigematsu, desperate to keep ahead of import shops Camps and Seas down the street, was constantly on the hunt for new American brands to sell.

The Ivy revival this time also captured the hearts of adults. Back in 1971, a middle-aged Japanese gentleman entered the New York location of famed Ivy League retailer J. Press and handed over $15,000 for every single piece of clothing in size 37 Short. Months later, lawyers called the Press family with news that Mr. 37 Short's employer, apparel giant Onward Kashiyama, wanted to license the brand for the Japanese market. The contract's terms were highly favorable, described by Richard Press, grandson of founder Jacobi Press, as "hitting a number on a roulette wheel." By the mid-1970s, Kashiyama's expansive development of the brand in Japan allowed men of all ages to buy faithful reproductions of J. Press's Ivy style at nearly every department store in the country.

As the decade progressed, Japan's high-end clothing market moved away from European labels, and instead championed traditional-minded New York designers such as Ralph Lauren, Alexander Julian, Alan Flusser, and Jeffrey Banks. Shopping mall PARCO came to dominate the Shibuya neighborhood thanks to an exclusive contract with Ralph Lauren's Polo line. The appearance

Young men in Preppy style on the streets of Tokyo, 1982. (©web-across.com, PARCO Co., Ltd.)

of these brands moved the trad scene away from domestic lines like Macbeth and New Yorker and toward American imports and licensed merchandise. Alexander Julian started selling in Japan after meeting a group of visiting Japanese retailers in New York. "I showed them my designs, the same designs which very few American buyers understood. To my great delight, they understood immediately! They got it! I was offered a contract on the spot! Their early understanding, support, and success allowed me to maintain and excel in the U.S.A., and then Europe. I owe my career to Japan."

When the 1978 VAN Jacket bankruptcy left a ¥40 billion ($708 million in 2015 dollars) void in the Ivy market, Brooks Brothers seized the opportunity to open its first Japanese store. Much like how VAN had originally copied Brooks' designs, the American brand now took a few cues from VAN when planning its arrival in Japan. Brooks Brothers placed its flagship Aoyama store in a former VAN retail space, on the same street as VAN's old headquarters. Brooks Brothers positioned its August 31, 1979 opening party—graced with an appearance from U.S. Ambassador Mike Mansfield—as a pivotal moment in Japan-America relations. Within a year of operations, Brooks Brothers had built up a clientele of ten thousand steady customers.

Japanese men capitalized upon the arrival of authentic brands like J. Press and Brooks Brothers as ammunition to fight lingering prejudices against personal style in the workplace. Former VAN employee Yoshio Sadasue explains the standard uniform up until the late 1970s: "You had to wear a navy blue suit with white dress shirt and black plain toe shoes. No wingtips, no penny loafers. You couldn't wear button-down collars. Wearing a pink shirt was inconceivable, and even blue was questionable." Crisp dress shirts in Japan are still called *wai*-shirts (or "Y-shirts"), derived from the fact that they were only permissible in white (*waito*).

In the 1970s, button-downs only made up 5 percent of the entire shirt market, and many department stores refused to make them for made-to-measure customers. As the original Ivy Tribe moved up the corporate ladder, however, they challenged these strict rules. Yoshio Sadasue recalls, "Button-downs finally received true citizenship in the early 1980s when Ivy fans all said, we want to wear them to work!" Of course, victory came easy when fighting for the least radical of causes—the right to dress like American bank managers. From the 1980s onward, men could proudly appear for their morning recitations of the company pledge in Brooks Brothers three-button sack suits. Navy blazers with gold buttons—once purely an item for "fashionable people"—became acceptable garb for corporate travel and parties.

Between teens shopping for Nikes at Beams, wives and mothers with Louis Vuitton handbags, and middle managers in their J. Press suits, Japanese fashion at the end of the 1970s completely refocused on imported goods and foreign labels. Everyone wanted the "real thing," not local imitations. But youth soon demanded more than just wearing classic American goods—they wanted to wear exactly what their peers in America were wearing.

THE INCREASE IN LUXURY CONSUMPTION AND MATERIALISM of late 1970s youth began to worry Japanese parents. Nothing encapsulated this social crisis more than the success of Yasuo Tanaka's debut novella *Nantonaku, Kurisutaru* (Vaguely, Crystal). The 1980 work nominally recounts the love life of a Tokyo college student and part-time fashion model named Yuri, but few readers paid attention to the plot. Tanaka's copious explanatory notes were the real draw—442 in just 106 pages—which offered pointed commentary on the hottest fashion brands, boutiques, record shops, songs, restaurants, neighborhoods, private schools, and disco clubs. For example:

> Note 112 • Lacoste – Brand with the crocodile mark famous for its polo shirts.
> Note 115 • Jaeger – English luxury knit brand, loved by Oscar Wilde and Bernard Shaw, with unique dyes for camel and flannel gray. Even in Japan, Jaeger is loved by people who understand real things.
> Note 117 • Aoyama – You shouldn't tell people you don't know well, "I want to live in Minami Aoyama San-chome." It's embarrassing.

The paperback version sold out on its first day and eventually moved over a million copies.

Tanaka intended his work to satirize Japanese youth's zealous consumption of foreign brand-name goods. Literary critic Jun Etō got the joke, commending Tanaka on "deconstructing Tokyo's urban space, seeing it as having turned into an accumulation of symbols." Teens, on the other hand, just wanted *Nantonaku, Kurisutaru* for its comprehensive list of trendy restaurants, clothing stores, brands, and Boz Scaggs singles.

Soon there was a national dialogue on the Crystal Tribe (*kurisutaru-zoku*)—teenagers who grew up post-Oil Crisis, and knew nothing but affluence. More broadly, the media called this generation the "New Breed" (*shinjinrui*) and criticized their seeming obsession with material things. Parents blamed magazines like *Popeye* and women's title *JJ* for both normalizing the expensive fashion styles of upper-class families and reducing pop culture into a list of purchasable goods. Writer Kōhei Kitayama contributed to *Popeye* in its early days but felt a sense of regret later in life: "*Popeye* was the magazine that pulled the trigger to start Japan's materialistic bubble."

Ivy was the de facto fashion style for New Breed males. *Men's Club* greeted the move back to East Coast campus fashion like a godsend. In the era of Heavy Duty, editors had put their models in tweed and heavy beards to make their Trad coverage more relevant. The 1978 Ivy revival meant the models could start shaving again and stop carrying around tent poles.

With this mandate to return to its roots, *Men's Club* promptly reintroduced the 1960s Ivy originators to a new generation. Now running his own shop, Cross & Simon, former VAN guru Toshiyuki Kurosu resumed his position as the national expert on traditional clothing. In 1980, he edited his own spin-off issue of *Men's Club* called *CrossEye*. That same year, Kazuo Hozumi's cartoon Ivy boy from the VAN poster starred in the dressing manual *Ivy Illustrated*. *Men's Club* reprinted Teruyoshi Hayashida's original *Take Ivy* photos and organized its own yearly university photo tours under the "Take Ivy" moniker. Even the Sixties street kids became heroes: a black-and-white photo spread in the August 1980 issue of *Men's Club* recreated the Miyuki-zoku look with contemporary models.

Men's Club and *Popeye* called this an Ivy revival, but actual teenagers at the time took more interest in Ivy's younger and more contemporary form, Preppy (or Preppie). *Men's Club* beat everyone—including most Americans—to the punch with a December 1979 cover story on "What is Preppie?" They stumbled on to the concept earlier that summer thanks to University of Virginia student Tom Shadyac's famed satirical poster "Are You a

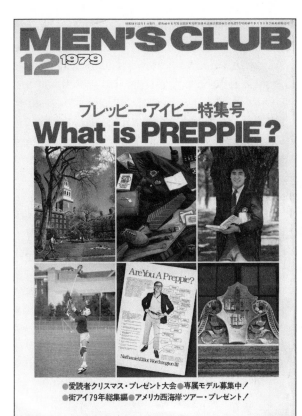

Men's Club covered Preppy fashion in its December 1979 issue, a few months before Lisa Birnbach's *The Official Preppy Handbook.* (Courtesy of Hearst Fujingahō)

Preppie?" which showed an archetypal prep, "Nathaniel Elliot Worthington III," in horn-rimmed glasses, button-down shirt over a popped Izod collar, baggy high-water khakis, and L.L. Bean duck shoes with no socks. *Men's Club* editors immediately understood Preppy and, in classic *Men's Club* fashion, boiled down American students' favorite apparel brands like Top-Siders into consumable lists. (The single style they questioned was teens' refusal to wear socks with loafers.)

A year later, Preppies went mainstream in the U.S. with the November 1980 publication of Lisa Birnbach's *The Official Preppy Handbook.* The cheeky guide to a prep life spent thirty-eight weeks in the number-one slot on the *New York Times* best seller list. The

Japanese translation appeared six months later and sold a hundred thousand copies. Birnbach's work examined the entire Preppy lifestyle—schooling, etiquette, language, careers, and summer vacation. Most Japanese just read the fashion chapter, which laid out proper Preppy style with *Popeye*-level precision. Birnbach's page of men's shoes—weejuns, L.L. Bean rubber moccasins, Brooks Brothers loafers, Gucci loafers, white bucks, L.L.Bean bluchers, Sperry Top-Siders and canvas deck shoes, Tretorn sneakers, wing tips, and patent leather opera pumps—was enough to fill a multi-year footwear agenda for an aspiring Japanese Prep.

Popeye and *Men's Club* sparked the so-called "Fourth Ivy Boom," but the flames spread to new audiences with *Hot Dog Press*—a young men's magazine from publisher Kōdansha debuting in 1979. The magazine borrowed everything from *Popeye*, down to the column formatting and cartoonish name. For primarily being a copycat publication, *Hot Dog Press* carved out a new niche of readers by targeting high schoolers rather than just college students. Editor Takanori Hanafusa decided to offer a laid-back version of East Coast style: "*Hot Dog Press*' high school and college readers did not know anything about the 1960s Ivy boom, so we decided to go Ivy for our fashion. But we didn't want to fall into the dogmatism of *Men's Club*." At the start of the 1980s, the nation's three young men's fashion magazines—*Men's Club*, *Popeye*, and *Hot Dog Press*—appeared on newsstands each month, telling Japanese young men how to dress in American traditional clothing.

Despite the editors' nostalgia for 1960s VAN, 1980s teens looked much closer to Birnbach's Preppies. A May 1980 issue of *Hot Dog Press* illustrated the changes in the style. A photo representing "Ivy '60" showed a stiffly-postured man with slicked-back Vitalis hair, a three-button suit with high button stance, a white oxford button-down shirt, a dark silk knit tie, a formal white pocket square, black plain-toe oxford shoes, a hard-cornered briefcase, and a slim black umbrella. His relaxed "Ivy '80" counterpart meanwhile looked straight off of the "Are you a Preppie?" poster:

June 25, 1981 issue of *Hot Dog Press* offered an exclusive look into *The Official Preppy Handbook*. (Courtesy of Kōdansha)

a loose navy blazer, a button-down oxford on top of a dark polo shirt, cuffed pleated khakis, and L.L. Bean duck shoes with no socks. The old Ivy style looked like someone in a high school production of *Death of a Salesman*, while the newer one looked like a guy you wanted at your raging kegger.

For being a style borrowed from the United States, Japanese Preppy did have its own innovations—namely, miniature bow ties and pom-pom-topped knit caps called *shōchan-bōshi*. The main difference between the two country's styles, however, was the context: Japanese teens wore Preppy clothing on urban streets, not in the shady lanes of idyllic college campuses. Every Sunday, Japanese Preppies would gather in the shopping neighborhoods of major cities, often with groups of friends in identical blazers or with girlfriends in matching ensembles of plaid and pastel oxford cloth.

Ripped from its original context and put into a metropolitan setting, Preppy clothing was no longer organic student attire but the intentional result of heavy styling and competitive shopping. In Aoyama, teens lined up for hours to purchase nautical-themed T-shirts and sweatshirts from the Japanese brand Boat House. They also raided Beams F for the latest imports: in late 1981, Shigematsu saw monthly revenue for his trad store hit ¥20 million ($250,000 in 2015 dollars). Borrowing a page from the Rollers, hardcore Preppies structured themselves into formal organizations. In 1983, there were more than sixty trad-themed social clubs across Japan with names like Three Piece, Square Knot, Nantucket, and Ivy Team Big Green.

The foremost fashion guru for the Preppy era was a familiar face—the seventy-year-old Kensuke Ishizu. Thanks to the *Popeye* issue on VAN, the once disgraced businessman retook his position as the highest authority on Ivy style. The January 25, 1982 "Kensuke Ishizu's New Ivy Dictionary" in *Hot Dog Press* helped the magazine outsell its rival *Popeye* for the first time. Just as before, Ishizu wanted teens to think about Ivy and Preppy clothing as part of a holistic lifestyle—not just a superficial fashion trend. And once again, he failed miserably.

Teenage lives began to revolve around shopping. In 1983, men twenty to twenty-four bought 46 percent more clothing than the average Japanese, and women of the same age bought 69 percent more. Adults lambasted teens for over-relying on magazines for lifestyle tips, dubbing them the "Manual Generation." Teens followed tutorials in *Popeye* and *Hot Dog Press*, to the letter, on how to dress, how to play sports, and how to go on dates. When the magazines advocated Ivy, teens dressed Ivy. When the magazines advocated Preppy, teens dressed Preppy. Women complained that their dates took them to the exact same set of restaurants, clubs, and then later, love hotels, where they performed the exact same plan of romantic moves in the same prescribed order.

In 1983, Hoichoi Productions, Japan's answer to *National Lampoon*, parodied these teens in a book called *The Official MIE Handbook* (*mie* meaning "looking good" in Japanese). The writers explained, "The way youth live today, 'What should I make of myself?' has no significant meaning. The important question is, 'How do other people see me?'" Young people of the Eighties were not interested in politics, nor the environment, nor in "discovering Japan." They simply wanted to look good, fit in, and have fun. And money became a necessary ingredient for social activity. Hoichoi astutely noted that skiing first came to Japan as a sport of solitude that pitted man against a harsh, snowy environment. In the 1980s, skiing was an excuse for women to scream down the slopes in mock fear so they could giggle about it later at the *après-ski*.

Preppy may have lacked a deeper spiritual resonance, but it remains important today as the landmark moment when Japanese culture began to experience global trends in real time. Hirofumi Kurino, former Beams employee and senior advisor of Creative Direction at UNITED ARROWS, explains, "What was most interesting is that Japan and America had the same exact fashion craze at that moment. There was no lag, no gap. The magazine *Popeye* played a big role in creating the word 'city boy.' New York, Paris, London, Milan, and Tokyo are all cities, right? Until then, the framework had been 'country' or 'nation.' But now city transcended nation. This would mark the start of what we now call globalism."

The loose concept of "city boy" spiritually connected Tokyo's elite youth to their urban counterparts worldwide, but those city boys relied on a fine-tuned network of media like *Popeye* and importers like Beams for the latest information and clothing to participate in global trends. Preppy style caught on in Japan concurrently with the U.S. thanks to Japanese magazines' constant and impassioned search for new developments in American collegiate fashion. In fact, *Men's Club* arguably beat *The Official Preppy*

Handbook—published by a slower, traditional publishing house—by an entire year in codifying the Preppy look.

Once Japanese teens could keep up with the rest of the world, the local fashion industry started to consider how to stay ahead of the curve. As the 1980s progressed, Japan's wealthy youth would grow bored with imitating the simple, laid-back clothing of American college students—they needed a more advanced sartorial direction.

IN 1981, BEAMS TOOK THE MONEY MADE FROM SELLING American trad and used it to open a new store, International Gallery Beams, located above the original shop space. The Gallery sold high-end designer brands previously unknown in Japan, including England's Paul Smith and Italy's Giorgio Armani. Compared to Beams proper, prices at International Gallery came with an extra digit. Young men shopping for California sportswear would wander upstairs, see the price tags on a suit, and run out of the shop traumatized.

No Japanese import shop had ever attempted to sell European designer clothing, and as with all of the Beams stores, consumers took a few years to catch up to Osamu Shigematsu's vision. By 1983, however, he looked prescient: Japanese youth had tired of American traditional clothing. Trad shops catering to the women's market—dressing couples in matching madras blazers and yellow button-down oxfords—were the beginning of the end for the Preppy look. Womenswear cycled through trends at a much faster rate than menswear, so when the women's fashion media started to tell the Ivy girls to ditch the stodgy prep look and try something more radical, girlfriends pulled their boyfriends along. By late 1982, writer Keiichi Baba was already noting, "Preppy quietly, quietly disappeared as if it had never existed. What *was* that exactly?"

As an early maneuver against this sea change, *Hot Dog Press* and *Popeye* expanded the previous definition of Ivy from only East Coast collegiate clothing to include any traditional American or

Avant-garde take on Ivy in "Ishizu Kensuke's New Ivy Book" from October 1983. (Courtesy of Kōdansha)

European style—"British Ivy," "French Ivy," and "Italian Ivy." Editors replaced the parochialism of button-down shirts and drab khaki pants with wild patterns, clashing fabrics, and conceptual designs. In the strange new universe of 1983, wearing a buffalo-checked flannel blazer, herringbone pattern shirt, and high-waist pleated cargo shorts could somehow still be considered "Ivy." Red suspenders went over off-white fisherman sweaters and tapered tartan pants. In just a few years, the styles promoted in Japanese magazines went from an approximation of a Brown University freshman to things that American coeds would wear in jest to a "tacky"-themed dance party.

Ivy's growing eccentricity had roots in the Japanese fashion revolution erupting in Europe. Avant-garde designers Rei Kawakubo of Comme des Garçons and Yohji Yamamoto made their joint Paris debut in 1981 with a show centered on the theme of "destitution." Their asymmetrical lines, intentional imperfections, and torn-up industrial-grade fabrics within a black monochromatic palette stunned the European fashion community. But the two designers' eventual success turned "Japanese fashion" into a full-fledged movement on the global stage and brought new attention to innovative predecessors Issey Miyake and Kenzō Takada. Before Paris, Kawakubo and Yamamoto ran respectably-sized businesses in Japan, but the attention from overseas transformed them into domestic superstars. From 1979 to 1982, Comme des Garçons' revenues tripled, hitting $27 million in global sales ($66 million in 2015 dollars). All four designer brands benefitted from "reverse importation." Just as foreign goods arrived in Japan with an automatic halo of legitimacy, these designers became godlike figures at home thanks to their critical acclaim in Paris.

By 1983, devoted worshipers of the Yamamoto and Kawakubo cult pranced around Tokyo and Ōsaka head-to-toe in the designers' work. Their layers of long solid-black garments, asymmetrical haircuts, provocatively natural makeup, and flat shoes prompted the press to label them the Crow Tribe (*karasu-zoku*). Never had Japanese women worn so much black outside of a funeral. In response, women's magazines quickly moved away from the girly, schoolgirl pastels of hamatora, Ivy, and Preppy and on to Parisian-Japanese styles. With Tokyo's most fashionable females decked out in European avant-garde designs, American clothing felt outmoded and jejune.

Japanese designer fashion appeared at the same time that the mainstream media took an unlikely interest in New Academism, an exploration of complex postmodern theory. In 1983, twenty-six-year-old Kyoto University assistant professor Akira Asada sold eighty thousand copies of his book *Structure and Power: Beyond Semiotics*—the "first systematic introduction of certain strands in French philosophical thought, starting with a consideration of Lacan and Althusser, and then moving on to an account of Deleuze and Guattari." Not exactly light reading. In similar fashion, Seiji

Tsutsumi—the head of the Saison retailing group behind department store Seibu and trendy shopping mall PARCO—earnestly explained his business strategy to shareholders "as a Baudrillardeian exercise in [the] embrace of simulacra and parody." College students latched on to these difficult intellectual ideas as though they were an exciting new fashion trend, though few actually learned the difference between Derrida and Foucault. Comprehension issues aside, the zeitgeist of 1984 went very highbrow and far beyond an ersatz American student life.

By 1985, the Crow Tribe's designer approach to fashion had subsumed the entire market, leading to a period known as the "DC Boom." These "Designer and Character brands" encompassed global powerhouses Comme des Garçons and Y's, as well as domestic favorites like Bigi, Pink House, and the derivatively named Comme ça du Mode. The DC boom began with womenswear but spread quickly across the gender divide. Kawakubo and Yamamoto's avant-garde concepts of fashion opened the gates for Japanese designers to reject traditional silhouettes, fabrics, and coordination. The previously standard monochromatic color scheme eventually expanded into a bolder palette of discordant hues.

Middle-class teens saved up to buy designer goods in Harajuku just as they had with VAN or Cream Soda. Only now, teens purchased avant-garde garments that had once been the exclusive purview of wealthy denizens of the art world. Comme des Garçons was significantly more expensive than VAN, but a booming economy and the proliferation of credit cards made the high-end labels just as pervasive.

The appetite for designer clothing during the DC boom also extended to import brands. By 1986, the once cutting-edge International Gallery Beams looked quaint. Tokyo offered standalone boutiques from agnes b, Jean Paul Gaultier, and Michel Faret, Joseph, Margaret Howell, and Katharine Hamnett. Ten years prior, the only place to buy a Lacoste polo shirt was in the mildewed back alleys of Ameyoko. Now the Harajuku and Omotesando area sold nearly any piece of foreign clothing a curious teen could want, each one displayed inside luxury boutiques like a precious work of art.

May 1986 saw the debut of a new fashion magazine, *Men's Nonno*, which focused on local and Parisian *mode* rather than traditional styles. *Popeye* and *Hot Dog Press* moved with the times and followed their new rival into the DC Boom. And with so many teens wearing Japanese designers, editors and consumers alike stopped looking overseas for "correct" ideas on fashion. Armed with a new faith in their own economy and culture, they championed and celebrated ideas of domestic origin. Japan had not just "caught up" to American fashion by the mid-1980s—Tokyo's fashion scene far exceeded the sophistication ever seen in the U.S.

The events of 1985 took these feelings of national pride into overdrive. On September 22, the major global economies met at the Plaza Hotel in New York to plan the devaluation of the U.S. dollar. Over the next two years, the yen's value rose from 200 to the dollar to 150. The subsequent increase in Japanese export prices caused a slight recession, but the government countered with expansionary monetary policies. This set off an asset price bubble: land values in big cities skyrocketed, and everyone—especially landowners and employees of elite businesses—felt incredibly rich. The real estate within Tokyo's Imperial Palace was worth more than all of California. The once poor, defeated nation was suddenly sitting atop an unprecedented stack of cash.

The second half of the 1980s thus became known as the Bubble Era, where unbridled economic optimism bred extravagant and decadent living. As America suffered from industrial decline, crack cocaine, and AIDS, everything was going right for Japan—expressed by Harvard professor Ezra Vogel's 1979 best seller *Japan as Number One*. In response, the nation collectively abandoned its postwar penny-pinching and went on a shopping spree. Sony bought Columbia Pictures, Mitsubishi purchased New York's Rockefeller Center, an insurance mogul bought a Vincent van Gogh for nearly $40 million, and a Japanese businessman forked over $841 million for California golf course Pebble Beach. (Similarly, in 1986, Onward Kashiyama bought J. Press outright.) Tokyo descended into a Gatsby-esque bacchanal of questionable taste. Burgeoning company entertainment budgets funded outrageous behavior at new international restaurants and high-end hostess bars, followed by dancing to Eurobeat with girls in tight dresses at secret clubs.

The Bubble years were especially kind to the fashion industry. Beams' business doubled between 1987 and 1988. A high yen made imported goods more affordable, which only increased the social expectation of high consumption. Magazine circulations soared as teens of all strata suddenly needed guidance on how to dress. Editors maintained that high-priced European designers and Japanese DC brands matched "number-one" Japan much better than sober American or British traditional clothing. By the late 1980s, more than half of Japanese people owned imported garments—over double the number from ten years prior.

In 1987, *Men's Club* published a book called *Juppie* ("Japanese yuppies") which categorized this proud segment of newly wealthy men into four clothing styles. In their research, 42 percent of Juppies liked American trad clothing, 27 percent wore trendy Japanese designers like Yohji Yamamoto, 18 percent preferred Italian suits, and 13 percent went with the British look of Paul Smith. Being that the survey was conducted by *Men's Club*, there is no surprise that Trad took a plurality, but note that over half of well-to-do men now rejected American classics for the exciting world of European and avant-garde suits. Economics, national confidence, and culture all moved in lockstep, and Japan's highs meant a new low for American style. America was in decline, Japan was on the ascent: Why would you want to dress like a loser?

OLD MONEY HATES NEW MONEY, AND THE BUBBLE ERA BRED a lot of New Money. And so the backlash against Japan's nouveau-riche styles came not from a bohemian counterculture, but among teenagers from Tokyo's wealthy suburban neighborhoods Setagaya and Meguro. Private school students from these two areas mocked provincial teens' slavish devotion to strange designer clothing in Harajuku. Rich Tokyo natives did not have to *study* fashion in magazines; they absorbed good style from their fathers and older brothers (who, of course, had learned it from *Men's Club*).

Seeking to distance themselves from the DC brands, Tokyo's rich suburban teens in the mid-1980s devised a new style called *amekaji* ("American casual")—comfortable clothing from classic brands such as Brooks Brothers, Levi's, and Nike. Amekaji was a return to American basics, but looser and sportier than Preppy. Affluent Tokyo youth dressed down like real urban Americans: print T-shirts, sweatpants, and athletic shoes, as well as key status items pulled from pop culture such as *Top Gun*'s Navy G-1 flight jackets and Run DMC's adidas Superstars sneakers. A tougher contingent wore leather jackets over white Hanes T-shirts, stonewashed Levi's 501s, and engineer boots.

After successfully guiding the Preppy and the Euro designer craze, Beams managed to also become the guiding spirit for amekaji. The chain—no longer an "import shop" but a "select shop"—allowed teens to mix up their own outfits rather than wear a single designer head-to-toe. UNITED ARROWS' Hirofumi Kurino explains, "The dominant concept became that you wanted to wear what you wanted to wear in the way you wanted to wear it. And at that time, select shops played a big part in being the partner in helping you choose what you wanted to wear." In the world of amekaji, anything American could be thrown together: East Coast prep, West Coast athletic, hip-hop, Hollywood, and Native American jewelry. (Yet *Time*, in the U.S., still thought the look too rote: "The ultimate way to look American may be not to look American at all.")

Between Beams and the Ralph Lauren Polo store inside PARCO, Tokyo neighborhood Shibuya became headquarters of the amekaji movement. The fashion elite had never considered Shibuya a major shopping district, but most private school students passed through the area to get home anyway. Compared to the apparel-centric Harajuku, Shibuya offered a wider selection of establishments: department stores, restaurants, fast food joints, and bars.

In the mid-1980s, a few enterprising high schoolers started to throw graduation-themed dance parties at Shibuya clubs in imitation of prom scenes in American movies. The party organizers huddled into official "teams" with names like the Funkies, Winners, Breeze, Warriors, and Yanks. From there, members became known as "Teamers" (*chiimaa*). Like any respectable club of the era, they wore matching uniforms, usually American-style varsity jackets with copious patches and the team logo on the back.

By 1988, amekaji morphed into a more distinct *shibukaji* ("Shibuya casual"). The archetypal look was a neat coordination of polo shirts, zip-up hoodies, down vests, rolled-up Levi's 501 jeans, moccasins, and an "ethnic" silver necklace. Shibukaji's futures rose just as DC Boom was imploding. After three years of buying designer brands, the mass customer base and bargain sales killed any cachet the designer brands once enjoyed. Desperate for a new look to advocate, the editors at *Hot Dog Press* and *Popeye* flocked to Shibuya for inspiration. The first mainstream coverage appeared in January 1989 with *Checkmate*'s cover story on "Perfectly Master Shibukaji!" followed in April by *Hot Dog Press*' "Thorough Shibukaji Research Manual" and *Popeye*'s "Pictorial of Shibukaji Coordination."

The media coverage cataloged, codified, and propagated wealthy Shibuya teens' unconscious style. Shibukaji was similar in nature to American Preppy—casual clothing worn by wealthy students naturally imbued with good taste. The teens' supreme self-confidence, however, ended up convincing the status-obsessed nation that shibukaji was an even more moneyed look than the DC brands. The socioeconomic background of the style was not lost on the magazines, which did not just break down how to dress shibukaji, but namechecked all the private schools that bred the look. This status helped shibukaji retain DC's focus on Japanese-born fashion legitimacy even though the ingredients were imports. As sociologist Kōji Namba notes, "Shibukaji was cool because of

An illustration of shibukaji style in *Hot Dog Press*' "Thorough Shibukaji Research Manual." (©Shūichi Kataoka)

Shibuya, not because of America. All the fashion items in shibukaji were American, but 'America' was not something that existed above them. It was something on their level."

Once sanctioned by the media, the shibukaji style became the hottest look in the country. The entire economy of Harajuku collapsed overnight. Out went hyper-fashion sensitivity and in came moneyed nonchalance. No one cared about designers, and no one wanted to wear a single brand head-to-toe. The formula for shibukaji was simply having the right brands without looking like you actually paid attention to the fashion world. The easy combination of classic American labels, loose-fitting clothing, and sneakers ultimately attracted more people into the apparel market than ever before. Unlike with the DC boom, teens did not need specialized knowledge, nor credit cards, nor a willingness to forgo personal comfort. The bar to being stylish had never been so low.

The Shibuya look went slightly more upscale in late 1989 with *kirekaji* ("neat casual")—white Brooks Brothers button-down shirts, penny loafers, and navy-blue blazers. The effect, however, looked nothing like Ivy: the shoulders were wide, the fit was relaxed. One of the main purveyors in Shibuya of this kirekaji look was UNITED ARROWS, a new select shop founded by former Beams employee Osamu Shigematsu. In 1988, Etsuzō Shitara retired from Beams and appointed his son Yō the new president. The company split into two factions, and in the summer of 1989, half walked away with Shigematsu to form UNITED ARROWS. The first UA store was designed to bring something completely new to the market. Shigematsu remembers, "We started the store as post-shibukaji—jeans with navy blazers. Like an older brother version of the look in suits." The robust apparel market in Shibuya helped UNITED ARROWS find quick success, and Beams also made a quick recovery despite losing most of its senior staff.

For most of the 1980s, select shops like Beams, UNITED ARROWS, and Ships dominated the retail scene, but they could not meet the growing demand for imported American goods through their slow process of placing seasonal orders with overseas brands. To fill the gap, new amekaji shops popped up weekly in Shibuya. Since most official importers maintained high wholesaling prices, these small shops found a lucrative niche in "parallel importing."

Shop proprietors flew to America on highly discounted airfares meant for students and bought products in stores at retail prices. They scooped up Levi's, Lee, Banana Republic, Gap, L.L. Bean, Oshkosh, Wrangler, Raybans, Timex, and jerseys from U.S. sports teams, wearing as many items on the plane as possible to get around paying import duties. In search of discounts, they descended like locusts upon Polo Ralph Lauren factory outlets and sneaker stores in suburban malls. American retailers eventually caught on to the racket and limited the number of items sold to each person. But even marking up from normal U.S. store prices could still be cheaper than the goods procured through official distribution channels. These products became known as *hando* in Japanese, from "hand carry."

Small import stores made Shibuya an even more popular shopping destination. But as youth poured into the neighborhood, bringing their own tastes and agendas, they changed the nature of shibukaji style. The second-wave of adopters preferred a more rebellious version of amekaji, mixing in silver jewelry, harder surfer influences, and a Guns'n'Roses Sunset Strip edge. The tougher amekaji could be seen in the savage second generation of Teamers, who outgrew throwing prom-like parties and moved into the drug trade. Violence erupted. The first major incident came in 1989 when students from two elite high schools held a knife fight over a girl—only one walked away alive. This promise of violence then attracted teens from rougher parts of the Tokyo metropolitan area, who, a decade earlier, would have become bōsōzoku or yankii.

The new breed of Teamers patrolled their small slice of Shibuya with four-wheel-drive SUVs and assaulted rival teams who waded into their territory. Influenced by the 1988 film *Colors*, they started to brandish butterfly knives and wear bandannas to indicate group affiliation. Writer Kenrō Hayamizu thinks American films were the clear influence: "Japan didn't have a culture of teenagers riding around in cars. Shibukaji guys were at first just imitating *The Outsiders*." Law enforcement cracked down on the entire neighborhood, pressuring clubs to stop working with underage party promoters. By 1993, the deviant Teamer image had completely annihilated the once moneyed ambiance of shibukaji. Trendy teens fled Shibuya the way they had fled Harajuku just four years earlier.

The rise and fall of Shibuya casual unfortunately echoed the arc of the entire Japanese economy. In December 1991, the Japanese stock market crashed, and over the next year, Tokyo land prices plummeted. The so-called Bubble popped, and individuals and companies alike woke up with unpayable debts. The culture of excess did not stop on a dime—incomes were still rising—but, by 1993, Japanese consumers started to sober up. At the time, no one knew how long the dip would last, but the downturn ultimately brought Japan into its "lost decade" of sluggish economic growth and intractable social malaise.

Fashion sales hit an all-time peak in 1991 at ¥19.88 trillion ($253 billion in 2015 dollars), and have drifted downward ever since. Select shops like Beams, UNITED ARROWS, and Ships, by contrast, continued to grow strongly in the 1990s. Their "editorial" format of curating international brands allowed them to flow with the changing styles while always being the go-to location for buying basics.

In the first years of the lost decade, the DC Boom and shibukaji both disappeared from the fashion scene—jettisoned as antiquated relics of a gilded age. The styles, however, introduced two important characteristics that would predict trends in the 1990s. Teens loved the exclusiveness and brand power of Harajuku designer fashion in the DC boom, and then found an equally compelling antithesis in Shibuya's effortless American casual. Brands that could synthesize these two positions in the 1990s would go on to amazing success—not just in Japan, but around the world.

EIGHT

From Harajuku to Everywhere

IN THE LATE 1970S, HIROSHI FUJIWARA WAS THE COOLEST kid in Mie Prefecture—skateboarding around on a homemade deck, listening to the Sex Pistols, playing in a rockabilly band. He may have even been the coolest kid in all of Western Japan. Certainly he was the only high school student writing letters to clothing stores in Ōsaka asking to buy Vivienne Westwood's Seditionaries line. He was so cool that when he moved to Tokyo at age eighteen, he was elected "best dressed" at an underground party London Nite and sent on a free trip to London. There he met his heroes Westwood and her partner, Malcolm McLaren, and when he returned to the U.K. a year later, he worked at their shop, World's End.

McLaren told Fujiwara to forget about punk and new wave and pointed him to a new musical genre coming off the streets of New York—hip-hop. Fujiwara recalled his subsequent trip to *Interview* in 2010: "The Roxy was really happening—Afrika Islam, Kool Lady Blue, that whole scene. I really got interested in the DJ side." He returned to Tokyo carrying the first crate of hip-hop records to grace the Japanese archipelago. He then showed the local club scene how to scratch and cut records with two turntables. But Fujiwara did not just want to be a DJ, so in 1985, he teamed up with Kan Takagi to form his own hip-hop unit, Tinnie Panx ("tiny punks"). The group was an integral part of the early Japanese rap scene, opening for the Beastie Boys' Tokyo concert in 1987 and cofounding Japan's first hip-hop label, Major Force.

With unrivaled connections to tastemakers in London and New York, Fujiwara appeared in Japanese magazines each month to introduce the latest in global trends. In 1987, Fujiwara and Kan started a column called "Last Orgy" in subcultural magazine *Takarajima* that mixed skateboarding, punk rock, art films, high fashion, and hip-hop all together into a single worldview—one that would later be formally codified as "street culture." Each month, Fujiwara and Takagi introduced their favorite new rappers, twelve-inches, clothing, films, and DJ equipment. In just his early twenties, Hiroshi Fujiwara was a living legend—cultural critic, DJ, rapper, breakdancer, and model.

Across the country, a small cult of young men started to hang on to every word of "Last Orgy" as gospel truth. This included Tomoaki Nagao, a high school student in Gunma Prefecture's sober capital Maebashi, who shared an eerie facial resemblance to Fujiwara. Soon Nagao switched his allegiances from rock 'n' roll to hip-hop. Each week, he and his friends videotaped the "Last Orgy" segment on late-night show FM-TV and watched it on repeat. When Tinnie Panx toured Gunma, Nagao waited around after the show to get Fujiwara's autograph.

Hoping to be a media guru like his idol Fujiwara, Nagao moved to Tokyo to enroll in a course for aspiring magazine editors at top fashion institute Bunka Fukusō Gakuin. In the school's music club, he met aspiring designer Jun "Jonio" Takahashi, who introduced him at London Nite to all the people he had read about in magazines for years. It was there that the head clerk of the punk-rockabilly boutique, A Store Robot, also noticed Nagao's resemblance to Hiroshi Fujiwara and gave him a nickname for the ages—*Fujiwara Hiroshi Nigō* ("Fujiwara Hiroshi Number Two"). Despite the slight mockery implied, young Nagao embraced it. Among friends, he was no longer "Tomo-kun" but "Nigo."

Within weeks, Fujiwara Number Two met his hero, Fujiwara Number One, and became one of his personal assistants. Plugged into the Fujiwara network, Nigo found a part-time job at *Popeye*, wrote a column with Jonio faithfully named "Last Orgy 2," styled musicians and TV talent, and DJ'ed at Fujiwara's weekly parties. At the age of twenty-one, Nigo was already living up to the Hiroshi Fujiwara Number Two name.

Where cultural icons of the past rose to fame on the power of their own creations, Fujiwara and his young pupils found success in the act of *curation*—choosing the best music, fashion, books, and consumer goods for magazines. Japanese media knew how to find trends on East Coast campuses and Parisian runways, but editors struggled in the mid-1980s to keep up with the rise of street culture. The knowledgeable, connected Fujiwara was the answer to all of their problems. But for Fujiwara to leave a lasting mark on culture, he would need to become more than a cultural clearinghouse. He and his crew needed to make something of their own.

HIROSHI FUJIWARA WAS THE FIRST JAPANESE MEMBER OF the International Stüssy Tribe—a loose network of like-minded creatives centered around Shawn Stussy's eponymous streetwear label. Fujiwara became friends with Stussy in 1986 after interviewing him for the magazine *Takarajima*, and after that, he started receiving boxes of Stüssy clothing in the mail.

Fujiwara disciple and graphic designer Shinichirō "Sk8thing" Nakamura had an itch to start a line of original T-shirts in the Stüssy mold. Fujiwara liked the idea of opening a streetwear brand, but wanted to do it right. He reached out to a young shop proprietor named Toru "TORUEYE" Iwai whom he had met while on tour in Kyūshū's gritty port city of Kokura. Iwai offered to help Fujiwara start his brand and made introductions to his own local backer, Nobuaki Ōkaji. The older gentleman agreed to act as a patron to Fujiwara's project, providing fashion industry know-how forged from many years selling VAN and American secondhand garments.

With this support, Fujiwara, Sk8thing, and Iwai launched Japan's first true streetwear brand—Goodenough. Launching in 1990, Goodenough appeared relatively early in the history of global streetwear, around the same time as pioneering labels FUCT and SSUR and predating other American counterparts such as X-Large. Borrowing from the Stüssy model, Goodenough focused on high-quality T-shirts and sportswear with bold graphic prints. The brand saw immediate success in Japan after *Popeye* and *Hot Dog Press* showcased it as part of the 1991 skateboarder fashion trend.

Fujiwara appeared each month in magazines wearing Goodenough, but he concealed his role in managing the brand. He explained to biographer Masayuki Kawakatsu, "If I told people that I was doing the brand, no one would actually look at the clothing. People who were going to buy it would just buy it, and people who hate me would ignore it." With the brand's origins obscured, Goodenough looked like an import from the U.S. like Stüssy, Freshjive, or FUCT. And henceforth, many young Japanese tourists got lost in Los Angeles trying to locate "the original" Goodenough store.

Capitalizing on Goodenough's success, Fujiwara tapped Nigo and Jonio to start the group's next apparel venture. The two twenty-somethings worked with Ōkaji to open a store in a quiet, non-commercial part of Harajuku, off of Omotesando Avenue but far from the main drags of Meiji-doori and Takeshita-doori. They called this quiet area *Ura-Harajuku* (*ura* meaning "back"). With the Harajuku neighborhood still reeling from the crash of the rock 'n' roll and the DC boom, Nigo and Takahashi represented a new generation who could lure teens back to the economically devastated neighborhood. In April 1993, they opened Nowhere, a hole-in-the-wall shop split into two sections. Takahashi sold his own punk brand Undercover on one side, while Nigo offered a mix of imported streetwear on the other.

After receiving magazine endorsements as part of the "neo-punk" trend, Undercover saw immediate traffic. But the other side of the shop remained quiet. Nigo soon realized that his own success hinged on creating an original brand. Sk8thing went off to think of an idea for the label and found his concept after watching a TV marathon of the five *Planet of the Apes* films. He lifted the films' iconic simian faces for the logo and slapped on an English slogan—A Bathing Ape in Lukewater [sic]—borrowed from a line in an underground Takashi Nemoto comic that described an old man "like an ape in a bath of lukewarm water." Nigo whittled down the official brand name to the first three words—A Bathing Ape—and printed up a few T-shirts and jackets in the style of American vintage garments.

In September 1994, Fujiwara, Nigo, and Jonio launched a new column, "Last Orgy 3," in Japan's first street culture magazine, *Asayan*. Like previous efforts, they used the space to introduce the latest goods from abroad. But now armed with their own brands and retail spaces, it quickly devolved into monthly acts of self-promotion. The second installment, in October 1994, for example, simply celebrated the opening of Harajuku Nowhere Ltd., a new store for Undercover's women's line. This media exposure lead to an immediate rise in sales. Thanks to *Asayan* readers, Fujiwara and Jonio's limited-edition AFFA (Anarchy Forever Forever Anarchy) line of MA-1 nylon bomber jackets with leftist political slogan patches sold out immediately.

As Goodenough, Undercover, and A Bathing Ape built up steady fan bases, more members of the Fujiwara crew created their own fashion lines. Former Major Force employee Shinsuke Takizawa started the punk/biker-themed brand Neighborhood in October 1994, and a month later, twenty-one-year-old pro skater Yoshifumi "Yoppy" Egawa founded the sporty line Hectic. Six months after that, Jonio's former bandmate, Hikaru Iwanaga, opened the punk-rock toy store Bounty Hunter.

To stand out from his peers, Nigo aligned A Bathing Ape closely with the indie hip-hop scene. He clothed his friends in rap group Scha Dara Parr just as they broke into the mainstream with their hit song "Kon'ya wa Boogie-Back." This track started a

An ape-patterned camouflage jacket and ape-head logo sweatshirt from the early years of A Bathing Ape. (©Nowhere Co., Ltd.)

national love affair with hip-hop that peaked in early 1995 when rap group East End X Yuri moved over one million copies of their song "DA.YO.NE." Nigo outfitted the group's female rapper Yuri Ichii in A Bathing Ape T-shirts, jackets, and sweaters just as she became a media darling. A Bathing Ape also styled Keigō Oyamada, who took his artist name Cornelius from the same 1993 *Planet of the Apes* marathon that gave birth to A Bathing Ape. In October 1995, Nigo produced Cornelius' tour shirts, and the star's fan base snapped up A Bathing Ape designs to follow their hero's fashion choices.

Nigo made his first international connections through London trip-hop record label Mo Wax. From the day Nigo met label boss James Lavelle, the British indie mogul started wearing A Bathing Ape on an almost daily basis. Back in Japan, A Bathing Ape's relationship to Mo Wax artists DJ Shadow and Money Mark gave the brand a massive boost of cachet among music nerds. Lavelle also introduced Nigo to New York graffiti legends Futura 2000 and Stash, who, in July 1995, faxed T-shirt designs over to Tokyo and later opened their own stores through the Fujiwara connection in Harajuku.

These alliances with the music world bolstered sales for A Bathing Ape and helped the passionate but small street fashion movement in Ura-Harajuku surface in the mainstream. In 1996, Nigo and Takahashi opened up a larger Nowhere around the corner from the original, causing queues that snaked through the backstreets all the way into the primary thoroughfares of Harajuku.

After the implosion of Shibuya Casual in 1991, the media spent the rest of the decade struggling to define a singular look for the era. Monolithic trends splintered into a variety of menswear styles, all categorized under the word *kei* ("style"). This included skater-kei, surfer-kei, street-kei, mod-kei, and military-kei. *Hot Dog Press* and *Popeye* filed Goodenough, Undercover, and A Bathing Ape under their own genre—*Ura-Harajuku-kei*. Boiled down to its essentials, Ura-Harajuku-kei was classic American casual items with neat presentation: camouflage jackets, crisp brand logo

T-shirts or striped skater shirts, rigid dark denim, Clark's Walla-bees, adidas Superstars, Nike Air Max '95s, and high-tech back-packs. The style was sporty and relaxed—a fashionable version of teenage boys' play clothes. Compared to other casual looks, how-ever, Ura-Harajuku-kei offered a much more compelling back-story: carefully defined brands, star personalities, and affiliations to musical artists.

By the end of 1996, Goodenough, Undercover, and A Bathing Ape were big enough to start taking the top spots in magazine polls of readers' favorite labels. An August 1996 survey in *Asayan* of readers' most admired male celebrities contained no movie stars or pop musicians, but instead, Hiroshi Fujiwara, Jun Takahashi, and Keigō Oyamada. Nowhere came in as the most popular shop. The media called Fujiwara and his crew *karisuma*—from the En-glish word "charisma"—denoting a nearly supernatural power to make followers buy anything they recommended. As sociologist Kōji Namba notes, "People did not necessarily imitate Hiroshi Fu-jiwara's personal style, but they jumped towards whatever he said was good."

In 1997, Ura-Harajuku officially graduated from subcultural fandom to complete domination of the entire Japanese men's fash-ion market. A September 1997 *Hot Dog Press* readers' poll ranked Ura-Harajuku-kei as the country's most popular style. Despite Goodenough and Undercover's early position as trend leaders, A Bathing Ape became the established entry point for newcomers. Young people more easily understood *Planet of the Apes*-inspired graphics on a T-shirt than Undercover leather bondage pants. And only hardcore devotees could get their hands on the extremely lim-ited supply of Goodenough.

With A Bathing Ape in the spotlight, Nigo began producing a full line of clothing each season. The rewards were instant: a No-vember 1997 *Hot Dog Press* poll of both Tokyo and Ōsaka listed A Bathing Ape as readers' number-one brand. On the street snap pages of fashion magazines each month, youth around the country proudly wore their Ape T-shirts and claimed to "worship" Nigo.

Fashionable teens of the 1990s did not just love the Ura-Hara-juku brands for their designs—they loved the hunt. Following the Stüssy model, Fujiwara and his disciples made too little product, sold at too few stores. But rather than frustrating consumers, these tactics elated any fans lucky enough to get their hands on the merchandise. A debate still rages over whether the brands' undersupply was a calculated marketing decision or an organic move to stay underground. The truth falls somewhere in between. Fujiwara never wanted to create a mass market brand or run a large company, often to the chagrin of his business partners. In 1995, at the very height of Goodenough's popularity, Fujiwara made the capricious decision that the brand would take a six-month hiatus. He also decided to cut the number of retailers from forty to ten. Nigo and Jonio took inspiration from this move, pulling their brands from stores in other cities and limiting point of sales to their own managed shops.

Although this retail method seems counterintuitive for a hit brand, it was a necessary move to maintain an exclusive image. Designer lines like Comme des Garçons used avant-garde designs and devilish prices to keep its products away from the masses. The Ura-Harajuku labels, on the other hand, sold basic, casual items that were relatively affordable. Getting Goodenough or A Bathing Ape to everyone who wanted them would torpedo the brands' cachet. The most obvious solution was to make less.

So Fujiwara, Takahashi, and Nigo made goods in numbers far below the market demand. This limited the brand to select audiences and simultaneously created a fierce consumer mania. They called the low production runs "limited-edition"—motivating teens to collect their clothing rather than simply wear it.

When Ura-Harajuku-kei became the top style in Japan, fans lined up in front of Nowhere and the other brands' shops each day. When Fujiwara opened a Harajuku retail base, Readymade, in 1997, to sell his own brands, hundreds of customers arrived before dawn. By that afternoon, teens had completely stripped the store of stock. In the first two days alone, the store saw $200,000 in sales, forcing Fujiwara to enlist a volunteer army of friends to transport the cash to the bank.

The constant cycle of limited-edition goods was highly profitable for Fujiwara and his disciples, but the practice also benefitted hundreds of unaffiliated resellers. The infamous queues inevitably included buyers from small provincial shops who purchased goods at retail prices and then resold at a high markup. Yet this shadow market continued to boost brand cachet. Stalls off Takeshita-doori in Harajuku offered sealed, mint condition A Bathing Ape T-shirts for five-times the regular cost. A three-year-old AFFA T-shirt sold for ¥79,000 in 1997 ($900 in 2015 dollars). The T-shirt—considered little more than underwear three decades before—was now a rare *objet d'art*. The promise of high resale value only encouraged further consumption. A teenager told *Asahi Shimbun* in 1997, "I don't care about the price. If I get sick of it, I'll just sell it off."

On a surface level, Ura-Harajuku clothing looked similar to American-inspired casual fashion of the past. But there was one fundamental difference: teens' most coveted brands no longer came from the United States, but originated in a specific neighborhood in Tokyo. In the 1990s, teens could choose from nearly every brand in the world—yet they preferred Japanese labels. Ura-Harajuku-kei provided the perfect compromise between Shibukaji and the DC brands: casual clothing with an air of exclusivity.

The Shibuya Casual boom had turned Harajuku into a shopping wasteland at the end of the 1980s. Less than a decade later, Ura-Harajuku was the most fashionable place in Japan—and perhaps the entire globe. Certainly there was more money pouring into Japanese streetwear brands than into similar brands in the U.S. Hiroshi Fujiwara turned everything he touched to gold, and his protégés were heroes to Japanese youth across the country. As the money rolled in, however, these young tycoons sat down to ponder the fundamental dichotomy of their existence: How could they continue being "underground" when they were on top of the world?

IN THE SUMMER OF 1998, AS OVER TWO HUNDRED JAPANESE youth waited patiently in the hot sun to enter Nigo's Busy Work Shop Harajuku, A Bathing Ape staff ushered inside a VIP—sunny-faced Ken Miyake of popular boy band V6. At the time, Miyake and his fellow group member Gō Morita wore Bathing Ape (or as it started to be called, Bape) shirts in all of their numerous TV and magazine appearances. Meanwhile, stylist friends of Nigo repeatedly put A Bathing Ape on the most popular male idol at the time, SMAP's Takuya Kimura.

These new Bape celebrity ambassadors—pretty faces with questionable talent who appeared nightly on teenage girls' favorite variety shows—were a far cry from indie gods Cornelius and James Lavelle. They gave A Bathing Ape broad exposure to teenagers who had never cracked open an issue of *Asayan*, let alone *Hot Dog Press*. A few months after Kimura's conversion to Ura-Harajuku fashion, police arrested two men in Ibaraki Prefecture making A Bathing Ape counterfeits, who simply knew the brand as one "worn by Takuya Kimura."

As A Bathing Ape gained traction inside the Japanese entertainment circuit, Nigo faced a stark choice—to stay half-hidden in the shadows like his mentor Fujiwara or push towards full mainstream success. At twenty-eight, Nigo decided to remove any artificial caps on his business. He abandoned limited production and exclusive access and aimed to make A Bathing Ape the most far-reaching and luxurious streetwear brand of all time.

In need of a new retail strategy, Nigo hired acclaimed architect Masamichi Katayama of Wonderwall to design a chain of identical Busy Work Shops around the country. Drawing on his unprecedented revenue stream, Nigo was able to create a luxury chain unlike anything seen in the U.S. or the U.K. The stores' modernist design motif—white walls, unadorned concrete, sleek glass, brushed steel, and bright lights—felt like a visit to a utopian future compared to the simple log cabin look of the original Nowhere.

In 1998, Nigo opened Busy Work Shops in Ōsaka, Nagoya, Sendai, and extremely rural Aomori, as well as a flagship Nowhere in his home prefecture of Gunma. These locations helped Bape sales hit ¥2 billion in 1999 ($22 million in 2015 dollars). That year brought new stores to Matsuyama, Fukuoka, Kyōto, and Hiroshima. A year later, Nigo took the brand upscale with a new flagship location called Bapexclusive in Aoyama, down the street from Comme des Garçons and Issey Miyake. In 2001, Nigo expanded his clothing empire into womenswear with Bapy.

Despite Bape's retail saturation in its home country at the turn of the century, the Ura-Harajuku phenomenon was still limited to Japan. The only people in the West who wore Goodenough, Undercover, or A Bathing Ape were Nigo's friends and touring Japanese musicians. Every once in a while, a few T-shirts showed up at New York boutique Recon or London store Hideout, but there was no reliable inventory. But, like in Japan, this very lack of supply made the brands red-hot with American and British fashion snobs. An August 1999 article in the *New York Times* introduced A Bathing Ape as one of the world's most exclusive "limited-edition" goods, quoting a magazine art director who went to London just to buy the brand's camouflage jacket: "It was worth it because all my friends wanted it, and I got there first." The same month, England's *The Face* placed A Bathing Ape on its list of greatest logo-based brands of all time, calling it "truly underground." What did Fujiwara and Nigo do in response? Absolutely nothing. With Japan emerging as the world's most sophisticated market for streetwear, they had no interest in catering towards foreign audiences.

The first baby step into international expansion came in 1999, when rapper Eric Kot and comedian/DJ Jan Lamb convinced Nigo to open a Busy Work Shop in Hong Kong. Bape solved any worries about gray market reimportation into Japan by forcing potential shoppers to apply for store membership using their Hong Kong passports. Appointments had to be made in advance—no walk-ins allowed. In spite of these exclusionary efforts, the Hong Kong expansion catapulted the brand into the wider Asian consciousness, and, within months, the entire Chinese-speaking world was coveting A Bathing Ape tees. Hong Kong teens snapped up

the Baby Milo line of childish cartoon print tees so enthusiasti-
cally that local TV news reported on the phenomenon. But simple
economics reigned supreme: the fundamental lack of supply
spurred every savvy counterfeiter in Asia to pump out fake A
Bathing Ape T-shirts. By 2001, American auction site eBay offered hundreds of "real Bape" shirts at a mere $15 a pop, with
dubious descriptions like "made for the Korean market."

As Bape became a global brand, Nigo could no longer keep
things under control or "exclusive." Bigger was the only move forward. In late 2001, Nigo joined with Pepsi Japan to wrap every
soda can in Bape camouflage. Just four years prior, youth had to
wait in line at a single store in Harajuku to buy A Bathing Ape
goods. Now they could stumble up to vending machines glowing
on an abandoned rural street at 3 a.m. and get something with a
Bape design for a few coins.

Nigo then moved into Napoleonic-levels of expansion: suddenly everything everywhere was "Bape." In 2002, after a few years
of quietly making tributes to Converse's Chuck Taylors, A Bathing
Ape produced candy colored sneakers called Bapestas in homage
to Nike's Air Force 1s. Nigo sold them in a new chain of innovative stores called Foot Soldier that displayed his footwear on con-
veyor belts. In 2003, Nigo invested in a hair salon called Bape
Cuts, as well as in a restaurant called Bape Café?! He opened a
children's wear store called Bape Kids and a short-lived space dedicated solely to Baby Milo goods. As the new century progressed,
Bape stores appeared in every remote area in Japan—Kanazawa,
Niigata, Shizuoka, Kagoshima, and Kumamoto. In Tokyo alone,
one could hit at least five A Bathing Ape locations in a twenty-
minute walk around Harajuku. Commercials for Nigo's cable television program, "Bape TV," rained down from huge jumbotrons at
the neighborhood's main intersection.

In 2003, Nigo completed work on his multimillion-dollar
house—a five-story concrete bunker guarded by dozens of security
cameras. He used the space as a museum of late twentieth century
pop culture—entire rooms dedicated to iconic Rickenbacker

guitars and the world's largest collection of *Planet of the Apes* toys. He used glass walls for his wood-floored garage so his Mercedes Benz SLR, Porsche, Rolls Royce, and Bentley would be visible from inside the house.

In contrast to Nigo's overexposure and public extravagance, Hiroshi Fujiwara found a comfortable niche as the quiet Godfather of Streetwear. Goodenough never strayed from the scale of its founding days, and a decade after its launch, Fujiwara cut all personal ties to the label. Fujiwara made his own fortune on a collaboration with Japanese bag maker Yoshida Kaban, called Head Porter—a series of bags made from the same nylon as American MA-1 flight jackets. Head Porter became the de facto bag, wallet, and fanny pack brand for Ura-Harajuku fans, even with teens who had never heard of Goodenough or Hiroshi Fujiwara. When Head Porter became a national phenomenon, however, the perpetual lone wolf handed off management to a friend. Fujiwara told *Theme* in 2005, "I didn't really want lots of people working for me, whom I have to take care of."

At the end of the twenty-first century, Fujiwara Number One and Number Two had taken their businesses into two completely different directions. In 2000, Fujiwara earned more between the two—paying ¥54.7 million in taxes ($700,000 in 2015 dollars) compared to Nigo's ¥45.3 million ($582,000). But when Fujiwara moved into a studio towards the top of luxury apartment Roppongi Hills Residence in 2003, Nigo took the penthouse.

From that apartment, Nigo looked each night over the city he conquered. He had it all in Japan—but the rest of the world was still there for the taking.

IN 2003, NIGO OPENED THE FIRST BAPE STORE IN LONDON. At the time, the Bapesta shoes were starting to get big in the West, but Nigo—who built his career on knowing global trends—felt out of touch with the global market. Former Mo Wax manager and lawyer Toby Feltwell joined Bape at the time to advise Nigo on the overseas business. Feltwell's first move was to help the Ape General rekindle his love for American hip-hop.

Feltwell and Nigo's favorite accessories designer, Jacob the Jeweler, schemed to match up Nigo and the most respected music producer of the era, Pharrell Williams. In 2003, Nigo offered Williams use of his Ape Studios to finish a recording while in Tokyo. Williams was vaguely familiar with the Bapesta shoe but was floored when he saw the full extent of the Bape empire. He told *Complex*, in 2013, "When I went to Nigo's showroom, it was the most amazing thing I had ever seen, ever. I just went crazy and he let me have whatever I wanted to." Despite needing to talk through an interpreter, Nigo and Williams became close friends, and, within hours, planned out a series of joint collaborations.

First up, Nigo stepped in to help design Williams's shoe line ICECREAM, eventually opening a store for the brand right above Busy Work Shop Harajuku. Nigo and Sk8thing then turned Williams's plan for a clothing line called Billionaire Boys Club into a reality, bringing together Ura-Harajuku retail prowess with American pizazz. In return, Pharrell acted as Nigo's conduit to mainstream American hip-hop. With new friends like Jay Z and Kanye West, Nigo finally felt the need to establish a retail presence in the United States. Nigo told *Nylon Guys,* in 2006, "Originally RUN DMC is what got me into fashion. I loved American casual. When I got into England, it's because I got bored of America. I think I've finally come back."

He opened Busy Work Shop New York in late 2004, introducing an entire generation of American youth to his brand. By the time the store opened, Bape had replaced the classic 1990s olive military patterns and standard logo bite T-shirts with a salvo of inventive camo hoodies and Bapestas in pastel colors. Asian shoppers lined up in droves, of course, but Nigo's connections to Pharrell helped make the store a hotspot for hip-hop royalty. To look the part of a true hip-hop impresario, Nigo asked Jacob the Jeweler to make him a series of diamond-encrusted pieces to wear around town—a wristwatch, a comical Flavor Flav-like clock pendant, and the *piece de resistance*, a full grill for his mouth.

Between the innovative product and the celebrity backing, A Bathing Ape instantly became the hottest brand in America. For four solid years in the mid-2000s, MTV transformed into a showreel of rappers wearing Bape. (Nigo himself made a guest appearance in Pharrell's video for the song "Frontin'.") Dozens of hip-hop tracks name-dropped Bape in their rhymes, starting on the East Coast and quickly spreading to regional upstarts. In his viral YouTube hit "Crank Dat," Mississippi's Soulja Boy bragged that "haters gettin' mad cause I got me some Bathing Apes."

Now firmly a global star, Nigo hit the society pages of *Vanity Fair* and *Vogue* posing with luminaries such as Karl Lagerfeld and David Beckham. In 2005, Nigo graced the cover of *Interview* biting onto a diamond-studded cross. A year later, Nigo and Pharrell Williams went together to the MTV Video Awards in matching red caps, white T-shirts, and heavy gold rope chains. But perhaps the clearest evidence of American success was the explosion in counterfeit merchandise—known colloquially as "fape." Fly-by-night urban gear stores in malls across America crammed hundreds of phony Bape shirts onto their hangers. Toby Feltwell one day got a call from United States Customs that two entire containers of counterfeit Bape were sitting offshore in Miami, Florida.

Sixty years after World War II, Americans clamored after the Japanese brand A Bathing Ape the same way that the Japanese had obsessed over American style in the preceding decades. This stunning achievement, however, was completely lost on Japanese youth. From the 1990s onward, a small subculture of hip-hop fans in Japan dressed in colorful baggy clothes in imitation of African-American rappers. Yet when their heroes in the U.S. started wearing a Japanese brand, they struggled with the cognitive dissonance and kept their distance from Bape. More broadly, the era of "reverse importation" was over: no one in Ja-

Pharrell Williams and Nigo at MTV Music Awards 2006. (©Jeff Kravitz / FilmMagic / Getty Images)

pan cared about A Bathing Ape because it was big overseas. The great irony is that teens learned to cherish local over global from the Ura-Harajuku crew, who gave them higher quality and more stylish Japanese product than what was coming from abroad.

Despite the lull in Japan, Bape's popularity overseas filled Nowhere's coffers to the tune of $63 million in sales for the 2007 fiscal year. Once Bape mania waned in the United States, however, the financial situation quickly began to deteriorate. After two years of declining sales and mounting debt, Nigo stepped down as CEO of Nowhere in 2009 and handed the Bape reins to a staid corporate executive formerly of Japan's largest fashion retailer, World. Busy Work Shops opened in Shanghai, Beijing, Taipei, and Singapore, making Bape as commonplace in Asia as global behemoths Nike or adidas. Unfortunately, the brand struggled in its original markets: stores closed in far-off Kumamoto and Kagoshima, and then Los Angeles.

On February 1, 2011, Japan awoke to the news that Hong Kong retailer I.T. Ltd. had snapped up 90 percent of A Bathing Ape parent company Nowhere for a mere ¥230 million—little more than $2 million. This was a pittance for a company still pulling in ¥5 billion ($62.5 million) in yearly revenue. The catch was that I.T. agreed to take on Nowhere's ¥4.31 billion ($52.79 million) in debt. Nigo could have easily followed the same path into bankruptcy as Kensuke Ishizu and VAN Jacket, but a Hong Kong buyout gave him a more graceful exit. He told *Women's Wear Daily* at the time, "I definitely didn't want to file [for bankruptcy] under the Civil Rehabilitation Law, and I didn't want to damage the brand. I had a strong feeling that I wanted the brand to survive, so the main thing was thinking what to do about that. I spent 20 years building it up, so it would be a real shame for it to disappear."

While the agreement with I.T. may have been a mixed bag for Nigo, it was a significant moment for the globalization of the Japanese fashion industry. No longer did cultural exchange flow in a single America-to-Japan direction. A Bathing Ape both burrowed straight into the heart of American pop culture and kicked off Japan's enduring fashion dominance over Asia, mirroring the way that America once influenced Japan. Companies in Greater China were placing big money on the table for the right to sell Japanese brands. And web-savvy Asian shoppers played an outsized role in modernizing the global streetwear scene. They shifted the streetwear ecosystem from a closed world of unobtainable Japanese brands written up in monthly printed magazines, to Hong Kong-based blogs like "Hypebeast," pumping out daily reviews of the latest products that could be purchased from anywhere, anytime through e-commerce.

The Bape bankruptcy offered a clear ending to the Ura-Harajuku era, but the movement's heroes still wielded a sizable influence on global culture. Nigo found his feet in no time, starting two smaller-scale brands, Human Made and a VAN-clone, Mr. Bathing Ape. He then signed on as Creative Director to UNIQLO's U.T. T-shirt line, and, in 2014, became an advisor to adidas Originals. Jun Takahashi has meanwhile enjoyed constant critical acclaim for Undercover since moving his whimsical, gothic fashion shows to Paris in 2002. More recently, Takahashi worked with Nike on an avant-garde running line called *Gyakusou* ("running backwards"), and collaborated with UNIQLO on a collection called UU.

Hiroshi Fujiwara is well-known as a creative consultant to Nike and works directly with CEO Mark Parker on special projects. When mainstream Japanese fashion magazines stopped following the Fujiwara crew's exploits, he started a curated selection of blogs called Honeyee.com. Overall, however, he maintains his mixed feelings about the globalized Internet—a medium that unraveled his one-time monopoly on introducing foreign trends to Japan. He told *Interview* in 2010 that our constantly connected world is "really convenient but kind of boring."

In comparison, the actual Ura-Harajuku neighborhood has deteriorated into irrelevance: Nowhere, Readymade, and Real Mad Hectic are all gone, replaced by second-rate brands and suspicious streetwear resellers. The spirit of the Ura-Harajuku movement, however, lives on unabated at a global scale—in Nike's hundreds of limited-edition sneakers, in pop-up stores within unmarked retail spaces, in heated comment threads of street fashion web forums, and in the long lines of shoppers who stand in front of New York's Supreme waiting for a chance to buy a single T-shirt. Former Stüssy Creative Director and current adidas Originals Creative Director Paul Mittleman does not mince words about the historical importance of Japanese street style, "If Stüssy started streetwear, Bape fucking blew it out of the water."

Despite their decades of unique experiences and hard-fought successes, Fujiwara and Nigo remain locked in the same teacher-pupil relationship that formed the first day they met in the late 1980s. In 2014, Nigo posted a photo on Instagram of the two with a *Star Wars*-inspired caption: "Master HIROSHI & Padawan NIGO." Yet both men changed the face of global fashion in their own ways. Hiroshi Fujiwara brought the underground straight into mainstream Japanese culture and put Japan on the map among the cultural elite. A Bathing Ape introduced Americans to the idea of paying top dollar for Japanese-made, American style. Thanks to both, the world's cultural leaders learned that keeping up with trends meant having to keep a constant eye on Japan.

NINE

Vintage and Replica

THROUGHOUT 1982, TWENTY-SIX-YEAR-OLD YŌSUKE ŌTSUBO withdrew cash each week from his bank in Los Angeles and hid the wad of bills in his socks. He then drove to the lesser-known South Gate neighborhood to visit his favorite clothing store, Greenspan's. The shop's dusty shelves offered an endless supply of garments from eras past: forgotten Levi's jeans, obscure denim jackets, pairs of socks from the 1950s. It was all "deadstock"—old merchandise in unworn condition no longer available from the manufacturer. During each visit, Ōtsubo uncovered new hidden gems, and over the year, he became the Greenspan family's favorite customer. He always cleaned up after himself and always paid in cash—pulled straight from his socks.

Each week, Ōtsubo then sent his haul to a small shop called Crisp in Tokyo's Ameyoko district. Crisp marked up the goods 100 percent above the American price tag. A $9 pair of Levi's 501s jeans went for ¥3,600. At these reasonable prices, *Popeye*-reading young shoppers snapped up most of the merchandise each week. Crisp needed constant restocking.

Ōtsubo found additional items at the Rose Bowl Flea Market by offering his sock-cash to random people on the street wearing vintage outfits. Ōtsubo recalls, "They would always say, no, this is my second skin. But if I offered $100, everyone sold me their treasure." Within a few years, the demand for vintage clothing in Japan became so great that Ōtsubo enlisted a team of "pickers" in Colorado and California to start hunting garments for him in their own territories.

Similar movements were afoot on the East Coast. In 1983, student Kōji Kusakabe received an assignment from a Tokyo used clothing store to travel around the U.S. and buy up American vintage pieces. Kusakabe spent the next decade driving through forty-nine of fifty states, scrounging in unpopular department stores and decaying western wear shops for any unsold merchandise. Kusakabe admits, "I knew little about clothing, but I loved to travel." He at least knew how to find the most important items— old Levi's 501 straight-leg jeans with an "XX" on the back patch, and unworn pairs of classic Converse and Keds sneakers.

Ōtsubo, Kusakabe, and other Japanese buyers in the 1980s were key players in the development of a growing segment of the Japanese apparel industry: vintage clothing stores. Masayuki Yamazaki's Cream Soda and Garage Paradise pioneered the sector in the mid-1970s by selling Fifties deadstock. At the end of the decade, stores such as Santa Monica, Dept, Banana Boat, Voice, and Chicago appeared in Harajuku and gave Japan its archetypal vintage shop format. While Beams and Ships sold new, expensive imported items, these stores provided cheaper, older versions of the goods seen in 1975's *Made in U.S.A.* catalog and each month's *Popeye*.

To keep goods in stock, vintage stores relied on individuals like Ōtsubo and Kusakabe to hunt for rare items across the Pacific and send them back regularly by boat. At a time when Americans flocked to shiny new shopping malls, these Japanese buyers haunted the American heartland's most antiquated and least profitable retailers. Old merchandise could only be found in shops without computerized inventory systems. Yet many of these dying retailers were reluctant to part with the jeans and shoes that had

A vintage store in Tokyo. (Photograph by Eric Kvatek)

gone unsold for decades. Kōji Kusakabe remembers, "Sometimes the owners wouldn't admit to themselves that their stock was old. Some places would only sell to locals. And there was a place where the guy only let me buy four or five items during a visit, so I had to come back 30 times to get what I wanted."

Japanese buyers all shared the same dream: unfettered access to stores' basements. Each store was a potential gold mine of vintage clothing laying fallow in pristine condition, piled up among musty chiffon lingerie and démodé cocktail dresses. Takeshi Ōfuchi, designer of vintage-inspired brand Post O'Alls and former buyer, suspected in the late 1980s that a deadstock motherlode sat in the basement of a Red Bank, New Jersey department store. He remembers, "I had to ask the employees to bring the clothes up for me, little by little. The owner was really moody and didn't look like she needed the money. I had to go back more than 20 times." Ōfuchi finally made traction by buttering her up with boxes of Godiva chocolates.

Vintage jeans were always the most lucrative garment for buyers. By the mid-1980s, Japanese brands such as Big John, Edwin, Bison, and Bobson had succeeded in outfitting everyone in denim—men and women, young and old, trendy and trend-adverse. This ubiquity, however, reduced the once magical blue cotton trousers to a cheap commodity. Over five thousand standalone jeans stores across the country sold stacks and stacks of every imaginable treatment and cut. Purists sick of stonewashed jeans in ultra-tapered fits longed to go back to the gold standard—the Levi's 501 straight-leg, button fly jean. This idea gained further momentum when fashion magazines such as *Checkmate* reported that Italians and French all used the 501 as the building block of their casual style.

Japanese interest in the 501 came at a time when Levi's American operations had moved its merchandising mix away from the classic fit and toward tight jeans, corduroys, and surfer pants. In 1984, Levi's Japan made a conscious break from this strategy and reinstated the 501 as the center of its promotional campaigns. This immediately boosted sales, and the Japanese love for classic Americana helped inspire Levi's U.S. to launch its "501 Blues" commercials leading up to the 1984 Los Angeles Olympics—a showcase of regular people on street corners wearing the iconic straight-leg jeans.

But as much as Japanese consumers loved the idea of Levi's 501s, the official pairs available from local retailers did not live up to the legend. A *Men's Club*'s jeans guide from the late 1980s noted, "The famed traditional Levi's 501, Lee 200, and Wrangler 13MWZ have changed quite a bit in terms of quality. For example, they are economizing on the dyeing process and using cheaper open-end spinning. They successfully increased manufacturing efficiency but have seen a decrease in quality. More was lost than was gained."

But there was not much that Levi's, Lee, and Wrangler could do. From the 1950s on, American jeans makers faced ballooning worldwide demand, which necessitated faster and cheaper production. They worked with textile mills to move away from the slower ring-spun thread to the faster open-end spun variety. This fundamentally changed the way the material absorbed indigo dye. Mills also replaced their fleets of narrow, slow-moving Draper shuttle looms with high-tech projectile looms. Ordinary Japanese consumers knew little about these particular manufacturing processes, but sensed that modern jeans lacked the magic of past incarnations. Takeshi Ōfuchi remembers, "The cover of the *Made in U.S.A.* catalog had a drawing of the Levi's 501. So I knew the color of new 501s was different than the original. We all thought, why is it so different?"

Vintage stores gave disenchanted denim customers a chance to return to superior old models of Levi's, Lee, and Wrangler. The strong yen of the Bubble era made American garments dirt cheap, and, by 1989, there was a full-fledged national craze for second-hand clothing. The movement got a style guide after struggling lifestyle magazine *Boon* reinvented itself with a vintage clothing fashion focus.

But the huge increase in demand drove up prices dramatically. In 1983, Harajuku's Banana Boat charged around ¥22,000 for 1960s model Levi's ($237 in 2015 dollars), but at the end of the decade, the store showcased its deadstock Levi's in glass cases tagged at ¥100,000 ($1,390, 2015). Newspapers incredulously reported on a pair of rare Lee cowboy pants on sale in Harajuku for ¥2 million ($28,000, 2015).

The promise of enormous profit margins then triggered an influx of Japanese buyers to the United States. Before leaving for America, young recruits received training on how to appraise denim through minute features. The most telling symbol was the *akamimi* "red edge" on the inside cuff—a reference to the red line on Levi's 501s' white hems made in the U.S. before 1983. American mills' old Draper looms produced denim with a self-finished edge—called a "selvedge" (or selvage) in industry lingo. Cone Mills distinguished its denim with a subtle red line on the selvedge, and this minor detail was the easiest way to distinguish older models of jeans made in the United States.

Selvedge was a must, but buyers also looked for even older design elements, including real leather patches (used until the mid-1950s), hidden rivets only visible on the inside of the jeans (1937–1966), and a "big E" on the red Levi's logo tag (1936-1969). These detail-oriented methods for dating denim first spread through word of mouth among retailers and buyers, but soon filtered down to consumers as well. Schoolyards swarmed with teens discussing techniques for dating antique jeans as if they were all armchair archaeologists of ancient raiment.

Meanwhile, in the United States, almost no one realized the potential value of old Levi's or Lee jeans. The handful of vintage stores in America ignored workwear for relics of classic Hollywood—Hawaiian shirts, bowling shirts, zoot suits, and colorful gabardine shirts. Thrift stores in New York City routinely cut off the legs of rare Levi's to make jean shorts in the summer months. Seth Weisser, co-owner of the SoHo vintage boutique What Comes Around Goes Around, told the *New York Times*, "Before the Japanese got involved, you just identified 40s, 50s and 60s jeans as different, but not necessarily more or less valuable. They were just all 'used jeans.'"

Photographer Eric Kvatek was one of the few Americans to hunt for vintage workwear at the time. After being offered $1,000 for a deadstock police jacket, he turned thrift store digging into a side business. Kvatek moved back to Ohio where an abundance of rare items was waiting for him. He explains, "Right in the early 1990s, a lot of the workers from that era started dying, and their clothing got pulled out of basements and moved into thrift shops." Ohio provided the "perfect storm" for vintage buying: plentiful product at low prices, cheap $1-per-gallon gas for endless driving, and $15 motel rooms. Kvatek contracted with a store in Sapporo, Hokkaidō as his primary client. To facilitate communications with the owner, Kvatek listened to Japanese conversation tapes while he drove across the Midwest.

While rummaging through secondhand shops, Kvatek took care never to reveal his mission to the Americans behind the

Eric Kvatek in front of Sapporo vintage store American Sugar. (Courtesy of Eric Kvatek)

counter. "Knowledge was gold," and buyers embraced a spy-like code of conduct lest they tip off thrift store owners to the value of their stock. To explain why he was purchasing two dozens pairs of jeans in various sizes, Kvatek told clerks that he was "outfitting a work crew." When he started to buy up old pairs of Nike Air Max 95s to supply the Japanese sneaker boom of the late 1990s, he pretended to be a track coach, bluffing about imaginary races like the "6-60" and the "10-40."

Right under the noses of Americans, Japanese, British, and French buyers descended upon the U.S. and smuggled out most of the country's deadstock. By the mid-1990s, there was very little left. Buyers then resorted to scooping up more commonplace items like used print T-shirts and nylon jackets to keep goods moving across the Vintage Silk Road. Japanese stores came to prefer these used garments to vintage, since they required no picking expertise and could be procured cheaply in bulk.

By the late 1990s, thousands of young Japanese entrepreneurs had joined the used clothing game. The original fifteen or so Harajuku shops in the 1980s faced growing competition from over a hundred other secondhand stores in the neighborhood. Across the country, there were an estimated five thousand stores specializing in used American clothing, a sector raking in hundreds of millions of dollars a year. Vintage store Harajuku Chicago alone saw revenues of ¥1.5 billion in 1996 ($20 million in 2015 dollars)—double its business ten years prior.

The scale of operations grew so large that the major Harajuku outlets organized their overseas pickers into veritable armies. One Japanese vintage store chain rented an apartment in Illinois to house salaried employees who would drive around the Midwest seven days a week and buy ten cartloads of old clothing at a time. Other chains just went straight to distributors—so-called "rag houses"—that packaged up unwanted thrift goods into shipping pallets for Third-World destinations. Many Japanese learned Spanish so they could sweet-talk Latina workers into granting better access to the good stuff. Harajuku's Voice struck deals with ten warehouses across the United States, buying old clothing by the gross ton and sorting it back in Japan. Voice then employed a large warehouse staff to wash the garments in nearby laundromats, clean up stains, fix zippers, and sew on loose buttons.

At the market's peak, in 1996, Japan purchased ¥1.3 billion worth of secondhand American clothing ($18 million in 2015 dollars), up from just ¥240 million in 1991 ($3.1 million, 2015). And almost all of the clothing coming into Japan was American. The raw tonnage of secondhand clothing from the United States in 1995 was twenty-three-times the next largest import source, Canada. Even though British fashion had always been influential in Japan, British imports lagged far behind the United States. Seventy-times more clothing came from America than England, despite a mere fourfold difference in population.

Japanese parents fretted that the boom in used American clothing revealed a morose recessionary mindset after the end of the Bubble Economy. But the youth themselves could not have disagreed more: old American clothes were not symbols of impoverishment, but a sign of cultural and economic progress. Nothing was more real, more American—and more expensive—than an actual pair of 1950s Levi's 501XX.

Vintage garments also brought an entirely new group of older male consumers into the apparel market. These men did not read *Popeye* or *Boon*, but instead followed an intense consumer goods magazine called *mono*. Its publisher, World Photo Press, spent the 1970s printing books on American jets, tanks, and nuclear submarines, but found a new niche in the 1990s photographing old workwear and military flight jackets. *mono* readers often guarded vintage jackets and jeans in their rooms as collectibles rather than to wear them. But their collections became a critical resource for helping magazines like *Boon* build comprehensive timelines of how Levi's jeans changed in each era. This then spread detailed knowledge down to rookie denim fans.

Ken Takahashi of Harajuku's Voice complained in 1997, "Originally what was good about secondhand clothing was that it was cheap. For very little money anyone could feel American—that was the point of used goods." But the rising demand for vintage from older collectors raised prices even further. And then, at the end of the 1990s, Americans caught on to what was happening in Japan. More experienced Japanese buyers knew to be discreet around American shop owners, but the jig was up after young Japanese from the countryside showed up at rag houses pointing to pictures of treasured items in *Boon*. The rag house owners noticed the prices in the captions and readjusted their rates for the Japanese, thus capturing more of the profits.

Around the same time, gentlemen buyers like Eric Kvatek, Kōji Kusakabe, and Takeshi Ōfuchi faced an even more formidable foe

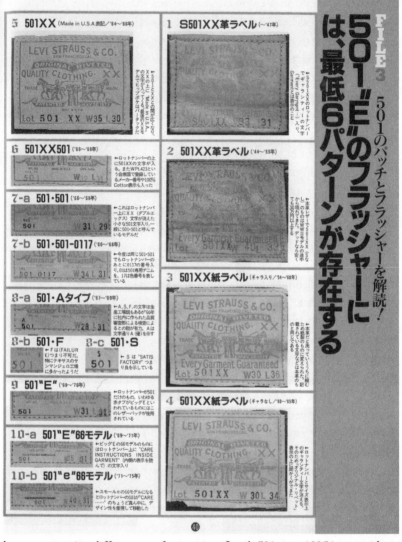

A page comparing different tags from various Levi's 501s in a 1995 jeans guide from magazine *Boon*. (Courtesy of Shōdensha)

than indiscreet newcomers—an enterprising businessman from Orem, Utah named John Farley. While living in Japan during the 1980s as a Mormon missionary, Farley received requests from a few store owners to send back vintage items from the U.S. This small favor blossomed into a full-fledged business called Farley Enterprises. His cousin Hugh Farley rented rooms in small town Radissons on the East Coast and advertised in the newspaper for people to bring by old Levi's and Nikes for sale. Hugh shipped the subsequent haul to John in Orem, who would take bids on a Web site from eight hundred Japanese store owners. At the peak, in 1996, Farley Enterprises sent six hundred pairs of rare American sneakers to Japan each week, racking up $3.2 million for his company of thirty employees.

Farley's ultra-efficient distribution system ruined the sport of clandestine thrift shop hunting. But he was not done yet. The Utah entrepreneur delivered the *coup de grâce* with a guide called "Wanted in Japan," which he sent to thrift shops across the entire United States. The booklet detailed what to look for in old garments and set standard prices for each item. Even if the best pieces did not end up at Farley Enterprises, they no longer ended up buried in piles on the shop floor.

With the rise of Farley Enterprises, a glut of young Japanese buyers over-sharing information with rag houses, the birth of Internet auction sites like eBay, and a tanking yen, the grand Japanese quest for American vintage clothing came to a halt at end of the twentieth century. The top Harajuku-based chains have remained an integral part of the Japanese fashion market, but many small companies disappeared overnight. Ultimately, the consumer rush for vintage clothing caused the largest ever transfer of garments from the United States to Japan—far beyond the postwar charity drives and military shipments or even contemporary brands' regular orders of new clothing. Although smaller in scale, this secondhand Silk Road continues today. Harajuku Chicago, for example, still imports vast amounts from America each month to stock its multiple outlets, requiring dedicated warehouses in downtown St. Louis and rural Ibaraki Prefecture.

Yōsuke Ōtsubo conservatively estimates that two-thirds of the rarest American clothing items, especially of the denim and

Berberjin store manager Yutaka Fujihara shows off a rare pair of 1946 "green stamp" 501s in the vintage jeans section of the basement.

workwear variety, remain in Japanese hands. Specifically, "the basement of Harajuku store Berberjin is definitely the most important place for vintage jeans in the entire world." In this tiny, subterranean room, Berberjin casually lines up Levi's from all eras; pairs from the 1930s, complete with decaying leather patches, go for around $10,000. Meanwhile, a single collector in Chiba Prefecture owns three thousand pairs. Thirty years after kicking off the cult of old Levi's, Banana Boat still fills its glass cases with dozens of deadstock 1966-model Levi's jeans in mint condition—currently for ¥200,000 each.

At these prices, normal teens could no longer afford to buy vintage, unworn Levi's 501s. But they stopped caring. No one needed the originals when there were even better replicas.

IN THE MID-1980S, ŌSAKA HIGH SCHOOL STUDENT MIKI-haru Tsujita could not afford designer brands like Men's Bigi or

Comme des Garçons, so he filled his wardrobe with flannel shirts and old pairs of Levi's 501s bought from vintage shops in the city's youth district, Amemura. Tsujita says, "American casual was fashion without spending money." He became a loyal customer of Lapine, one of the first clothing stores in Ōsaka to sell imported deadstock.

During one of his routine visits to Lapine in early 1989, store manager Hidehiko Yamane told Tsujita of a radical plan to make new jeans that closely reproduced the unique features of vintage American models. Sourcing vintage from the U.S. was becoming too expensive, and Yamane thought he could just make new jeans in the "old taste." Tsujita wanted in; he quit his advertising job and joined Lapine. Tsujita and Yamane both knew all the hallmarks of great vintage jeans—a leather patch, copper rivets, chain-stitched hems, and, of course, selvedge denim. Now they just had to figure out how to make new jeans with these old features.

The first task was to find a supply of selvedge denim. When Japanese mills first moved into denim production in the 1970s, they started with modern Sulzer projectile looms. So there was no custom of making selvedge denim in Japan. The first attempt came in 1980 when Big John asked its fabric supplier, Kurabō, to make denim on old Toyoda shuttle looms normally used to make sailcloth. They then used the selvedge denim as the selling point for Big John Rare—an ¥18,000 ($225 in 2015 dollars) pair of jeans with imported Talon zippers, real copper rivets, and a label made from traditional *washi* paper. At three times the cost of a normal pair, Big John Rare found few customers. Moreover, its failure scared off other mass manufacturers and mills from experimenting with selvedge denim.

Kurabō instead focused its spinning prowess on recreating the unique touch-and-feel of classic American denim. In 1985, the mill debuted *mura-ito*, a "slubby" yarn that used cutting-edge technology to replicate the unevenness common to fabrics before the era of mass production. Denim made from this yarn faded in vertical lines known as *tateochi*—one of jeans purists' most valued traits. Andrew Olah, a veteran denim merchant who worked at Kurabō for many years, explains, "For jeans until the 1950s, ring-spinning technology was very poor. They tried to make the yarn straight but they couldn't. When the indigo faded, you saw all these faults all over the fabric. But instead of considering it a fault, the Japanese saw it as the main feature of the product. So they replicated uneven faults. The industry as a whole moved to open-end spinning because it was cheaper, cleaner, faster, and solved a lot of problems. The Japanese never really endorsed that."

Instead of supplying the Japanese market, Kurabō sold the first batch of its mura-ito denim to French lifestyle brands Et Vous, Chevignon, and Chipie. The slubby Japanese denim worked as a perfect complement to the brands' Continental 501 homages. These French models, in turn, triggered the next Japanese attempts to clone old jeans. Vintage collector and fashion industry veteran Shigeharu Tagaki came upon French denim brands in the early 1980s when he worked in Paris for Jean-Charles de Castelbajac and Pierre Cardin. Returning to Japan in 1985, Tagaki founded a brand with a pseudo-French name, Studio D'artisan, and set out to make premium jeans that captured the essence of prewar models.

His masterpiece, the DO-1, debuted in 1986 with features not seen on jeans for decades, such as the back-buckle from 1930s-era Levi's. Parodying the iconic Levi logo, the DO-1's patch showed two pigs, rather than horses, pulling apart a pair of jeans. The DO-1's ¥29,000 price tag ($268 in 2015 dollars) shocked both the fashion industry and consumers. And like Big John Rare six years before, Studio D'artisan's jeans sold poorly. But Tagaki kept pressing on. He worked with Okayama denim mill Nihon Menpu to make premium textiles on tiny 3-foot-wide selvedge looms, dyed with the traditional *hon-aizome* natural indigo.

At the exact same time, retro French jeans were inspiring a much more established denim company in Tokyo—Levi's Japan. Executive Hajime Tanaka encountered a pair of classic 501 copies in a Parisian store window and decided that Levi's needed its own vintage re-creation line. Wanting to go the full mile for discerning Japanese customers, Tanaka requested to have Cone Mills restart production of selvedge denim, but headquarters balked at the request. He eventually discovered that the French jeans' denim came from Kurabō, and asked the mill for an exclusive supply. In 1987, Levi's Japan debuted its first replica model, the 701XX—a reproduction of the 1936 501XX with a back-buckle—a year before Europe and two years before America made their own vintage remakes.

Yamane and Tsujita were well aware of these prior efforts when they started work on their jeans for Lapine. They sold Studio D'artisan jeans in the store and also paid close attention to the Kōbe brand Denime, whose designer, Yoshiyuki Hayashi, created jeans that closely copied the 501's 1966 model. But where Denime and Studio D'artisan filtered their admiration for American vintage through a chic European disposition, Yamane and Tsujita wanted to make something classically American.

Just as Lapine finally put out its first replica jeans model, Yamane quit to form his own denim brand—Evis. The name was a cute joke, dropping the "L" from Levi's as a way to spell out *ebisu*, the Japanese god of fishermen and good fortune. Yamane hoped to make jeans "just like I bought at surplus stores when I was in middle school"—a loose waist meant to be cinched with a belt, tapered legs, and draped bottom. He made three hundred pairs, and, wanting to look like he had more product options, hand-painted a "seagull" arch in white on the back pockets of half his supply, right where Levi's put its iconic arcuate stitch. Yamane says now, "The paint was half joke. I never thought there was anyone who would buy them." To his surprise, the painted pairs sold out, so he painted the arch on the remaining pairs. Evis was now in business, and Tsujita quit Lapine to help Yamane handle the surging demand.

Each week, the small scene of vintage-inspired jeans makers in Ōsaka—workers at Studio D'artisan, Hayashi of Denime, as well as Yamane, Tsujita, and college-aged twin brothers Kenichi

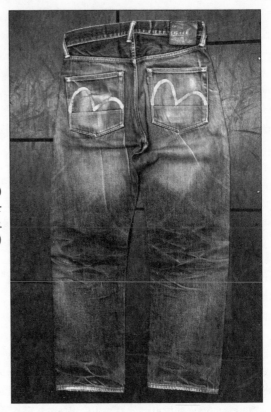

Evisu Lot.2000 straight fit jeans after long-term wear. (Courtesy of Evisu)

and Kenji Shiotani from Evis—met up to drink at Yamane's office and trade production hints. As time went on, however, opinions started to diverge. Tsujita and the Shiotani brothers pushed Yamane to make the jeans closer to early American models. Yamane defended his design: "It's easy to make them exactly like vintage. Anyone can do that. But that'd just be a copy. I have to make an original that only I can make." The idea was not to just "rip off America," but, as he explains, "offer the feeling of seeing America as a Japanese person." Tsujita was not convinced: he did not like the painted seagull and wanted to make something "more serious, more pure."

Tsujita dug into his cardboard box of vintage Levi's and ripped them all apart, thinking something inside would explain why they felt so much better to wear than modern jeans. He carefully considered every detail, every stitch. After unraveling the fabric to examine the yarn, Tsujita eventually concluded that old jeans used cotton with a much longer staple. By the 1990s, industrial spinning techniques could produce high-quality yarn from short staple cotton, making long staple an unaffordable premium. After much research, Tsujita imported an obscure and relatively inexpensive long staple cotton from Zimbabwe. With the help of a mill in Okayama, he became the first person worldwide to turn this cotton fiber into denim.

Tsujita called his brand Full Count, and the first jeans went on sale in 1993. But at the time, many vintage stores were still skeptical about modern replicas. He remembers, "Everyone on the phone said, *I don't want fakes.* But when they saw them in person, they said, *Wow, what's this!*" The Ōsaka jeans not only fit well into these stores' overall merchandising mix—they offered a vintage-like product that could be easily reordered.

In 1995, former Evis employees Kenichi and Kenji Shiotani opened their own brand Warehouse to make even more detail-obsessed vintage re-creations. This made five major independent jeans brands in Ōsaka—Studio D'artisan, Denime, Evis, Full Count, and Warehouse—known today as the "Ōsaka Five." After *mono* introduced Evis to its vintage-rabid readers, Yamane started to sell two thousand pairs each month. Magazines like *Boon* spread the Ōsaka Five brands to the masses by styling their jeans with T-shirts from Ura-Harajuku. Teens stopped lusting over the ¥100,000 deadstock behind the glass at Banana Boat and instead picked up comfortable, well-sized pairs of replica jeans for one-fourth the price.

By 1996, Full Count was selling a hundred thousand pairs a year. Evis had enough demand to open its own factory in Okayama. Edwin, at this point the largest jeans maker in Japan, also threw its weight behind retro denim—spending millions on a series of TV commercials for the "new vintage" line 505 with American actor Brad Pitt. Harajuku's sea of light blue, faded vintage 501s darkened as youth walked stiffly in the deepest indigo of rigid, unwashed denim.

As teens devoured vintage styling from small brands and mass manufacturers alike, new companies jumped on the trend by replicating old garments beyond five-pocket denim pants. In the late 1980s, the Real McCoy's of Kōbe made a nearly perfect re-creation of the American A-2 flight jacket. Once complete, they expanded into a wide variety of American military uniforms and jackets. Tōyō Enterprise in Tokyo, meanwhile, reproduced similarly reverent American flight jackets under the name Buzz Rickson.

American Air Force pilots surely wore jackets just like these in 1945 when they bombed every single centimeter of urban Japan. Was this interest in U.S. military gear Stockholm Syndrome on a national scale? A sales clerk at Voice Harajuku once said of the used clothing boom, "This is all because Japan lost the war. If Japan had won, Americans right now would probably be competing to wear kimonos." But these jackets were not necessarily a knee-jerk embrace of American cool. For a certain set of middle-aged Japanese men, American military gear invoked both a universal machismo as well as nostalgia for the Occupation—an iconic period of *Japanese* history in which Americans just happened to appear. Faux flight jackets also allowed middle-aged men to take a "healthy" interest in military affairs without breaching the taboos of Japanese wartime memorabilia.

The sheer number of vintage stores and replica lines in Japan at the end of the 1990s allowed consumers to buy practically any quintessential American garment, either old or new. The Ōsaka Five and their followers came to premium jeans from a deep admiration for American denim, hoping to bring back the magic of Levi's glory years. But at the same time, others in Japan were ready to break the mold of classic American styles and try something new. Denim was about to become much more Japanese.

GROWING UP IN KŌBE, TOSHIKIYO HIRATA NEVER ONCE TRIED on a pair of jeans. He was a jock, preferring martial arts to the counterculture: "There was no one I hated more than the long-hairs." At a karate tournament during the 1970 Ōsaka Expo, foreign visitors encouraged Hirata to teach martial arts overseas, so he boarded a Brazil-bound ship docked in Kōbe's harbor and hopped off in Hawaii—without papers. Hirata first worked at a gym, and then a network of Japanese expatriates supported him on a grand adventure across the United States. During his travels hitchhiking in the early 1970s, he realized that jeans were for everyone, not just hippies. He bought himself a pair.

Back in Japan, Hirata met his wife after college, and, in 1975, the young couple moved to her hometown of Kojima, Okayama. Needing a job, Hirata applied at all the major blue jeans makers and ended up at John Bull. Hirata claims, "I had no interest in jeans. I was fine with whatever," but after a few years, he became a local sewing legend. As his skills improved, however, he lost patience with the Kojima brands' over-reliance on American trends: "I was just miserable that the companies continued to copy America more and more as they grew."

In 1985, Hirata left John Bull to form his own company, Capital, hoping to make jeans that surpassed the American original. In contrast to the other Kojima manufacturers, Hirata wanted to make "jeans so distinct that you could tell the brand without looking at the stitch on the seat pocket." He bought himself a vintage Union Special sewing machine and told friends he wanted to make something as radical as jeans with an extra leg. After extensive experimentation with materials, sewing, and treatments, Hirata finished a set of (two-leg) prototypes that re-created the aged patina of secondhand garments in new jeans.

Hirata got his big break from Gen Tarumi, the owner of popular Tokyo clothing store Hollywood Ranch Market. After bumming around California on VAN Jacket's dime in the 1970s, Tarumi started one of Japan's first used clothing stores, Gakurakuchō (Bird of Paradise). This morphed into the wildly successful shop, Hollywood Ranch Market, which sold a mix of used American clothing and original brands, all with a rustic and vaguely

Toshikiyo Hirata, founder of Okayama denim brand Kapital. (Photograph by Eric Kvatek)

traditional Japanese flavor. At the time, stonewash was just coming into style, and Tarumi instantly took a liking to the handiwork on Hirata's samples. Tarumi told him, "Let's make something *Japanese* that leaves an impression on people." The resulting jeans—a mix between vintage American aesthetics and superior Japanese crafts-manship—were a hit.

Capital grew throughout the late 1980s and early 1990s, man-ufacturing jeans for Tokyo brands like Hysteric Glamour, as well as Kansai denim lines Studio D'artisan and Denime. Hirata later found a new soulmate in 45rpm, a brand with a unique aesthetic blending American vintage, French resort wear, Italian tailoring, and traditional Japanese craftsmanship. With Hirata's son Kiro working as a designer, 45rpm threaded these different styles to-gether under the concept of *wabisabi*—the Zen Buddhist concep-tion of finding beauty in imperfection. Hirata's pre-distressed jeans realized 45rpm's vision: decayed printing on the jeans' leather patch and broken-in denim which retained its rich indigo color. To further reinforce a Japanese origin, 45rpm's jeans models took names from ancient Japanese history such as "Jōmon," the hunter-gatherer occupiers of the archipelago from 12,000 BCE.

In 2000, 45rpm opened a store in New York's SoHo district to sell its premium denim to Americans. On foreign soil, the brand played up its Japanese roots to an even greater degree, emphasizing its use of organic fabrics and artisanal dyeing processes. The brand invited American photographer (and former vintage buyer) Eric Kvatek to shoot its catalogs and materials, using craftspeople in the ancient capital city of Nara as the models. Kvatek remembers, "To help me better understand the essence of Japanese quality, they took me to Nara to explore shrines and temples. We spent time with a tea ceremony master, visited a natural indigo dye workshop, and spent time with an expert on antique Japanese textiles." 45rpm, with both the elder and younger Hiratas' help, seamlessly tied pseudo-vintage American garments to centuries-old forms of Japanese craftsmanship. The two concepts have been entangled ever since.

Later that year, Toshikiyo Hirata called his son back from 45rpm to start an original brand, Kapital. Based in downtown Kojima, Kapital further fused American bohemianism with Japanese traditions of *monozukuri* craftsmanship. Their logo is two blue hands, the semi-permanently stained palms of a Japanese indigo dyer. Kapital has always played with the tension between indigenous identity and American style—using the eighth-century technique of *kakishibu* persimmon tannin dyeing while producing pacifist parodies of modern U.S. ARMY T-shirts that read "FARMY." Since 2005, Eric Kvatek has photographed the brand's semiannual catalogs, showing models in Kapital's patched-up, military-inspired, Japanese-fabric clothing frolicking in pastoral spaces all around the world. The catalog titles alone construct a fantasy planet of global vagabonds: Sea Gypsies, Azure Anarchy, Deniming for Sunken Treasure, Colorado Hippies.

Long before 45rpm or Kapital, Evis (which later became Evisu to defend against Levi's legal team) was the original pioneer in selling classic Americana abroad through a defiantly Japanese identity. Back in 1994, Yamane partnered with British business-man Peter Caplowe to make the white seagull jeans a must-have for DJs, celebrities, and streetwear fans in New York and London. Paparazzi caught soccer player David Beckham in a pair, and Beckham later bought a limited-edition model made with gold thread and 18-carat gold buttons. Meanwhile, in the U.S., Jay-Z gave a nod to Evisu in his 2001 single "Jigga That Nigga," and Atlanta's Young Jeezy requested to be entombed in Evisu in "Bury Me A 'G.'"

Evisu's trick was to use Oriental design motifs to position its jeans as more *authentic* than modern American jeans. Their jeans told a story of superior Japanese craftsmen working hard to make the things that Americans could no longer make themselves. The press in the late 1990s invariably reported that Yamane bought up old "Levi's looms" thrown away in the American brand's mindless pursuit of efficiency and profit. This was untrue in multiple ways: Levi's never owned looms, Cone Mills' older Draper looms were sold off for scrap rather than to the Japanese, and Japanese denim mills already owned higher-quality Toyoda selvedge looms. Nev-ertheless, the myth persisted because the story sounded logical for a Japanese denim company sparing no expense in re-creating vin-tage details.

And once Evisu, 45rpm, and Kapital established the principle of Japanese denim superiority, the next wave of jeans brands natu-rally looked at their own nation's history for inspiration. Ōsaka's Samurai called its models Geisha, Yamato (the first Japanese na-tion), and Zero (the World War II fighter plane). Okayama sprouted a brand called Momotaro Jeans—named after the local myth of a boy floating down the river in a giant peach. Sensing this growing pride in Japanese denim, the city of Kojima asked small brands to open shops on its shuttered shopping arcade, which it renamed "Jeans Street" to much fanfare. Visitors could even buy "denim colored" blue ice cream.

Overseas, Japanese denim became its own distinct product category. In late 2006, two stores opened in the U.S. dedicated to jeans from Japan: New York's Blue in Green and San Francisco's Self Edge. Back in the mid-1990s, Kiya Babzani of Self Edge stumbled into Evisu's Yamane Salon on a trip to Hong Kong, and found the 1950s-style jeans that he had always longed for as a rockabilly fan. He recalls, "I became completely obsessed with the idea that the Japanese were reproducing vintage fashion and that the quality level was of something not seen even on the original garments." But when he asked the brands to sell in the U.S., many resisted: "They would say to me, 'Why do you want our brand when you have Levi's?'" Babzani eventually assembled an expansive list of small Japanese labels for the California store—Iron Heart, The Flat Head, Strike Gold, Dry Bones, and Sugar Cane—most of which would never have considered a retail presence abroad.

Nagano's The Flat Head epitomizes the extremes to which this third wave of replica manufacturers take their pursuit of vintage details. Founder Masayoshi Kobayashi ran a used clothing and repair shop in rural Nagano where he studied lost manufacturing techniques which could be reclaimed for modern production. The Flat Head demands denim mills use particular yarn twist styles and dye with twenty shallow dips in indigo rather than the usual twelve deep ones. The brand makes each part of the jeans—legs, back pockets, belt loops—in separate, specialized Kojima factories. Kobayashi even developed a proprietary rivet that is longer than standard models. With all this attention, there is no surprise the final product starts from $300.

Despite insanely high import prices, Self Edge found a ready-made audience for The Flat Head and like-minded brands among the growing number of fashion nerds lurking on Internet message boards Style Forum and Superfuture. But business steadily grew among customers who knew nothing of Japanese replica jeans: "A large chunk of people buy because of quality. Aesthetics come second. That's why we sell so many basics. The entire idea that it's vintage-inspired has now taken a backseat."

The entrance of high-end Japanese jeans to the U.S. led to a new discipline and seriousness about clothing among Americans. Denim fanatics started trading photos and secrets online about how to get "whisker" fades on the front and "honeycomb" fades behind the knees. In their descriptions, posters dropped unabashedly Japanese terms like "tateochi." Commenters looking for tips on the perfect fade weighed the merits of ocean soaks, freezer stints, vinegar baths, or no wash at all.

Mikiharu Tsujita of Full Count does not understand how Americans picked up these practices: "It's not cool when guys get too into the fade. The whole point is that jeans should be easy-to-wear, durable, and no-stress." Babzani agrees: "If you ask Japanese brands how they take care of their jeans, they kind of look at you in a funny way: *We just wash them... in the washing machine.*" These stresses about washing denim suggest a peculiar historical reversal: Americans have become just as anxious about wearing their jeans "correctly" as the Japanese were about Western clothing in the 1960s.

Beyond the expansion in retailers and the epidemic of rancid unwashed jeans, the Japanese replica brands reached a new level of respect in the global market in January 2007 when Levi's Strauss found it necessary to sue Studio D'artisan, Iron Heart, Sugarcane, Oni, and Samurai for trademark infringement. Levi's re-asserted its ownership of the arcuate stitch, vertical tabs on the back pocket, and waist patches with moving animals or objects pulling jeans apart. In response to the legal crackdown, the brands refrained from including these details on export models. Arguably, this did not amount to a major loss; the brands provide a value far beyond an identical arch shape on the seat of the pants. The exercise mostly revealed that Japanese brands no longer need to be slaves to vestigial remnants of 501 re-creations.

Back in Japan, however, replica brands faced a much larger issue than litigation—the collapse of the premium denim market. Youth spent the 1990s deciding between pairs of Evisu, Full Count, Hollywood Ranch Market, and 45rpm, but the next generation, who knew nothing of the Bubble nor the culture boom of the Nineties, were satisfied with cheap jeans from mass retailers like UNIQLO at a fraction of the cost. In 2009, UNIQLO's sister brand, g.u., made headlines with a pair of jeans for only ¥990. Vintage aficionados in their thirties and forties remained core consumers of the replica lines, but the companies could no longer count on adding new ranks of young Japanese men and women. Fortunately, the brands found salvation in increased exportation to the West, Greater China, and Southeast Asia. Japan indisputably sparked the world's interest in vintage denim and workwear, and now Japanese brands are sustaining their businesses by satisfying that demand around the globe.

One clear proof point for Japan's role in reviving vintage American styles is the rise of the selvedge as universal shorthand for premium denim. There is no question that Japanese brands and denim mills were the ones who brought this particular feature back from the dead. As Self Edge's Babzani says, "If the Japanese hadn't done it, I don't know who would have been so obsessed to set up these mills dedicated to making older styles of fabric for jeans." For the first decade of the twenty-first century, menswear enthusiasts scoffed at wearing any denim without a selvedge on the cuff. The feature's cachet, however, is plummeting: UNIQLO makes pairs with that distinctive white hem from Kaihara denim and charges a mere $49.90. Generic store brands have cheated by sewing a selvedge onto low-quality denim later in the process.

In 1970, Japanese denim pioneer Tetsuo Ōishi told *Shūkan Asahi*, "Jeans were born in America, but I want to get to the point where Japan can dominate the market." Forty-five years later, Japanese denim may not command the world, but the country does set the global standard for luxurious fabrics, high-quality sewing, innovative production techniques, and ingenuous treatments. After Japan lost its edge on consumer electronics, semiconductors, and even video gaming consoles, denim gave Japan a new arena for national pride. Many brands try to conjure up an imaginary past where eighth-century Japanese artisans somehow made sturdy pants from indigo-dyed twill cloth, but certainly the country's ancestral craftsmen would have been impressed with the handiwork of their descendants.

TEN

Exporting Ametora

On May 24, 2005, VAN Jacket founder Kensuke Ishizu passed away at the age of ninety-three. At the time of his death, millions of Japanese men—students, employees, executives, and retirees—were following Ishizu's principles of Ivy as their basic style. Ishizu taught the 1960s generation how to dress up, and they have since passed down those sartorial lessons to their own children.

Ishizu did not just kick off the culture of Japanese menswear, but also helped create the modern menswear industry. Former employee Yoshio Sadasue explains, "After the bankruptcy in 1978, 1,000-1,500 really well-trained people at VAN went into other apparel companies. These companies didn't really understand fashion very well, and suddenly, they had someone from VAN Jacket, who was treated like a god." Sadasue is one of the most successful cases. In 1993, he opened up his brand, Kamakura Shirts, to provide well-made dress shirts at reasonable prices. With Ivy in his blood, 40 percent of the company's shirts are button-downs—a far higher proportion than his competitors.

By any measure, the most successful brand to come out of the VAN Jacket family is the $36 billion, global apparel giant Fast

Retailing. Its marquee chain, UNIQLO, has over fifteen hundred stores in eighteen countries, and is on the verge of $15 billion in yearly revenue. Founder Tadashi Yanai is often ranked as Japan's richest person. His father ran a small VAN franchisee called Ogōri Shōji in the industrial town of Ube, Yamaguchi, which Ishizu renamed "Men's Shop OS" to attract a younger crowd. Sadasue remembers, "Yanai knows VAN and Ivy really well. And when VAN went belly up, Yanai realized that he couldn't keep Men's Shop OS like it was."

In May 1985, Tadashi Yanai opened a large-scale shop for casual basics in Hiroshima called "Unique Clothing Warehouse"—abbreviated as UNIQLO. While many of UNIQLO's best sellers over the years have not necessarily been Ivy items—most notably, brightly colored down jackets, fleece, and Heattech thermal underwear—Yanai's dedication to selling unisex basics at reasonable prices echoes the original mission of VAN Jacket. Towards the end of his life, Kensuke Ishizu visited a UNIQLO store and told his son Shōsuke, "This is what I wanted to make!"

Even if Yanai is not explicitly channeling Kensuke Ishizu, the American traditional look sits at the heart of UNIQLO design. In the late 1980s, Yanai called a breakfast meeting with GAP Inc.'s CEO, Mickey Drexler, and told him, "You are my professor. I follow everything you do." Meanwhile, Senior Vice President of Global Research and Design Yukihiro Katsuta has tastes firmly rooted in Heavy Duty, often referencing his obsession with L.L. Bean as a teenager.

Today, UNIQLO has a store on Manhattan's Fifth Avenue and Kamakura Shirts operates one on Madison Avenue. Ishizu and the Japanese of the 1960s imported the styles of the East Coast, and now Ishizu's disciples are exporting their modified versions back. To be fair, most shoppers at UNIQLO are not specifically looking to re-create traditional Ivy style. But when a legion of young American men took a new interest in 1960s Ivy League style at the end of the 2000s, they looked right to Japan for guidance.

Tamiko and Yoshio Sadasue in front of Kamakura Shirts' New York store (©Shukan NY Seikatsu/ New York Seikatsu Press, Inc.)

THE JAPANESE ECONOMY MOVED OUT OF RECESSION IN THE mid-2000s, but most of the spoils went to the top. *Kakusa shakai*—"stratified society"—was the era's defining buzzword as a once egalitarian Japanese society divided into "winners" and "losers." The affluent revelled in a flamboyant lifestyle reminiscent of the 1980s Bubble, while part-time workers subsided on the unsold leftovers from their doughnut shop jobs. Women's magazines offered advice on which outfits would help the wearer snag a fiancé from the ranks of doctors, investment bankers, and entrepreneurs. With a zeitgeist of conspicuous consumption and capital accumulation, European luxury brands dominated the fashion scene.

This all came crashing down in the 2007–2008 financial crisis. As the public lost its appetite for vulgar displays of wealth, fashion editors needed something practical, something classic. As illustrator Kazuo Hozumi says, "If no one knows what is in style, they always come back to Ivy and Trad." In 2007, Japanese menswear titles and select shops uncovered a movement brewing among tradition-inspired brands in the United States—namely, Thom Browne, Band of Outsiders, and Michael Bastian. This kicked off the "Fifth Ivy Boom," where *Popeye* and *Men's Nonno* taught a new generation of youth about cricket sweaters, candy-striped button-down oxford shirts, regimental ties, seersucker and pincord suits, ribbon belts, and shell cordovan oxfords.

This time, however, the industry did not just import the latest in American style; somehow, a Japanese ethos had infused America's "neo-trad." New York designer Thom Browne, with his *Right Stuff* haircut and cropped gray wool suit, personified the new wave of Americana in the Japanese press. For all his novelty, Browne felt very familiar to Japanese readers. Almost like an old issue of *Men's Club*, he provided customers with strict rules for wearing his clothing: "The last button on the cuff of the jacket should be left unbuttoned." / "Please do not iron the oxford shirts after washing." And his high-water, ankle-revealing pants eerily resembled the Miyuki Tribe's shrunken trousers. On meeting Browne for the first time, Engineered Garments' Daiki Suzuki remembered thinking, "I've never seen an American dress in such Japanese style." Browne denies taking literal inspiration from Japan, but his business has always been strongly connected with the country. When Browne faced possible bankruptcy in 2009, Okayama-based firm Cross Company came to the rescue by acquiring a 67 percent stake.

Browne partially intended his aggressive suit silhouette—an extremely short jacket and show of ankle—to shock complacent American men out of sloppy dress. *Popeye* Editor-in-Chief Takahiro Kinoshita says, "I think Tom's great achievement is showing again how a guy in a suit could look cool." In the 1990s, the United States took on the ignoble distinction of being the First World's most casual country. For many men, dressing poorly became a badge of honor. Suit jackets slumped off the shoulders, and pant cuffs collected in a rippled muddle above the shoe. Ivy League students attended classes in stained sweatpants and flip-flops.

The tech boom of the 2000s gave unkempt appearances further legitimacy: Nerd billionaires saw the necktie as a "noose." Google proclaimed in its founding manifesto, "You can be serious without a suit." One could argue that America has rejected ostentatious and ornate clothing since its founding days—Yankee Doodle only put a single feather in his ragged hat to be "Macaroni"—but early twenty-first century style was a complete and unprecedented rejection of propriety.

In response to the disheveled elites, a style counter-assault bubbled up on the Internet. Web sites Superfuture and Hypebeast gave streetwear fans their first digital home. Gentlemen looking to relearn the lost art of dressing up headed to Web forums Ask Andy and Styleforum to crowdsource expertise on hem lengths, jacket buttons, and necktie knots. And then Scott Schuman's photo blog "The Sartorialist" came along to provide daily visuals of stylish people on the streets of New York. Facing this knowledge vacuum, the early movers in online menswear media veered towards pedagogy over artistic exploration. Web sites Valet, Put This On, and even GQ.com lectured fashion beginners through numbered lists and concrete steps to explain the assembly of a classic wardrobe.

In this menswear resurgence, America in 2008 uncannily resembled Japan in 1964. During both historical moments, a small autodidactic vanguard fought against social taboos around male interest in clothing. To bring others into their cause, both VAN Jacket and American menswear blogs explained the basics, emphasized traditional clothing over designer trends, and showed real-life examples of style on the streets. Valet's serious tutorials on garment care and suit fit are nearly identical to things Toshiyuki Kurosu wrote in *Men's Club*. And in a sense, "The Sartorialist" is a contemporary version of "Ivy Leaguers on the Street." Of course, these Americans started their media ventures without ever seeing the 1960s Japanese originals, but their mission to evangelize fashion to a heathen population led them to the same methods of proselytization.

With such common goals, the English language blogosphere was destined to discover Japan's forty-year head start on the studied mastery of American style. May 19, 2008 may be the exact date for that encounter—the day when Michael Williams posted a few scans of *Take Ivy* on his site "A Continuous Lean." Men's fashion blogs were hunting for archival photos of classic collegiate styling and wardrobes, and *Take Ivy* was a dream come true: documentary evidence of how real American students used to dress in the glory days. The students' slim pants, tweed jackets, skinny ties, and crewneck sweaters perfectly matched the styling on modern blogs. A few months later, menswear blog "The Trad" posted scans of the entire *Take Ivy* volume. In a flash, the entire world could view the once unknown Japanese book online.

Unfortunately, American fans hoping to buy an actual copy of *Take Ivy* were out of luck. In Japan, even 1970s reprints went for $300. In America, one sold on eBay for the outrageous sum of $1,400. Designer Michael Bastian told the *New York Times* that a cult had developed around the Japanese book: It was "more influential as a myth or Holy Grail that no one could get their hands on." Designer Mark McNairy admitted to the *Times* that he owned a copy: "When I first started at J. Press and went to Japan, they had an original copy there and I flipped out. I got them to photocopy the whole book for me and I used that for a couple years."

With the book in such high demand, Brooklyn publisher powerHouse licensed the content and translated the text into English. When it was rereleased in Spring 2010, the once obscure VAN Jacket project was suddenly everywhere, selling more than fifty thousand copies. The influence went far beyond units moved. Ralph Lauren and J. Crew stores used *Take Ivy* in their bookshelf displays. The Gap's one-time designer Rebekka Bay proudly showed her copy to *Elle* to explain her influences. *Take Ivy* even made Ivy League students rethink their own clothing: two students at Dartmouth and Princeton founded a brand, Hillflint, just to re-create the graduation-year sweaters seen in the book.

The authors of *Take Ivy* in 2010 — from left, Teruyoshi Hayashida, Toshiyuki Kurosu, Shōsuke Ishizu, Hajime "Paul" Hasegawa. (Courtesy of the Ishizu family)

Take Ivy revealed the degree to which Japan's deep interest in American style kept the knowledge alive while Americans spent decades rejecting their own legacy of dress. Few Americans in the 1960s thought to take pictures of college students any more than they would take pictures of hamburgers, highways, or oak trees. On the other hand, the Japanese—in their examination of Ivy League style as an alien culture—needed reference materials and photographic evidence. Years later, when fashion brands like The Gap, J. Crew, and Ralph Lauren foraged for authentic historical records, they discovered the Japanese documentary material as the best source for photos of student clothing from Trad's golden years.

Beyond *Take Ivy*, Japan's cataloging of American culture has played a major role in helping U.S. brands return to their roots. Levi's Japan revitalized the 501 before its American headquarters thought to do so, and was the first global unit to make vintage reproductions. Kurabō and Kaihara's work in selvedge denim nudged Cone Mills to also pull out its own old looms.

American companies have also relied on Japanese retailers to keep their brands in good business health. Clothing company J. Peterman's origin story tells of selling a few classic horseman's duster jackets around the U.S.—only to have a "mysterious gentleman" from Japan order two thousand. Few shoe companies remain in the United States, but Alden continues to produce its high-quality leather loafers, bluchers, and boots in Massachusetts thanks in part to bulk orders from select shops like Beams, UNITED ARROWS, Ships, and Tomorrowland. Ralph Lauren signals its dedication to the Japanese market by leasing a 24,000 square-foot white-columned mansion in Omotesando on top of prime real estate valued at $300 million. Former Creative Director of Stüssy, Paul Mittleman, says, "Without Japan, Stüssy probably would have gone out of business. When all was grim, everyone waited for that order from Japan to say, Alright, let's start making clothing."

In the twenty-first century, it is now conventional wisdom that the Japanese "do Americana better than Americans." Michael Williams of "A Continuous Lean" declared to his readers after a trip to Tokyo in 2009, "I stick to my belief that menswear in Japan is leaps and bounds ahead of what we get here in the States." His colleague, Jake Gallagher, praised Kamakura Shirts: "The [oxford button-down] shirt has remained an icon of American style for over a century, which is why it only makes sense that arguably the best oxford on the market right now comes straight from Japan." The Gap's Bay told *Elle*, "The Japanese men's magazines have a much better understanding of what is true, authentic American than do the Americans." More broadly, Tyler Brûlé of *Monocle* has spoken of Japan as a place that retains what other countries have lost: "Japan has somehow held on to, not just Japanese traditions, but everything that happened in the postwar period. ...You still feel like you're walking onto a stage set. Everything is done exquisitely and perfectly."

Inside the book *Fuck Yeah Menswear*, authors Kevin Burrows and Lawrence Schlossman parody Japanese magazines with "Cheer Up! Pony Boy." (Illustration by Ben Lamb)

Likewise, the American fashion media have lionized their Japanese peers. Photos on "The Sartorialist" made international style icons out of Japanese fashion industry leaders such as *Popeye*'s Takahiro Kinoshita, fashion critic Takeji Hirakawa, Ships executive Haruo Suzuki, and UNITED ARROWS' Hirofumi Kurino, Yasuto Kamoshita, and Motofumi "Poggy" Kogi.

Kevin Burrows and Lawrence Schlossman meanwhile dedicated a portion of their satirical volume *Fuck Yeah Menswear* to a parody of a Japanese magazine called "Cheer Up, Pony Boy," complete with faux Kazuo Hozumi art and silly nonnative English captions. Schlossman laughed to *Esquire*, "It's so funny to think how, for the ultimate men's-wear nerd, Japanese magazines are seen as this gold standard. But nobody has any idea, for the most part, what's being written."

The most popular Japanese title in the U.S. among menswear enthusiasts has been *Free & Easy*—a "Dad's Style" magazine devoted to "rugged" traditional American clothing for older men. Compared to similar titles, *Free & Easy* has looked not abroad to Naples or Los Angeles, but pulled directly from the history of American fashion in Japan. The magazine ran multi-part stories on VAN Jacket and the Heavy Duty craze, recruited Yasuhiko Kobayashi and Kazuo Hozumi to draw covers, and asked VAN's Paul Hasegawa and Shōsuke Ishizu to reminisce about the old days. Hasegawa thinks that the magazine may be over-idolizing the past, but "fashion is glamour. They're doing exactly the same ludicrous stuff that we used to at VAN." Just this time, they are glamorizing their own history.

By the beginning of the 2010s, neo-trad American designers and the Japanese heritage mixed, meshed, and merged to the point where it was unclear who was following whom. Nigo from A Bathing Ape dressed head-to-toe in the Thom Browne-designed Brooks Brothers' Black Fleece. Beams ran an interview with *Monocle*'s Tyler Brûlé on its Web site about his collaborations with Japanese brand Porter. San Francisco's Unionmade boutique built a reputation with Americans by selling Japanese brands Kapital, Ships, and Beams+—but now Japanese select shops look to the store for inspiration.

In his first appearance in *Men's Club* in 1959 with his fellow Traditional Ivy Leaguers, Toshiyuki Kurosu made the prescient statement, "A magazine in the U.S. like *Esquire* should cover us: 'Look what exists over in Japan.' And then they'll send us money for the voyage and say, you should definitely come visit us." It may have taken over fifty years, but Kurosu's dream of American magazines obsessing over Japanese finally came true.

JEANS, NAVY BLAZERS, AND SNEAKERS MAY TELL A UNIQUELY American story, but after seven decades in Japan, the Japanese have added their own social meanings to each garment. As Engineered Garments' Daiki Suzuki says, "Who is to say traditional American styles are American? The Japanese have definitely made them their own." The Japanese version of Ivy is now a rich, living set of practices, distinct from 1950s Ivy League campus fashion. Toshiyuki Kurosu explains: "Ivy is a lot like *tonkatsu* (breaded pork cutlet). It was originally German but now it's just part of Japanese cuisine. You serve it with rice and miso soup and eat it with chopsticks. I think Ivy is becoming like tonkatsu. It may have originally come from America 60 years ago, but after 60 years of being in Japan, it's been arranged to better fit us." The Japanese at first shortened the words "American traditional" to *Ametora*, but now an entire set of Ametora practices stands as its own separate tradition.

So what makes Ametora distinct from the original? Both Japanese and foreign observers commonly point to a specific set of characteristics—rule-driven, studied, gender-normative, and high quality. Many assume these traits are extensions of the Japanese national character, but most of the quirks can be traced to the specific historical circumstances in which American style entered the country.

For example, why have the Japanese been so interested in fashion—arguably far beyond other cultural fields? As Japanese teens built up their own youth culture, they always prioritized fashion over music, automobiles, furniture, and cuisine. Masayuki Yamazaki's Garage Paradise failed as a furniture shop but boomed as a clothing store, and there were always more faux *oka* fashion surfers than real surfers. As a start, urban consumers did not need nice interior goods because no one entertained in their cramped apartments. And between a lack of facilities and little free time from work, sports have not been a major part of adult life. By contrast, fashion worked well with the busy, crowded Tokyo lifestyle. UNITED ARROWS' founder and Honorary Chairman Osamu Shigematsu explains, "Clothes have always had the highest return on investment because, unlike other kinds of culture, they're seen by others, and the Japanese care a lot about that. Clothes can express personal identity and also act as a communication tool."

Meanwhile, Japanese fashion's emphasis on "rules" in fashion comes directly from the country's importation of an entirely new clothing system. American college students in the 1960s—whether Ivy-styled fraternity members or radical hippies—looked to their peers for clues on the "right" things to wear. No one needed to verbalize the rules. As fashion critic Shōzō Izuishi points out, "There's no 'Dictionary of Trad' in America, because you have older brothers, fathers, and grandfathers."

But to help Japanese teens start being stylish from scratch, VAN Jacket and *Men's Club* needed to take these unspoken precepts and turn them into explicit commandments. Kensuke Ishizu admitted in the 1980s, "When Ivy was introduced to Japan, we had to really drill the rules into people, because they had absolutely no knowledge about fashion. I am partly responsible for the fact that Ivy became taught in the style of 'You must do this.'" Ishizu's students, however, were not always cognizant of this alteration to Ivy culture; they just came to believe that rules were integral to the fashion experience.

Strict, rule-based fashion then incentivized followers to build up comprehensive knowledge. UNITED ARROWS' Hirofumi Kurino says, "When it's your own culture, you tend to stop learning mid-way through. But we kept studying until we got to the very edge of knowledge." As Kurino explains, an American looked at a button-down collar and thought, "I have to attach these buttons," but the Japanese in the 1960s thought instead, "Why does this collar have buttons?" One question led to another for over fifty years, resulting in a nation with an unprecedented collective understanding of American fashion.

Before VAN Jacket, chauvinistic traditions in Japan disparaged male fashion as feminine (a needless vanity) and lecherous (intended to attract women). But the detail-heavy, tradition-minded introductions for dress in *Men's Club* triggered neither taboo.

Western clothing fans looked like studious model train enthusiasts rather than social outlaws. By the 1980s' heyday of materialism, no one belittled well-dressed men. The U.S. menswear resurgence has also reversed prejudices through a similar focus on details, rules, heritage, and collector mentality. Designer Michael Bastian told *GQ*, "There are these straight guys in their 20s, who are very obsessive about their clothes. It's so fascinating to me because I never realized this group of guys existed, who follow designers and clothing like a lot of guys might follow baseball. And it's not an affront to their masculinity at all."

Finally, there is Japan's respect for craftsmanship and high quality. Their particular excellence in fashion production starts with the postwar government's support of the textile industry as a quick, low-tech way to boost exports. This created an expansive infrastructure of fabric mills, sewing houses, and treatment facilities. As adidas Originals' Paul Mittleman reminds us, "People underestimate that Japan has a base of production. Europe doesn't really have that. In Japan, you'll find someone with 200 yards of khaki twill and a factory that can make the material into pants, and they will be perfectly made." Japanese brands are able to prioritize high-quality garments, because, for the last seventy years, there have been craftsmen who can create those high-quality garments.

And consumers are willing to pay. The Flat Head can request that the back pockets and belt loops for its jeans be made by specialists in different factories, because someone will pay $300 for that luxury detail. American fashion has always been incredibly expensive in Japan—from the first pairs of jeans in Ameyoko in the late 1940s to VAN jacket button-downs in the 1960s to a $5,000 Thom Browne suit in 2010. During the Economic Miracle, the top brands in Japan could dream up the highest quality goods without having to compromise because consumers could either afford it or were willing to sacrifice.

This is no longer true. Japanese incomes have suffered since 1998, and the fashion market has declined in tow. Globalization, however, is helping on two fronts. UNIQLO (and a surprising amount of high-end chains) can provide Japan with high-quality, low-cost clothing by manufacturing garments outside of the country. Also, the growth in affluent consumers across Greater China has allowed many boutique labels to maintain a high enough price point to keep making clothing with the top crafts-people in Japan.

While these economic and historical factors made Japanese fashion what it is today, we cannot downplay the role that specific individuals played in introducing American styles and concepts to the apparel market. Without Kensuke Ishizu, the bespoke business suit would have likely retained its dominance in the postwar. If Big John did not pledge to make authentic jeans or if Kurabō and Kaihara did not experiment with antique, selvedge denim, few Japanese brands would have exported their creations to the world. Japanese fashion owes a tremendous debt to all of these rebels and mavericks who fought against conventional wisdom and dominant market forces to change the way people dress.

Certainly many "traditional" cultural norms shape fashion in Japan, and perhaps they manifested most obviously in the behavior of Japanese consumers. The history of American fashion in Japan reveals generations of teenagers always looking to media authorities for instruction on how to wear new styles. Teens liked Ivy's rules because they provided a foolproof recipe for how to wear clothing "properly." In 2001, Undercover's Jun Takahashi told *The New Yorker*, "Japanese people read magazines as their bibles, and when they see images in them they have to have them and will pay anything. Generally, Japanese people can't make up their own minds and have to have an example to follow." *Popeye*'s catalog magazine format thus became the industry standard because it legitimized more goods each issue. And this tendency towards organized mimicry is even seen among delinquent subcultures: the bōsōzoku started imitating Eikichi Yazawa from Carol, and, by the early 1990s, all wore identical right-wing-inspired tokkōfuku uniforms.

From the widest perspective, Japanese fashion certainly shows that cultural behavior is not an expression of eternal national characteristics passed down from generation to generation in an unbroken line. American fashion came to Japan in the hands of social misfits hungry for change and business success. It then blended with local customs and practices. The ecosystem was always changing, moving, and adapting—and going forward, we should expect the same thing to happen. The Ametora tradition will not stand still, but will continue to be shaped by the passage of time.

FOR THE MOST PART, THE ORIGINATORS OF AMETORA profiled in this book understood their life's work as the pursuit of incremental improvements upon a "copy" of the United States. This echoes the popular narrative around Japan's electronics industry: Sony begged Bell Labs to license transistors for radios, and then pushed the technology into unseen directions. Toshiyuki Kurosu frames his own work in a similar way: "In the 1950s and 1960s, we just imitated Ivy exactly. We tried to stay exactly in step with the American model. But I think Ivy has evolved with the times. It's not the model it was sixty years ago."

There is a precedence for this idea of "copying towards innovation" in the pedagogy of traditional Japanese arts. In flower arrangement and martial arts, students learn the basics by imitating the *kata*, a single authoritative "form." Pupils must first protect the kata, but after many years of study, they break from tradition and then separate to make their own kata—a system described in the term *shu-ha-ri* ("protecting, breaking, and separating").

This model fits the development of Japanese fashion after World War II. VAN's Kensuke Ishizu and Toshiyuki Kurosu pieced together the proper way to wear American style. The fashion magazines like *Men's Club* taught this kata to readers with the unbending strictness of a karate master—a severe and long list of dos and don'ts. Teens, in turn, followed the instructions to the letter, with the most obsessed among them becoming masters of the details. Many of these young fashion fans grew up to create their own brands, and it was this learned focus on minutiae that pushed them to make better quality and more "authentic" versions of American styles. They wanted to get closer and closer to the kata.

The kata-mindset, however, is conservative at its core—finding legitimacy only at the origin rather than in new ideas. Fashion critic Shōzō Izuishi, for example, still refuses to believe that "real jeans" could be made outside of the U.S. Likewise, *Popeye*'s Kinoshita admits, "The thing that people want out of American traditional brands is that they are made in the U.S.A." In today's gleefully superficial postmodern culture, these rigid beliefs on authenticity can feel quaint. But more importantly, they ignore that the clearest kata for American style may exist now in Japan rather than in America.

Japan's heritage of American-styled clothing now surpasses the United States on many measures. Collective knowledge about how to "dress properly" is more widespread and deeper in Japan than in the United States, where it exists only within a small coterie of dedicated men. To learn how to properly dress in America, one can no longer just be an obedient son imitating his father, but must become a devoted archivist of past generations. Harvard students learning to dress today through *Take Ivy* are further removed from the primary source than Japanese men were in 1965.

Japan, meanwhile, has convinced significant numbers of foreigners that their versions of American clothing are *more* authentic than anything being made in the U.S. American brand PRPS touts the "authenticity" of its jeans by proclaiming an exclusive use of Japanese selvedge denim. In the past, jealous Americans castigated Japanese perfection as superficial mimicry lacking a *soul*. But even that has become outdated slander. Self Edge's Kiya Babzani says, "The brands I sell have massive amounts of soul. When you pick it up, you feel something that you don't feel when you pick up any other garment. Even if it's someone who knows nothing about any clothing, when they come in and touch a shirt, they think, there's something different about that shirt. It has a life to it."

Japanese designers, however, mostly envisage their own work within the narrow context of the domestic market—where the clothing is worn by teens living far from "authentic" American lifestyles. Shōzō Izuishi points out, "It's sad, but in Japan culture and fashion aren't linked. It's just floating above without any connection. Fashion is supposed to come from a lifestyle, but most Japanese don't try to understand that." Yasuhiko Kobayashi once compared Japanese fashion to "dress-up dolls"—systems of clothing put together for fun in a predictable way that can be put on and taken off without any deep meaning.

While these criticisms often ring true, this superficiality hearkens back to the fact that they are *imported* styles. By virtue of their foreign origin, any corresponding lifestyle must follow from the clothing rather than vice versa. Fashion thus became an expressive form of play in Japan. Society allowed teenagers to indulge in subcultural looks as long as they cleaned up for job interviews later. A connected and deep fashion may have been too disruptive in Japanese society and never caught on.

Moreover, American fashion's permanent alien status only drove fashion obsessives to move closer towards owning and creating "real things." Japanese creativity in clothing for so long has been a manifestation of anxiety around authenticity—is this thing *real* enough?

This may only be a twentieth century phenomenon, however. The latest crop of Japanese designers have learned from American fashion without being crushed by the weight of its legacy. Daiki Suzuki of made-in-America brand Engineered Garments admits that history is a "great, useful reference," but is always subverting expectations with his original designs and bold patterns. Suzuki's extensive knowledge is present in his work, but he is wholly disinterested in replica. He once asserted, "The Japanese point of view on American style is not something I relate to."

Junya Watanabe of Comme des Garçons Homme meanwhile works frequently with traditional brands such as Brooks Brothers and Levi's, but is hired specifically to desecrate their classic items.

In 2009, for example, he made a reversible Brooks Brothers navy blazer with red gingham check lining. He told *Interview*, "Western clothes are our everyday wardrobe [in Japan]. I don't think that it makes much of a difference anymore whether you're Japanese or American or European." The difference, of course, is that the Japanese version comes to market framed as a luxury. Watanabe tweaked a $100 denim jacket from Tennessee-based workwear label Pointer Brand and charged $800.

Hiroki Nakamura's high-end streetwear line, visvim, has abandoned references to Ivy and American denim and delved instead into ancient folk customs. After obsessing over Heavy Duty items as a teenager, Nakamura was shocked when he moved to Alaska, "I was head-to-toe in American heritage brands—Levi's 1955, WWII-model, the most rare Red Wing you can find. No one cared!" After a stint at Burton Snowboards and becoming friends with Hiroshi Fujiwara, Nakamura started a shoe line in 2002 that fused high-tech American sneakers with Native American moccasins. As he expanded visvim into a full clothing line, he became the Indiana Jones of the apparel world, uncovering heavy wool coats in Tibet, reindeer-skin boots from Norway's Sami tribe, colorful folk art in Guatemalan villages, hand-dye blankets on Navajo reservations, and kudu pelts in Africa. He incorporated these elements not just as visual design but studied age-old techniques to pick up clues on bolstering functionality.

Visvim customers do not just pay for the high costs of premium materials, but for the "story" sewn into every product. Thanks to his use of rare materials and nods to traditional folk ways, Nakamura can spin epic yarns about every piece in his collection. In his emphasis on how products are created, Nakamura became the patron saint of the twenty-first century's "Cult of Production," where customers want to know exactly where and how their products are made. Nakamura believes this is the future: "The Japanese market is getting more mature. The consumers are getting older. People don't need so much product. They want to have something that has meaning and lasts long. They realize that material things alone don't bring happiness. We try to produce less. We try to sell less."

Suzuki, Watanabe, and Nakamura have taken the concept of tradition to new places, but many younger designers want to completely unchain themselves from any bonds of history. Kō-suke Harada, a former planner at John Bull, now runs the men's bottoms brand TUKI out of the Okayama Research Park Incubation Center. While selling small lots of pants to select shops, Harada and his wife also conduct research into vintage textiles and the history of clothing production. Despite this interest in garment history, Harada is tired of all the "storytelling" in men's apparel: "I hate when there is too much emphasis on the 'story' in clothing. People should wake up and want to put on my pants because they feel great."

Desiring an "antithesis" to the over-proliferation of replica denim in Japan, TUKI created an ultra-minimal pair of jeans with non-selvedge denim, dark navy blue inner stitching, chrome rivets and buttons with no marking, and a pure navy blue leather patch on the back. The design removed all vestiges of the Levi's 501 that others continue to blindly imitate. Harada's calculated rejection of heritage may be an extreme reaction to the current trend. But now that Japanese designers have learned all the secrets of clothing history, perhaps there is less value in always looking back to move forward. Harada does not want to preserve the traditional kata nor make an avant-garde reaction against it; he just wants to separate and create something new.

FRAGMENTS FROM JAPAN'S FASHION HISTORY STILL LITTER the contemporary pop culture landscape. Even in death, Kensuke Ishizu retains his Zeus-like status, and former VAN employees still refer to him in conversation as *sensei*—"teacher." Big John and Edwin have faced financial trouble in the last decade, but Okayama and Fukuyama are still home to sewing factories, treatment houses, and world-class denim mills. *Popeye* is stronger than ever, under

Okayama brand TUKI's minimalist jeans.

the editorial direction of "The Sartorialist"-regular Takahiro Kinoshita.

Rock 'n' roll guru Masayuki Yamazaki passed away in 2013, but Pink Dragon's neon still glows each night in Harajuku. On certain Sundays, the Tokyo Rockabilly Club meets to twist around a boom box in Yoyogi Park—even though the youngest member of the crew is over fifty. Yankii culture experienced another mainstream media moment in 2008 with an indulgent bad taste even further divorced from the subculture's roots in imitating American soldiers. Beams has seventy-four stores across Japan, while UNITED ARROWS has over two hundred. The Japanese and American flags still fly high at Brooks Brothers' flagship in Aoyama. Once veteran collector of vintage Levi's, Yōsuke Ōtsubo runs Levi's Vintage Clothing in Japan. A Bathing Ape's Nigo is now Creative Director of UNIQLO's T-shirt line U.T.

Japanese brands have shown their skill in producing and improving upon American fashion, but the next decade will be the true test. After seventy years of borrowing style ideas from the United States, the Japanese have absorbed all possible ideas from American history. The kata for Ametora may have started in the United States, but now it has settled comfortably in Japan. Going forward, the world will likely imitate the healthy Japanese example rather than the moribund American original. After so many years of being the pupil, Japan has an opportunity to be the teacher.

Japan will have to rely on its own heritage for new fashion ideas, but thankfully the country has the richest, most diverse contemporary fashion scene in the world. As Japan provides its versions of American traditional style to the globe, we now must wait to see how Japan reacts when other countries start exporting their own versions of Ametora back to Japan.

ACKNOWLEDGMENTS

In September 2010, I was watching my old cordovan oxfords get polished at Tokyo's "shoeshine bar" Brift H, when a middle-aged man walked in and pulled out an original 1965 print of *Take Ivy*. I leaned over and mentioned that I had just wrote a piece about Kensuke Ishizu of VAN Jacket. He introduced himself as former VAN employee Kazufumi Ōshiba and wanted to set me up with Ishizu's son Shōsuke. The next week I made a formal visit to Ishizu Office, where son Shōsuke and grandson Rui have been keeping the VAN founder's legacy alive. Mr. Ōshiba then introduced me to more VAN employees, and I realized there was an amazing and mostly unknown story that linked VAN's importation of American fashion in the 1960s with the research I had done at college on A Bathing Ape.

I spent the next few years rushing to interview the key people in bringing American fashion to Japan. The good people at Kamakura Shirts set me up with both founder Yoshio Sadasue as well as Toshiyuki Kurosu. Takahiro Kinoshita, Editor-in-Chief at *Popeye* magazine, helped me get in touch with Yasuhiko Kobayashi, while TUKI's Kōsuke Harada introduced me to Kapital and Kaihara. Sometimes I was too late: *Take Ivy* photographer Teruyoshi Hayashida was in the hospital when I asked for an interview and passed away a few months later. The book also became a good excuse to interview major influences on my own writing over the years: social critic Kenrō Hayamizu, subcultural scholar Kōji Namba, and fashion historian Shōzo Izuishi.

The completion of this book required much help from many people, and I want to offer my gratitude. First, I want to thank my wife Utako for her constant support and putting up with my disappearance into my study each weekend morning for two years. Same goes for my two children, whom I cruelly prevented from coloring all over stacks of printouts from the National Diet Library. I also thank my parents for sending me to Japan as a high school student, and my siblings for putting up with seventeen years of droning on and on about Japanese fashion.

I want to thank all those who made introductions and gave me guidance through the process, including the Ishizu family, Kazufumi Ōshiba, Takahiro Kinoshita, Eric Kvatek, Kōsuke Harada, Christian Chensvold, Mayumi Horiguchi, Daisuke Kawasaki, Kaori Nakano, Souris Hong, Scott Mackenzie, Michiko Tamaoki, Kevin Burrows, Kenshi Kawano, Ayako Kōno, Craig Mod, Gideon Lewis-Kraus, Audrey Fondecave, Junko Sakamoto, and Philomena Keet, as well as those who provided me with deep knowledge on many parts of the book, including Ryō Wagatsuma, Bruce Boyer, Matthew Penney, Paul Trynka, and Toby Feltwell.

Through the power of Google Docs, I had a superstar squad of readers and proofreaders: thank you to Matt Alt, Emily Balistrieri, Matt Treyvaud, Robin Moroney, Cassandra Lord, Connor Shepherd, Josh Lambert, and my Dad.

Thanks goes to my agent Mollie Glick and original editor Alex Littlefield for making this all possible, as well as publisher Lara Heimert, editors Katy O'Donnell and Leah Stecher, and everyone at Basic for making the book readable. And special thanks to Wes Del Val for helping me think broader with the initial idea.

A big thank you to Néojaponisme co-founder Ian Lynam for his help with the art and design (including scanner privileges) and Jane Chun for tons of advice and uncovering amazing anecdotes around the intersection of Japanese and American brands. And thank you for your time, Sara Jew-Lim, for an unsuccessful search through the Princeton archives for the still enigmatic Lieutenant O'Brien. I've always been grateful for the years of support from Benjamin Novak, Chess Stetson, Trevor Sias, Patrick Macias, and Ryan Erik Williams. And Sean Boyland, I haven't forgotten that I still owe you a game of *go*.

NOTES AND SOURCES

Mabuchi (1989) is a key source throughout the book on the history of Japanese youth culture. Additional notes on postwar fashion culture in Kimura (1993), Across Editorial Desk (1995), and Satō (1997).

Personal interviews (in alphabetical order): Kiya Babzani, Toby Feltwell, Kazuyoshi Fukuda, Kōsuke Harada, Hajime "Paul" Hasegawa, Kenrō Hayamizu, Takeyoshi Hayashida, Takeharu Hirakawa, Toshikiyo Hirata, Kiro Hirata, Kazuo Hozumi, Shōsuke Ishizu, Shōzo Izuishi, Yoshiharu Kaihara, Takahiro Kinoshita, Masayoshi Kobayashi, Yasuhiko Kobayashi, Kōji Kusakabe, Toshiyuki Kurosu, Eric Kvatek, Paul Mittleman, Hiroshi Morinaga, Kōji Namba, Takeshi Ōfuchi, Andrew Olah, Kazufumi Ōshiba, Yōsuke Ōtsubo, Richard Press, Yoshio Sadasue, Osamu Shigematsu, Yuichi Suenaga, Mikiharu Tsujita, Tadayoshi Yamada, and Hidehiko Yamane. Email interviews with Alexander Julian, Daiki Suzuki, and Paul Trynka. Consulted past personal interviews with Hirofumi Kurino, Hiroki Nakamura, Nigo, and Jun Takahashi. Hiroshi Fujiwara politely declined.

INTRODUCTION
Quotes about Miyuki-zoku from *Asahi Shimbun* articles ("A net to catch Ginza's 'Miyuki Tribe," "100 Miyuki Tribe taken into custody"). PARCO quip from Gibson (2003).

CHAPTER ONE
Prewar fashion in Tozaka (1972) and Slade (2009). *Mobo* raids in Ambaras (2005). Tianjin liberation in Shaw (1960). "*Tsurushinbo*" slur from Gordon (2012). Ōe quote in Duus/Hasegawa (2011). Dower (1999) is the canonical work on Occupation culture, while Tanaka (2002) provided further notes on Pan Pan Girls. "Oh Mistake!" incident covered in Mabuchi, Dower, as well as Iwama (1995).

All biographical details for Kensuke Ishizu in autobiography Ishizu (1983), his testimonies in Tashima (1996), online museum at ishizu.jp, as well as Sayama (2012) and Udagawa (2006).

CHAPTER TWO

Kurosu (2001) provides autobiographical details as well as good information on postwar clothing culture and early VAN. Key VAN stories also in Baba (1980), Hanafusa (2007), and *Eien no Ivy-ten* (1995). Kurosu and Hozumi repeatedly recalled their history in *Men's Club* taidan discussions. Portrait of VAN on the verge of success in *"Kimi wa VAN-tō ka, JUN-tō ka?"* (1964). Sales numbers in Baba as well as Urabe (1982). The history of *Heibon Punch* in *Heibon Punch no Jidai* (1996), Namba (2007), and Akagi (2004).

CHAPTER THREE

Teens confused about Ivy in Ishizu (*"Aibii-zoku"*, 1965). Yasuoka's confusion in Yasuoka (1975). Olympic blazer anecdotes in "Sports and Art" (2007). The Take Ivy behind-the-scenes stories in Shōsuke Ishizu et. al (1965) and "The Trad" interviews. Quote from Ivy Tribe member in *Asahi*'s "Around one hundred taken into custody." "Beggar" slang and police quotes recalled in *"Aibii to Nihon no Wakamono."* Ishizu's speech extrapolated from Ishizu (*"Aibii-zoku,"* 1965) and Sayama. Anti-Ishizu article in *Shūkan Gendai*'s "The Reputation of Mr. Kensuke Ishizu." Sadasue story in *Dankai Punch*.

CHAPTER FOUR

Basic history of Japanese jeans in Saeki (2006), Koyama (2011), *Denim no Hon* (1991), Hori (1974), Kitamoto (1974), and Kurosu (1973). Reporting on Kojima and Maruo Clothing in Sugiyama (2009) and Inoki (2013). Cotton details in Sugihara (1999). Ameyoko jeans and Shirasu story in Izuishi (2009) and Izuishi (1999), as well as "Jeans: This Chic Fashion" (1970). Ameyoko background in Mahi (1960) and Shiomitsu (1982). Kobayashi jeans story in Kobayashi (1966) and Kobayashi (1996). Counterculture from Mabuchi and Across Editorial Desk. "Non-political" VAN in Sayama. Kurosu anti-U.S. quote in Satō (1997). Bell bottoms in Kobayashi (1972). Pehda's quote from "Gaijin Teaches Young Jpnz. Good Manners."

CHAPTER FIVE

"Illustrated Reportage" notes in Kobayashi (2004) and Kurosu (1990). Interviews with Kobayashi, Ishikawa, Kinameri, Terasaki, Uchisaka, and other *Popeye* editors in Akata (2002). Public poll numbers in NHK (1982). Mabuchi, Across Editorial Desk, and Urabe (1982) round out social history. Further notes on *Made in U.S.A* in Namba (*Social History of Debut Issues*, 2009). History of *Popeye* in Akata and Shiine (2010). Heavy Duty "system" idea from Kobayashi (1978) and (2013). Urabe (1982) on Heavy Duty market. Early history of surfing in Nishino (1971) and Suzuki (1981). VAN bankruptcy in Udagawa, Sayama, Baba (1980), and *Eien no Ivy-ten*, as well as Tsuzuku (1980).

CHAPTER SIX

Masayuki Yamazaki's biographical details in Morinaga (2004) and Yamazaki (2009). Yamazaki quotes from Cream Soda publications *Rock 'n' Roll Connection* (1977), Yamazaki (1980), *Teddy Boy: Rock'n' roll Bible* (1980). *Gurentai* in Ōnuki (1999) and Dower. "Yokosuka jumpers" in *Sukajan* (2005). "Colonialist chic" line in Kobayashi (1972). *Bōsōzoku* in Satō (1991). *Yankii* culture in Namba (*Evolution of Yankii*, 2009), *An Introduction to Yankii Studies* (2009), and *Big Yankii Collection* (2009). Rollers in *Hātō wa Teddy* (2003). Two anti-tsuppari girl quotes in "The Harajuku '78." Harajuku sundays in *"Wakai Hiroba Harajuku 24 jikan."* Dave Barry quotes from *Barry* (1992).

CHAPTER SEVEN

Early Beams and Shigematsu story in Kawashima (2008), Yamaguchi (2006), "Beams de ichiban sugokatta…," and Yō Shitara's *Senken Shimbun* series. Luxury market in Urabe (1982). Kitayama quote in Akata. American brands and Preppy boom in Baba (1980) and Baba (1984), as well as *Ishizu Kensuke's New Ivy Book* (1983). Brooks Brothers in Nakamuta (1981) and *Eien no Aibii-ten*. *Hot Dog Press* backstory in Akata, Namba (Social History, 2009), and Hanafusa. Hoichoi in Hoichoi Production (1983). *Nantonaku, Crystal* quotes from Tanaka (1980) are my translation. Money as social ingredient in Fujitake (1977). Youth consumption stats in Sano (1986). Comme des Garcons sales numbers in Chimura (2001) and Roy (1983). Foreign product ownership numbers from "Challenges for the fashion business leading up to 2020." Juppies in Iwata (1987). *Time* quote from Hillenbrand (1989). Shibukaji in Namba (2005), Chimura, and Koike (2004). Teamers in Nakano (1997). Shibuya import shops in Koike. Shibu-kaji style details in "Thorough Shibukaji Research Manual."

CHAPTER EIGHT

Fujiwara, Ōkaji, and company in Kawakatsu (2009). Nigo and Takahashi details from interviews in *Nylon for Guys*. Lesser-known Nigo details in "The true face of Nigo from 14 fragments." *Hot Dog Press* reader polls in September 25 and November 10, 1997 issues. Ura-Harajuku-kei as the most popular style in *Hot Dog Press'* readers poll a year later. AFFA T-shirt price and teenager quote in "The non-individualistic vintage boom." Nigo and Fujiwara's tax payments (previously public information) in Okajima and Ogasawara (2001). Pharrell quotes in Blagrove et. al. (2013). Sales numbers and bankruptcy details in Wetherille (2011).

CHAPTER NINE

Stories of vintage buying from personal interviews with Ōtsubo, Kvatek, Kusakabe, and Ōfuchi. Industry perspective in Ishikawa (1994), "Multiplicative game continues for imported second-hand clothing" (1996), and "Cultural Theory of Recycling" (1997). Saeki again for jeans history and Levi's Japan. Koike and Nakano for *Boon* and consumer demand. Quote about decreasing quality from *The Jeans* (1988). Weisser quote in Bunn (2002). Quotes about Latina workers and from Voice Harajuku in "The non-individualistic vintage boom." Farley story in "Fads: The Nike Railroad" (1997), Bunn (2002), Frisch (1997), and Uhlman (1997). The growth of replica lines in *Nippon no Jiinzu: Made in Japan* (1998). Mura-ito in Saeki. Some additional Yamane quotes from Yamane (2008). Evisu's success overseas in Tredre (1999). Real McCoy's in Koike. Kapital in Sugiyama. Levi's lawsuit in Barbaro and Creswell (2007). Ōishi quote in "*Gpan kono iki na fasshon*" (1997).

CHAPTER TEN

Ishizu death and legacy in Udagawa, *Eien no Ivy-ten*, Hanafusa, Kobayashi (1996), and Sadasue interview. Pressler (2010) has Yanai/Drexler story, while Burkitt (2012) talks about Katsuta. Colman (2009) is full of good details, including Daiki Suzuki's quote on Thom Browne. Trebay (2010) on *Take Ivy* popularity. Fifty thousand sales number in Jacobs (2010). Bay anecdote and quote from Swanson (2014). Browne denied his "literal" inspiration in Kohl (2013). "A Continuous Lean" quotes in Williams (2009) and Gallagher (2013). Tyler Brûlé in Bartlett (2013). Rise of American menswear blogging and Bastian quote in Greenwald (2011). Schlossman quote in Evans (2012). Suzuki's denial of "Japanese point of view" from Dugan (2013). Watanabe quotes in "Sentimental Journey" and his Pointer Brand work in Horyn (2013). PRPS point from Keet (2011). Ishizu quote in "New Ivy Text '82." Ralph Lauren's Omotesando store price in Fujita (2014).

BIBLIOGRAPHY

For reference, I have added English titles for Japanese works in parentheses. Most are my own translation but some were provided by the Japanese author.

"*14ko no danpen kara naru Nigo no sugao*" (The true face of Nigo from 14 fragments). *Asayan*. Vol. 85. January 2001: 19.

Across Editorial Desk. *Street Fashion 1945-1995*. Tokyo: PARCO, 1995.

"*Aibii no ditēru*" (Ivy details). *Men's Club*. Vol. 43. June 1965: 82-83.

"*Aibii riigā no kinō, kyō, ashita*" (Ivy Leaguers of yesterday, today, tomorrow). *Men's Club*. Vol. 43. June 1965: 42-46.

"*Aibii riigāzu ōini kataru*" (We talk a great deal with the Ivy Leaguers). *Men's Club*. Vol. 14. April 1959: 88-93.

"*Aibii to nihon no wakamono*" (Ivy and Japanese youth). *Men's Club*. Vol. 12. June 1965: 216-223.

Akagi, Yōichi. *Heibon Punch 1964*. Tokyo: Heibonsha, 2004.

Akata, Yūichi. *Shōgenkōsei "Popai" no jidai—aru zasshi no kimyō na kōkai* (Based on witness testimony, the "Popeye" era: the strange voyage of a certain magazine). Tokyo: Ohta Books, 2002.

Ambaras, David R. *Bad Youth*. Berkeley: University of California Press, 2005.

Asada, Akira. "A Left Within a Place of Nothingness." *New Left Review*. No. 5. September-October 2000.

Baba, Keiichi, ed. *Ivy Goods Graffiti*. Tokyo: Rippū Shobō Publishing, 1984.

Baba, Keiichi, ed. *VAN Graffiti*. Tokyo: Rippū Shobō Publishing, 1980.

"*Baibai gēmu wo tsuzukeru yu'nyū — kifurushi ga kakko ii!?*" (The multiplicative game continues for imported second-hand clothing — shabbiness is cool?!). *Tōyō Keizai*. August 24, 1996: 40.

Barbaro, Michael, and Julie Creswell. "Levi's Turns to Suing Its Rivals." *New York Times*. January 29, 2007.

Barry, Dave. *Dave Barry Does Japan*. New York: Ballantine Books, 1993.

Bartlett, Myke. "Tyler Brûlé makes Monocle." *Dumbo Feather*. Second Quarter 2013. http://www.dumbofeather.com/conversation/tyler-brule-makes-monocle/

"'Bathing Ape' T-shirts land duo in hot water." *Daily Yomiuri*. (Tokyo) 16 October 1998: 2.

Be 50's: Book around the rock 'n' roll. Tokyo: Shinsensha, 1982.

"'Beams de ichiban sugokatta no wa nanika naa' wo kataru" (We talk about what was the most amazing at Beams). *relax: Beams Mania special edition*. April 1998: 46-47, 68-69.

Birnbach, Lisa, ed. *The Official Preppy Handbook*. New York: Workman Publishing Company, 1980.

Blagrove, Kadia et. al. "The Oral History of Billionaire Boys Club and Icecream." *Complex*. December 3, 2013. http://www.complex.com/style/2013/12/oral-history-bbc-icecream

"*Bōkoku no dezainā Ishizu Kensuke-shi no hyōhan*" (The reputation of Mr. Kensuke Ishizu — a "designer who will lead to national ruin"). *Shūkan Gendai*. October 13, 1966: 128-132.

Bunn, Austin. "Not Fade Away." *New York Times*. December 1, 2002.

Burkitt, Laurie. "The Man Behind the Puffy Purple Coat." *Wall Street Journal*. March 16, 2012.

Chaplin, Julia. "Scarcity Makes the Heart Grow Fonder." *New York Times*. September 5, 1999.

Chapman, William. *Inventing Japan*. New York: Prentice Hall Press, 1991.

Chimura, Michio. *Sengo fasshon stōrii—1945-2000* (The postwar fashion story—1945-2000). Tokyo: Heibonsha, 2001.

Colman, David. "The All-American Back From Japan." *New York Times*. June 17, 2009.

Cooke, Fraser. "Hiroshi Fujiwara." *Interview*. 2010.

De Mente, Boye, and Fred Thomas Perry. *The Japanese as Consumers*. Tokyo: John Weatherhill Inc., 1968.

Denim no Hon (Book of denim). Tokyo: Urban Communications, 1991.

Dower, John. *Embracing Defeat*. New York: W. W. Norton & Company, 1999.

Dugan, John. "Daiki Suzuki." *Nothing Major*. June 19, 2013. http://nothingmajor.com/features/60-daiki-suzuki/

Duus, Peter, and Kenji Hasegawa. *Rediscovering America Japanese Perspectives on the American Century*. Berkeley: University of California, 2011.

"*Eiga 'Take Ivy' ni tsuite katarō*" (Let's talk about the 'Take Ivy' film). *Oily Boy: The Ivy Book*. November 2011: 66-67.

Eien no Ivy-ten (The everlasting Ivy exhibition 1995). Tokyo: Nihon Keizai Shimbunsha, 1995.

English, Bonnie. *Japanese Fashion Designers: The Work and Influence of Issey Miyake, Yohji Yamamoto and Rei Kawakubo*. Oxford: Berg, 2011.

Etō, Jun, and Shigehiko Hasumi. *Old Fashioned — Futsū no Kaiwa*. Tokyo: Chūōkōronsha, 1985.

Evans, Jonathan. "Q&A: The Guys Behind the Fk Yeah Menswear Book." *Esquire: The Style Blog*. November 7, 2012. http://www.esquire.com/blogs

/mens-fashion/kevin-burrows-lawrence-schlossman-fuck-yeah-menswear
-110712

"Fads: The Nike Railroad." *New York Times*. October 5, 1997.

Fasshon to fūzoku no 70nen (Seventy years of fashion and culture). Tokyo: Fujingahōsha, 1975.

"Fasshon bijinesu 2020nen he no chōsen" (Challenges for the fashion business leading up to 2020). *Fashion Han-Bai*. May 2014.

Frisch, Suzy. "Growing Yen For Old Things American." *Chicago Tribune*. December 05, 1997.

Fujita, Junko. "Mitsubishi Corp in final talks to buy Tokyo Ralph Lauren building for $342 million: sources." *Reuters*. Jan 30, 2014.

Fujitake, Akira. "Hordes of Teenagers 'Massing.'" *Japan Echo:* 4.3 (1977): 109-117.

"Gaijin Teaches Young Jpnz. Good Manners." *The New Canadian*. July 1, 1977.

Gallagher, Jake. "Classic Ivy Oxfords Straight From Japan." *A Continuous Lean*. December 3, 2013. http://www.acontinuouslean.com/2013/12/03/classic-ivy-oxfords-straight-japan/

Gibson, William. *Pattern Recognition*. New York: G: Putnam's Son, 2003.

"Ginza 'Miyuki-zoku' ni Hodō no Ami" (A net to catch Ginza's "Miyuki Tribe"). *Asahi Shimbun*. September 13, 1964.

Gordon, Andrew. *Fabricating Consumers: The Sewing Machine in Modern Japan*. Berkeley: University of California, 2012.

"Gpan kono iki na fasshon" (Jeans: this chic fashion). *Shūkan Asahi*. February 27, 1970: 36-39.

Greenwald, David. "Reblog This: The Oral History of Menswear Blogging." *GQ*. December 13, 2011. http://www.gq.com/style/profiles/201112/menswear-street-style-oral-history

Hanafusa, Takanori. *Aibii wa eien ni nemuranai* (The IVY doesn't sleep through all eternity). Tokyo: Sangokan, 2007.

Hara, Hiroyuki. *Bubble Bunkaron* (A theory of Bubble culture). Tokyo: Keio Gijuku Daigaku Publishing, 2006.

Hāto wa Teddy—Japan's Rock 'n' rollers Revival-ban (Teddy in our hearts). Reprint. Tokyo: Daisanshokan, 2003.

Hayashida, Teruyoshi et. al. *Take Ivy*. Trans. Miho Ayabe. New York: Powerhouse, 2010.

"Heavy-Duty Ivy-*tō senden*" (Manifesto of the Heavy-Duty Ivy Party). *Men's Club*. Vol. 183. September 1976: 151-155.

Heibon Punch no Jidai (The era of Heibon Punch). Tokyo: Magazine House, 1996.

Hillenbrand, Barry. "American Casual Seizes Japan." *Time*. November 13, 1989: 106-107.

Hisutorii — Nihon no Jiinzu (History: Japanese jeans). Tokyo: Nihon Sen'i Shimbunsha, 2006.

Hoichoi Productions. *Mie Kōza* (A course on looking good). Tokyo: Shōgakkan, 1983.

Hori, Yōichi. *Jiinzu: Owari no nai ryūkō no subete* (Jeans: Everything about a trend with no end). Tokyo: Fujingahō, 1974.

Horyn, Cathy. "A Tennessee Clothing Factory Keeps Up the Old Ways." *New York Times*. August 14, 2013.

"Hyakunin-amari wo Hodō, Ginza no Kōmori-zoku-gari" (Around one hundred taken into custody — Tsukiji Police Station hunting for Ginza's Umbrella Tribe). *Asahi Shimbun*. April 25, 1965.

Inoki, Masami. *Sen'i Ōkoku Okayama Konjaku* (Past and present of Okayama, textile kingdom). Okayama: Nihon Bunkyō Publishing Okayama, 2013.

"Interview with Teruyoshi Hayashida. I of III." "The Trad." October 6, 2010. Accessed November 19, 2014. http://thetrad.blogspot.com/2010/10/interview-with-teruyoshi-hayashida-i-of.html.

"Hayashida & Take Ivy on 16mm - Part II of III." "The Trad." October 7, 2010. Accessed November 19, 2014. http://thetrad.blogspot.com/2010/10/hayashida-take-ivy-on-16mm-part-ii-of.html

"Hayashida & 'Nioi' Part III." "The Trad." October 8, 2010. Accessed November 19, 2014. http://thetrad.blogspot.jp/2010/10/hayashida-nioi-part-iiii.html

Igarashi, Tarō, ed. *Yankii bunkaron josetsu* (An introduction to Yankii studies). Tokyo: Kawade Shobo Shinsha, 2009.

Ishikawa, Kiyoshi. *"Mijuku na yokubō" wo akinau gendai no yamishōnin"* (Modern-day black marketeers who peddle 'immature desires'). *Ushio*. July 1994.

Ishizu, Kensuke. *"Aibii-zoku wa ze ka hi ka"* (Is the Ivy Tribe right or wrong?). *Men's Club*. Vol. 47. November 1965: 25-28.

Ishizu, Kensuke. *"Anata mo Gpan, boku mo Gpan"* (You're in jeans, I'm in jeans). *Heibon*. Heibon Publishing. September 1961. 134-136.

Ishizu Kensuke daihyakka. Accessed March 1, 2013. http://ishizu.jp.

Ishizu, Kensuke. *Ishizu Kensuke ōru katarogu* (Ishizu Kensuke all catalog). Tokyo: Kōdansha, 1983.

Ishizu, Kensuke. *Itsu, dokode, nani wo kiru?* (When, where, what to wear). Fujingahōsha, 1965.

Ishizu, Kensuke. *"Kore ga honba no aibii"* (This is Ivy in its habitat). *Men's Club*. Vol. 18. April 1960: 62-65.

Ishizu, Kensuke. *"Watashi no oshare jinsei"* (My stylish life). *Men's Club*. Vol. 31. Spring 1963: 115-117.

Ishizu Kensuke's New Ivy Book. Tokyo: Kōdansha, 1983.

Ishizu, Shōsuke, Toshiyuki Kurosu, and Hajime Hasegawa. *"Aibii tsuā kara kaette, sono 1"* (Back from the Ivy Tour, part one). *Men's Club*. Vol. 45. September 1965: 11-15.

Ishizu, Shōsuke, Toshiyuki Kurosu, and Hajime Hasegawa. *"Aibii tsuā kara kaette, sono 2"* (Back from the Ivy Tour, part two). *Men's Club*. Vol. 46. October 1965: 11-14.

Iwama, Natsuki. *Sengo wakamono bunka no kōbō* (A beam of light from postwar youth culture). Tokyo: Nihon Keizai Shinbunsha, 1995.

Iwata, Ryūshi. *Jappii — kimi wa otona ni nareru ka* (Juppies: Can you become an adult?) Men's Club Books No. 55. Tokyo: Fujingahōsha, 1987.

Izuishi, Shōzō. *Burū jiinzu no bunkashi* (The cultural history of blue jeans). Tokyo: NTT Publishing, 2009.

Izuishi, Shōzō. *Kanpon burū jiinzu* (Complete textbook of jeans). Tokyo: Shinchōsha, 1999.

Jacobs, Sam. "Take Ivy, The Reissue Interview." *The Choosy Beggar*. August 19, 2010.   http://www.thechoosybeggar.com/2010/08/take-ivy-the-reissue -interview/

The Jeans. Men's Club Books No. 20. Tokyo: Fujingahōsha, 1988.

Kawai, Kazuo. *Japan's American Interlude*. Chicago: University Of Chicago Press, 1979.

Kawakatsu, Masayuki. *Oka no ue no panku*. (Tink Punk on the Hills). Tokyo: Shōgakukan, 2009.

Kawashima, Yōko. *Beams senryaku*. (Beams strategy). Tokyo: Nihon Keizai Shimbun Shuppansha, 2008.

Keet, Philomena. "Making New Vintage Jeans in Japan: Relocating Authenticity." *Textile:* 9:1 (2011): 44–61.

"Kimi wa VAN-tō ka, JUN-tō ka?" (Are you pro-VAN or pro-JUN?). *Heibon Punch*. Vol. 6 June 15, 1964: 7-14.

Kimura, Haruo. *Fukusō ryūkō no bunkashi* (The cultural history of clothing trends). Ōsaka: Gendai Sōzōsha, 1993.

Kitamoto, Masatake. *Jiinzu no hon* (The jeans book). Tokyo: Sankei Books, 1974.

Kobayashi, Yasuhiko. *Eien no Toraddo-ha* (Everlasting Trad). Tokyo: Nesco, 1996.

Kobayashi, Yasuhiko. *"HD wa traddo ni hajimaru"* (HD starts with Trad). *Men's Club*. Vol 213. December 1978: 188-191.

Kobayashi, Yasuhiko. *Hebii dūtii no hon* (The book of Heavy Duty). Reprint. Tokyo: Yamakei Bunko, 2013.

Kobayashi, Yasuhiko. *Irasuto rupo no jidai* (The era of Illustrated Reportage). Tokyo: Bungeishunjū, 2004.

Kobayashi, Yasuhiko. *Wakamono no machi* (Youth streets). Tokyo: Shōbunsha, 1972.

Kobayashi, Yasuhiko. "Yokosuka Mambo story." *Punch Deluxe*. November 1966.

Kohl, Jeff. "An Interview With Thom Browne." *The Agency Daily*. May 2013. http://www.theagencyre.com/2013/05/thom-browne-interview-tokyo -flagship/

Koike, Riumo. *Daihitto zasshi no GET shirei* (The "get"-captain of a hit magazine). Tokyo: Shinpūsha, 2004.

Koyama, Yuko. "Who Wears Jeans? Acceptance of Jeans in the Showa Era of Japan Viewed from Generations and Genders." Japanese language. *Journal of History for the Public* 2011 (8): 14-33.

Krash Japan. "Kojima: Holy Land of Jeans." Accessed on August 14, 2013. http://www.krashjapan.com/v1/jeans/index_e.html

Kurosu, Toshiyuki. "*Aibii arakaruto*" (Ivy à la carte). *Men's Club*. Vol. 45. September 1965: 18.

Kurosu, Toshiyuki. "*Aibii arakaruto*" (Ivy à la carte). *Men's Club*. Vol. 46. October 1965: 15.

Kurosu, Toshiyuki. *Aibii no jidai* (The Ivy era). Tokyo: Kawade Shobo Shinsha, 2001.

Kurosu, Toshiyuki, ed. *City Boy Graffiti*. Men's Club Books Super Edition. Tokyo: Fujingahōsha, 1990.

Kurosu, Toshiyuki. "Ivy Q&A." *Men's Club*. Vol. 43. June 1965: 142-145.

Kurosu, Toshiyuki. *Traddo saijiki* (Trad almanac). Tokyo: Fujingahōsha, 1973.

"*Kurutta 'gaitō rēsu' Toyama*" (Toyama: crazy street racing). *Asahi Shimbun*. June 19, 1972.

Lee, John, and Jeff Staple. "Hiroshi Fujiwara: International Man of Mystery." *Theme*: Issue 1, Spring 2005. http://www.thememagazine.com/stories/hiroshi-fujiwara/

Mabuchi, Kōsuke. "*Zoku*"-*tachi no sengoshi* (The postwar history of the tribes). Tokyo: Sanseido, 1989.

Made in U.S.A. Catalog. Tokyo: Yomiuri Shimbunsha, 1975.

Mahi, Mari. "*Horidashimono techō*" (Bargain notebook). *Men's Club*. Vol. 20. October 1960: 84-87.

Manabe, Hiroshi. "*Tokai no kirigirisu*" (Urban katydids). *Asahi Shimbun*. September 20, 1965.

Marx, W. David. "Future Folk: Hiroki Nakamura." *Nylon Guys*. Fall 2008.

Marx, W. David. "Jun Takahashi." *Nylon Guys*. Fall 2006.

Marx, W. David. "Nigo: Gorillas in Our Midst." *Nylon Guys*. Spring 2006.

Marx, W. David. "Selective Shopper: An interview with fashion guru Hirofumi Kurino." *Made of Japan*. September 2009.

Matsuyama, Takeshi. "The Harajuku '78." *an·an*. February 5, 1978: 43-57.

Mead, Rebecca. "Shopping Rebellion." *The New Yorker*. March 18, 2002: 104-111.

"*Miyuki-zoku' hyakunin hodō*" (100 Miyuki Tribe taken into custody). *Asahi Shimbun*. September 19, 1964.

Morinaga, Hiroshi. *Harajuku gōrudo rasshu – Seiunhen* (Harajuku gold rush). Tokyo: CDC, 2004.

Motohashi, Nobuhiro. "*VAN no shinwa: Kamakura Shātsu ni miru VAN no idenshi*" (The myth of VAN: Seeing VAN's DNA in Kamakura Shirts). *Dankai Punch*. Vol. 2, July 2006: 96-112.

Mystery Train. Film. Directed by Jim Jarmusch. Original Release Year: 1989. Mystery Train Inc.

Nakabe, Hiroshi. *Bōsōzoku 100nin no shissō* (Bōsōzoku – 100 people speeding along). Tokyo: Daisanshokan, 1979.

Nakamuta, Hisayuki. *Traditional Fashion*. Tokyo: Fujingahōsha, 1981.

Nakano, Mitsuhiro. "Teenage Symphony." *Baburu 80s to iu Jidai* (A story of the Bubble Eighties). Tokyo: Aspect, 1997.

Nanba, Kōji. "Rethinking 'Shibu-Kaji'." Research Note. Kwansei Gakuin University Sociology Department Bulletin. No. 99. October 2005: 233-245.

Nanba, Kōji. *Sōkan no shakaishi* (The social history of debut issues). Tokyo: Chikuma Shinsho, 2009.

Nanba, Kōji. *Yankii shinkaron* (The evolution of yankii). Tokyo: Kōbunsha, 2009.

Nanba, Kōji. *Zoku no keifugaku – yūzu sabukaruchāzu no sengoshi* (The genealogy of tribes: a postwar history of youth subcultures). Tokyo: Seikyūsha, 2007.

"New Ivy Text '82." *Hot Dog Press*. January 25, 1982.

NHK Broadcasting Culture Research Institute. *Zusetsu – Sengo yoronshi* (Charts – the history of postwar public opinion). Tokyo: NHK Books, 1982.

Nihon no Retoro Sutairu Bukku 1920-1970 (Japan retro style Book 1920-1970). Tokyo: Oribe Publishing, 1990.

Nippon no Jiinzu: Made in Japan (Japan's jeans: Made in Japan). Tokyo: World Photo Press, 1998.

Nishino, Mitsuo. *Tanoshii sāfin* (Fun surfing). Tokyo: Seibido Shuppan, 1971.

Okajima, Kaori, and Itaru Ogasawara. "*Nigo to iu yamai*" (The illness called Nigo). *Cyzo*. August 2001: 95-97.

Olah, Andrew. "What is a Premium Jean?" *Apparel Insiders*. November 2010. http://www.apparelinsiders.com/2010/11/1619018243/

OLD BOY SPECIAL Eien no VAN (Eternal VAN). Ei Mook 138. Tokyo: Ei Publishing, 1999.

Ōnuki, Setsuo. "*Warera, Shinjuku Gurentai*" (We were the Shinjuku gurentai). *Gurentai Densetsu*. Tokyo: Yosensha Publishing, 1999.

"*Otoko no futatsu no ryūkō wo kataru aivii riigu ka Vsutairu ka?*" (We talk two men's trends: Ivy or V-style?). *Men's Club*. Vol. 6. October 1956: 121-125.

Packard, George R. "They Were Born When the Bomb Dropped." *New York Times*, August 29, 1969.

Pressler, Jessica. "Invasion of the $10 Wardrobe." *GQ*. December 2011.

Purototaipu na jīnzu 200 (Prototype denim 200 pairs). *Boon Extra*, Vol 1. Tokyo Shōdensha, May 20, 1995.

"*Risaikuru no Bunkaron 7 — Amerika no Gomi*" (Cultural theory of recycling #7: America's trash). *Gekkan Haikibutsu*. October 1997: 88-95.

Rokkunrōru Conekushon (Rock'n'roll connection). Kyoto: Shirakawa Shoin, 1977.

Roy, Susan. "Japan's 'New Wave' Breaks on U.S. Shores." *Advertising Age*. September 5, 1983.

"*Ryūkō ni Oinukareru Aseri no VAN-Kyōso Ishizu Kensuke*" (VAN guru Kensuke Ishizu is feeling the heat as trends pass him by). *Shūkan Bunshun*. January 13-20, 1969: 138-140.

Saeki, Akira. *"Wagakuni no Jiinzu Sangyo Hatten Ryakushi"* (An abbreviated history of the development of the Japanese jeans industry). *Hisutorii – Nihon no Jiinzu*. Tokyo: Nihon Sen'i Shimbunsha, 2006.

"Sannin yoreba: MC Hyōshi Sunpyō-kai" (If you ask those three: A quick review meeting about MC covers). *Men's Club*. Vol. 280. June 1984: 22-37.

Sano, Shinichi. *"Dan'ihōshoku jidai no furugi būmu"* (Second-hand clothing boom in an era of luxury). *Chūō Kōron*. November 1986: 254-267.

Sasaki, Tsuyoshi, ed. *Sengoshi Daijiten — 1945-2004 Zōho Shinpan* (Encyclopedia of postwar history, 1945-2004 new, expanded edition). Tokyo: Sanseido, 2005.

Satō, Ikuya. *Kamikaze Biker: Parody and Anomy in Affluent Japan*. Chicago: University of Chicago Press, 1991.

Satō, Yoshiaki. *Wakamono Bunkashi* (Postwar 60's, 70's and recent years of fashion). Tokyo: Genryūsha, 1997.

Sayama, Ichirō. *VAN kara tōku hanarete* (Far removed from VAN). Tokyo: Iwanami Shoten, 2012.

Seidensticker, Edward. *Tokyo: from Edo to Showa 1867-1989*. Tokyo: Tuttle Publishing, 2010.

"Sentimental Journey" (Junya Watanabe). *Interview*. 2009.

Shaw, Henry I. Jr. *The U.S. Marines in North China, 1945-1949*. Historical Branch, Headquarters, USMC, 1960.

"Shibukaji, sono fasshon kara seitai made, tettei kenkyū manuaru" (Thorough shibukaji research manual — from the fashion to the ecology). *Hot Dog Press*. April 10, 1989.

Shiine, Yamato. *Popeye Monogatari—Wakamono wo Kaeta Densetsu no Zasshi* (The Popeye story '76-'81). Tokyo: Shinchōsha, 2010.

Shiomitsu, Hajime. *Ameyoko Sanjūgonen no Gekishi* (Ameyoko's 35 years of extreme history). Tokyo: Tōkyō Kōbō Shuppan, 1982.

Shitara, Yō. "America no seikatsu uru mise hiraku" (We opened a shop to sell the American lifestyle). *Senken Shimbun*. Date unknown: 7.

Shitara, Yō. "Nagare yomi bijinesu ga kakudai" (Expanding the business by reading the flow). *Senken Shimbun*. Date unknown: 11.

Ski Life. Tokyo: Yomiuri Shimbunsha, 1974.

Slade, Toby. *Japanese Fashion: A Cultural History*. Oxford: Berg, 2009.

"Sports and Art #5 Kurosu Toshiyuki." Japan Olympic Committee (JOC). July 26, 2007. Accessed November 19, 2014. http://www.joc.or.jp/column /sportsandart/20070726.html

Stock, Kyle. "Why Ralph Lauren Is Worried About a Weakened Yen." *Businessweek*. June 05, 2013.

Sugihara, Kaoru. "International Circumstances surrounding the Postwar Japanese Cotton Textile Industry." Graduate School of Economics and Osaka School of International Public Policy (OSIPP), Osaka University, May 1999.

Sugiyama, Shinsaku. *Nihon Jiinzu Monogatari* (The story of Japanese jeans). Okayama: Kibito Publishing, 2009.

Sukajan: Japanese souvenir jacket story and photograph. Tokyo: Ei Publishing, November 2005.

Suzuki, Tadashi. *Surfin'.* Tokyo: Kōdansha, 1981.

Swanson, Carl. "The New Generation Gap." *Elle.* January 15, 2014.

Tanaka, Toshiyuki. *Japan's Comfort Women: Sexual Slavery and Prostitution during World War II and the US Occupation.* London: Routledge, 2002.

Tanaka, Yasuo. *Nantonaku, Kurisutaru.* (Vaguely, crystal). Tokyo: Shinchōsha, 1980.

Tashima, Yuriko. *20-seiki Nihon no Fasshon* (20th-century Japanese fashion). Interviews by Junko Ōuchi. Tokyo: Genryūsha, 1996.

Tedi Boi: Rokkunrōru Baiburu (Teddy Boy: Rock'n'roll bible). Tokyo: Hachiyōsha, 1980

Toi, Jūgatsu, ed. *Tomerareru ka, oretachi wo.* (Can you stop us?). Tokyo: Daisanshokan, 1979.

Tozaka, Yasuji. *Genroku kosode kara minisukaato made* (From genroku kosode to the miniskirt). Tokyo: Sankei Drama Books, 1972.

Traddo kaiki to pureppii (Preppie and the return of Trad). *Men's Club.* Vol. 225. December 1979: 139-143.

Trebay, Guy. "Prep, Forward and Back." *New York Times.* July 23, 2010.

Tredre, Roger. "Jeans Makers Get the Blues as Sales Sag." *New York Times.* January 13, 1999.

Trumbull, Robert. "Japanese Hippies Take Over a Park in Tokyo." *New York Times.* August 26, 1967.

Tsuzuku, Chiho. *"Boku wa sandomo muichimon ni nattemasu yo — Ishizu Kensuke."* (I have gone rags-to-riches three times now — Kensuke Ishizu). *STUDIO VOICE.* Volume 61. December 1980.

Udagawa, Satoru. *VAN Sutōriizu—Ishizu Kensuke to Aibii no Jidai* (VAN stories: Ishizu Kensuke and the Ivy era). Tokyo: Shueisha Shinsho, 2006.

Uhlman, Marian. "There May Be Money In Your Air Jordans. Japanese Buyers Pay Big For Old Sneakers." *The Philadelphia Inquirer.* July 21, 1997.

Urabe, Makoto. *Ryūkō Uragaeshi* (Upside-down history of trends). Tokyo: Bunka Fukusō Gakuin Shuppankyoku, 1965.

Urabe, Makoto. *Zoku • Ryūkō Uragaeshi* (Upside-down history of trends, continued). Tokyo: Bunka Shuppankyoku, 1982.

"VAN Ōkoku Suitai ni Aegu Ishizu Ikka no Rōhi" (The Ishizu family extravagance that will lead to the ruin of the VAN kingdom). *Shūkan Shinchō.* January 4, 1969: 42-44.

Wakai Hiroba Harajuku 24 jikan (Young plaza: 24 hours in Harajuku). NHK. 1980.

Wetherille, Kelly. "Nigo Opens Up About Bape." *Women's Wear Daily.* February 7, 2011.

Williams, Michael. "That Autumn Look | Turning Japanese." *A Continuous Lean.* September 21, 2009. http://www.acontinuouslean.com/2009/09/21/that-autumn-look-turning-japanese/

Yamaguchi, Jun. *Biimuzu no kiseki* (The Beams miracle). Tokyo: Sekai bunka-sha, 2006.

Yamane, Hidehiko. *Tateoti.* Tokyo: Ei Publishing, 2008.

Yamazaki, Masayuki. *Kuriimu Sōda monogatari* (The Cream Soda story). Tokyo: JICC Publishing, 1980.

Yamazaki, Masayuki with Hiroshi Morinaga. *Takara wa itsumo ashimoto ni.* (The treasure is always under your feet). Tokyo: Asuka Shinsha, 2009.

Yankii daishūgō (Big yankii collection). Tokyo: East Press, 2009.

Yasuoka, Shōtarō. "*Noshiaruku 'Aibii-zoku' ni Monomousu.*" *Yasuoka Shōtarō Essei Zenshū,* Volume 8. Tokyo: Yomiuri Shimbunsha, 1975.

"*Zasshi, tarento ni odorasareru 'botsu' kosei-ha no furugi būmu*" (The *non*-individualistic vintage boom that's making magazines and celebrities dance). *Aera.* September 22, 1997: 30.

INDEX

The photo section is indexed as *p1,p2,p3* etc. since there are not actual page numbers for it

activism, 85–87

AFFA (Anarchy Forever Forever Anarchy), 179, 184

aibii (Ivy). *See* Ivy League style

aivii riigu moderu (Ivy League model), 27

amekaji (American casual), 149, 168–169, 171–172

American Graffiti (film), 135, 138

Ameyoko district, 76–77, 78, 80, 149–151

Ampo Japan-U.S. Security Treaty, 85–86

anti-pollution movement, 102

antiwar demonstrations, 85–86

Aoyama, 155, 160

apure/Après, 24–25, 126

architectural style, 7, 21, 59–60, 185

"Are You a Preppie" (poster), 156–157, 158

Army uniforms, 138

Asada, Akira, 164–165

Asama-sansō, 91

Asayan (magazine), 179, 182

authenticity, 119, 236

avant-garde fashion, 163–165, 163 (photo)

aviator sunglasses, 25, 126

baby boomer generation, 66, 72

Baby Milo, 187

Babzani, Kiya, 217, 218, 219, 236

Bamboo Shoot Tribe. *See* takenoko-zoku

bankruptcy
    Bape, 192–193
    of VAN, 118–120, 153–154, 221

Bape. *See* A Bathing Ape

Bapesta shoes, 187, 188, 189

Barry, Dave, 147

baseball, 8, 114, 128

Bastian, Michael, 224, 226, 233

A Bathing Ape, 179, 180 (photo), 181–182, 189, 191, 241
    bankruptcy, 192–193
    Busy Work Shop and, 185
    celebrity ambassadors and, 185, 190
    counterfeits, 190
    in Hong Kong, 186–187
    London, 188

Beams, 150–151, 152

Beams F, 152, 160, 168, 171, 173, 241

The Beatles, 71, 131

bell-bottom jeans, 92, 221

"Big Ivy Meet Up," 65

Big John jeans, 84–85, 84 (photo), 94, 239
    advertisements, 90, 90 (photo), 101–102
    Heavy Duty boom and, 110–111, 111 (photo)
    hippies and, 90–91

bikers, 142–143, 145
    See also bōsōzoku bikers; motorcycles

Birnbach, Lisa, 157–158, 159
Black Cats, 123, 146
blazer, Ivy League, 50–51, 51 (photo)
blue jeans. *See* jeans
Bobson, 92, 94, 198
Boon (magazine), 199, 203, 204 (photo),
    211
bōsōzoku groups, 132–133, 133 (photo),
    139–140, 142, 143, 145
Brand, Stewart, 97, 99–100
Brooks Brothers, 152, 153–154, 237–238
Brown University, 58, 163
Browne, Thom, 224, 230, 233
Bubble Era, 166–167, 173, 199, 203
Busy Work Shop, 185–186, 189,
    191–192
button-down shirts, 28–29, 33, 54, 154

California lifestyle, 112–114, 118
Canton Mills denim, 81–82
"Cape Cod Spirit" (sales campaign), 69,
    70 (photo)
Carol (band), 130–132, 131 (photo), 144
catalogs, 106, 107, 115
    See also Made in U.S.A.; *Whole Earth
    Catalog*
chinos, 43, 83
C.I.A., 117
"city boys", 124, 161
Coca-Cola, 35, 70, 120, 134
Columbia University, 58
Cone Mills, 81, 83, 92, 93, 99, 209, 216
Continental style, 52, 70–71, 85, 98–99
Converse's Chuck Taylors, 187
Cornelius, 181, 185
Cornell University, 58
cotton, 75, 81, 211
countercultures, 85
    American, 98
    changes in, 134
    jean market and, 88–89
    Maruo Clothing and, 91
    in Shinjuku, 86–88
counterfeits, 185, 186–187, 190
craftsmanship, Japanese, 215, 219–220,
    233
Cream Soda, 123, 139, 147
    delinquency and, 146

Harajuku and, 136–137, 141–142
Crisp (store), 195–196
CrossEye (magazine), 156
Crow Tribe, 164–165
Crystal Tribe, 155–156
currency controls, 55–56

Danshi Senka (magazine), 17, 23
Dartmouth, 57, 110, 226
DC boom, 165–167, 169, 171, 173
deadstock, 196, 197, 199, 201–202
delinquent style, 126, 132, 139, 141–142,
    147–148
    American, 146, 147–148
    Fifties movement and, 142
    iconic, 147–148
    Japanese, 146
demonstrations, student, 85–86
denim, 209
    American supply of, 92
    Canton Mills, 81–82
    demand for, 94, 198–199
    French brands, 208
    imports of, 80–81
    Japanese, 93, 216–217
    Maruo Clothing and, 83–85
    milling of, 217
    mura-ito (slubby denim), 207–208
    one-wash, 82–83
    retro, 211
    Seibu and, 84–85
    selvedge, 199–200, 207, 219
    sewing and, 81–82
    supply of, 92
    vintage stores and, 199
    washed-out, 79
denim market, Japanese, 93–94
denim mills, 81–82, 219, 239
designer fashion
    European, 162
    Japanese, 164–165
"Dictionary of Men's Fashion Terms," 27
disco, 141, 155
"Discover America" (sales campaign), 69
DO-1 (Studio D'artisan jeans), 208,
    cover (photo)
Dower, John, 12
down vests, 110, 169

drugs, 87, 116
    See also thinner huffing

East End X Yuri (rap group), 181
economy, Japanese, 166–167, 173, 234
    Oil Crisis and, 102–103
    recession and, 223
    See also Bubble Economy
Edwin, 83, 90, 94, 198, 211, 239
Eikō Shōji, 78
Emperor Meiji, 1–3, 3 (photo)
European suits, 70–71
Evisu, 209–210, 210 (photo), 211 216, 219
exercise, 100–101

fabric
    denim, 81–82
    kimono, 14
Farley Enterprises, 204–205
Fast Retailing, 221–222
    See also UNIQLO
Feltwell, Toby, 188–189
Fifties movement, 137–138, 139, 142,
    145–146
The Flat Head, 217, 233
flight jackets, 168, 203, 212
food shortages, 8, 10–11
45rpm, 214–215, 216, 219
Free & Easy (magazine), 230
French denim brands, 208
Fuck Yeah Menswear (Burrows and
    Lawrence), 229, 229 (photo)
Fujin Gahō (magazine), 17
Fujingahōsha (publisher), 60–61, 62
    See also Take Ivy photo book
Fujiwara, Hiroshi, 179, 181
    as DJ, 175–176
    Goodenough and, 178, 188
    Head Porter and, 188
    International Stüssy Tribe, 177
    Nigo and, 193–194
    Nike and, 193
    success of, 184
Fukuyama, Hiroshima, 92–93, 239
Full Count, 211, 218, 219

gakuran uniforms, 23–24, 24 (photo), 25
Garage Paradise (store), 139, 196, 231

Ginza, ix–xii
    Ivy League style and, 35, 43, 63–65
    police and, 5–6, 64
globalization, 192, 193, 234
Goodenough (brand), 178–179, 181–
    183, 188
Grease (movie), 139
greasers, 130, 132, 143, 145, 147
Greenspan's (store), 195
gurentai (band of thugs), 126

Hair cast arrests, 91
Haircut Edict, 2
hairstyles, 2–3
    Kennedy cut, xi, 127
    Miyuki Tribe and, 45
    pompadour, 126, 127, 129, 140
    regent, 132
    rockabilly singers and, 126–127
hamatora (Yokohama traditional),
    151–152, 164
Hanover, New Hampshire, 57–58
Harada, Kōsuke (designer), 239
Harajuku Chicago (store), 202, 205
Harajuku district, 123, 150
    bōsōzoku groups in, 139–140
    Cream Soda, 136–137, 141–142
    designer goods in, 165
    foreign clothing and, 165–166
    Yamazaki and, 134–135, 146
    youth fashion and, 139
Harvard University, 56–57, 236
Hasegawa, Hajime "Paul", 20–21, 55–56,
    59–61, 70, 118–119, 227 (photo),
    230
Hawaiian shirts, 21, 25, 126, 127
Hayashida, Teruyoshi (photographer),
    55–57, 59 (photo), 60, 156, 227
    (photo)
Head Porter, 188
Heavy Duty (style), 238
    Heibon Planning Center and,
    111–112
    imports, 150
    Ivy style and, 109, 110, *p9*
Heavy Duty Book (Kobayashi), 110
Heavy Duty boom, 109–111, 111
    (photo)

"Heavy Duty Ivy Party Manifesto"
(*Men's Club* piece), 110
Heibon Planning Center, 103–106,
110–112
Heibon Publishing, 103, 116–117
Heibon Punch (magazine), 41–46, 54, 124
American lifestyle and, 101
dumbed down, 103
Ivy fashion and, 63
Hepburn, Audrey, 17
hip-hop music, 175–176, 179, 181
hippies, 87, 90–91, 100–101, 134
hippie-zoku (Japanese hippies), 87–88,
p6
Hirata, Toshikiyo (Kapital), 92, 212–215
Hiyama, Ken'ichi , 76–77, 80, 81
Ho, Jeff, 106, 116
Hoichoi Productions, 161
Hollywood-style jacket, 26–27
Hong Kong, 186–187, 192, 217
"*Honmono sagashi tabi*" (column), 109
Hot Dog Press (magazine), 158, 159
(photo), 162–163, 169
Hozumi, Kazuo (illustrator), 31 (photo),
229, 230

Ichii, Yuri (rapper), 181
illustrations, 36, 41–42, 42 (photo), *p2*
imitations, 29, 146–147, 235
Imperialist era, 24, 142–143
imported clothing, 2, 14, 152, 171–172
American jeans, 78–80
denim and, 80–81
European designer, 162
Heavy Duty, 150
import stores, 171–172
Maruo Clothing and, 81–82
regulations on, relaxed, 78–79
vintage clothing, 205
indigo dying, 81, 93, 199
International Gallery Beams, 162
Internet, 193, 225, 226
Isetan, 82–85
Ishikawa, Jirō
America and, 97–98, 99
in Europe, 98–99
Heibon Punch and, 103
Kinameri and, 104

Popeye magazine and, 112–114
Whole Earth Catalog and, 97–98
Ishizu, Kensuke, 1, 36
bankruptcy and, 118–119
childhood of, 3–4, 4 (photo)
death of, 221
Heibon Punch and, 41–42
Ivy League and, 22, 31–32
as Japanese Olympic team designer,
49–51
legacy of, 221, 239
menswear industry and, 221–222
mobo-moga life and, 4–6
Otoko no Fukushoku and, 17–21
police and, 64–66
Preppy era and, 160
retail store transformations and, 37
rules of Ivy and, 232
son of, 31–32
in Tianjin, China, 6–8
TPO and, 40–41, 49–50
United States, first visit to, 21–22
Ishizu, Shōsuke, 36
Ivy film project and, 54–56, 58
Ivy League clothing and, 31–32
Ishizu, Yūsuke (Wrangler), 102
I.T. Ltd. (Hong Kong retailer), 192
"Ivy Boy" (illustration), 36, 156, *p2*
"Ivy Club" (radio show), 69
Ivy League model, 27
Ivy League style, 31–32, 31 (photo), 227
in America, 60
avant-garde take on, 163–164, 163
(photo)
ban on, 46
blazer and, 50–51, 51 (photo)
button-down shirts and, 154
college campuses and, 54–58, 60–63
as conventional fashion, 89
dos and don'ts of, 38–40
eccentricities of, 163–164
film project and, 54–58, 60–63
Ginza and, 35, 43, 63–65
Heavy Duty and, 109, 110, *p9*
Heibon Punch and, 63
Hozumi and, 28–30
image of, 49
Japanese version of, 230–231

Kurosu and, 27–30, 89, 230–231
Men's Club and, 34–40, 40 (photo)
Miyuki Tribe and, 43–47
as nationwide trend, 67–68
Olympics and, 63
radicals and, 89
rebellious subculture and, 47
reputation of, 65–66
rules of, 232
students and, 21–22
tailors and, 28–29
Take Ivy and, 62–63
TPO and, 40–41
"Ivy Leaguers on the Street" (column in
    Men's Club), 35–36
"Ivy Q&A" (column), 38–39
Ivy revival, 152, 156
Ivy Tribe, 63, 65, *p4*
Iwai, Toru "TORUEYE" (Goodenough),
    177, 178

J. Peterman, 228
J. Press, 152, 154
jackets
    flight, 168, 203, 212
    gold buttons on, 34, 39
    Hollywood-style, 26–27
    souvenir (sukajan), 128
    wool, 23–24
    See also blazer, Ivy League; sport coats
Jaeger (brand), 155
Japan Airlines, 91
Japanese factories, 33
Jarmusch, Jim, 147
jazz musicians, 26–27, 28
jean makers, 80–81, 92, 198–199, 213
jeans, 76, 81, 84, 219–220
    American, 216
    Americans and, 83, 95
    bell-bottom, 92, 221
    countercultures and, 88–89
    film and, 78
    as foreign import, 78–79
    French, 208
    guide in *Boon*, 204
    high-end, 217–218
    hippies and, 90–91
    Hirata and, 212–214

Ivy style and, 89
Kobayashi and, 79
leftists and, 90–91
minimalist, 239, 240 (photo)
pre-distressed, 214–215
as rebellious clothing, 85
sizing and, 78
straight-leg, 198
as unifying factor, 88
vintage, 198, 205–206
washing, 82
women and, 95
"Jeans Controversy," 95
jiipan (G.I. pants), 76–77, 82
jogging, 100–101
John Bull, 92, 94, 213
JUN, 68, 70
Juppie (*Men's Club* publication), 167

Kaihara, 93, 219, 228, 234
Kaijin 20 Mensō (bar), 129–130, 132
Kamakura Shirts, 67, 221–222, 223
    (photo), 228
Kapital, 213–216, 230
Kashino, Shizuo (Big John), 76, 84
    jean making and, 80–81
    one-wash denim and, 82–83
kata-mindset, 235–236
    Heibon Punch and, 41–42
    illustration of, 36
    "Ivy Boy" and, 36, *p2*
    Ivy League style and, 28–30
    Kurosu and, 28–30, 45, 46
Kawakubo, Rei, 163–164, 165
KD-8 denim, 93–94
Kennedy, John F., xi, 69, 84
    See also Kennedy cut
Kennedy cut, xi, 127
Kent, 71
Kentucky (faux American brand),
    14–15
Kinameri, Yoshihisa (editor)103–104,
    106, 112–114, 117, 120
King Kong (bar), 134–135
Kinoshita, Takahiro (editor), 224, 229,
    236, *p13*
kirekaji style (neat casual), 171
kitten photographs. *See* Nameneko

Kobayashi, Yasuhiko
America and, 97–98, 99, 103
in Europe, 98–99
Heavy Duty boom and, 109–111
jeans and, 79
at *Men's Club*, 109
skiing and, 104–106
Whole Earth Catalog and, 97–98, 106
Yankee style and, 128–129
Kojima, 75, 92, 93
kokuminfuku (citizen clothing), 8, 77
"Kon'ya wa Boogie-Back," 179, 181
Korean War, 13–15, 26, 78
Kurabō textile mill, 93–94, 207–209, 228, 234
Kurosu, Toshiyuki, 23–24, 24 (photo)
essays of, 54
Hollywood-style jacket and, 26–27
Hozumi and, 28–30, 45, 46
Ivy film project and, 54–58
"Ivy Leaguers on the Street" and, 35–36
Ivy revival and, 156
Ivy style and, 27–30, 89, 230–231
jazz music and, 26, 28
Men's Club and, 30, 31 (photo)
VAN and, 32–33, 72–73
Kurino, Hirofumi (United Arrows), 101, 161, 168, 229, 232
Kusakabe, Kōji, 196, 197, 203–204
Kvatek, Eric, 200–201, 201 (photo), 203–204, 215

labor strikes, 92
Lacoste, 152, 155, 165
Lapine (store), 207, 209
"Last Orgy" (column), 176
"Last Orgy 2" (column), 177
"Last Orgy 3" (column), 179
Lee jeans, 78–79, 94, 199
leftists, 5, 85–86, 88, 90–91
Levi Strauss & Co., 93–94, 206
501s, 77, 108, 198, 204 (photo)
big E, 200
imported, 78–79
lawsuit and, 218
vintage re-creation line, 208–209, 241
Levi's Japan, 198, 208–209, 227

limited-edition goods, 183–184, 186
L.L. Bean, 109–110, 152, 157–159
Lod Airport attack, 91–92
logo
on bags, 71
sweatshirts, 152
on T-shirts, 69
VAN and, 33–34, 33 (photo), 43–44, 44 (photo), 47, 71
London, 188
looms, 199, 207, 216
Louis Vuitton, 151, 154
luxury goods, 151–152, 154–155
Lynn, Vivienne, 135

Made in U.S.A. (catalog), 106–110, *p7*
magazines, 167
catalog, 115
lifestyle and, 160–161
for men, 17–18, 228
mail-order catalogs, American, 106
Mambo style, 126–127, 128, *p10*
See also Yokosuka Mambo
mansion makers, 134
manufacturing techniques, 217
Marines, U.S., 9
martial arts, 132, 212–213, 235
Maruo Clothing, 76, 78, 89
Big John jeans and, 84–85
Cone Mills and, 92
countercultures and, 91
denim and, 83–85
imports from U.S., 81–82
jean manufacturing and, 80–81
Maruseru (store), 76–77, 78, 80
Marxist student movement, 85–87, 91, 99, 117
Masayuki Yamazaki, 123–124, 127, 130 (photo)
death of, 240
delinquent fashion and, 126
Fifties style and, 139, 146
gangs and, 133–134
growing up, 125–126
Harajuku and, 134–135, 146
imitations and, 146–147
Ivy and, 129
Kaijin 20 Mensō and, 129–130

Lynn and, 135
rockabilly empire, 148
rock'n'roll and, 125
sukaman look and, 129
vintage clothing store, 136–137
masculinity, xi, 15–16, 72, 233
materialism, 102, 103, 108
backlash and, 85
Popeye and, 116, 156
McLaren, Malcolm, 135, 175
Meiji Era, 1–3
Men's Club (magazine), 19–20, 21, 30, 31 (photo), 54, 156, 158
Heavy Duty Ivy and, 110, *p9*
imported American jeans in, 80 (photo)
Ivy style and, 34–40, 40 (photo)
preppy fashion and, 156–157, 157 (photo)
revival and, 156
VAN and, 34–35, 36
Mister VAN (brand), 70–71
Miura & Sons, 150, 151
See also Ships
Miyake, Issey, xiii, 164, 186
Miyake, Ken, 185
Miyuki Tribe, ix–xii, xi (photo), *p3*
hairstyles and, 45
high-water pants and, 45
Ivy style and, 43–47
VAN and, 45–46
Mo Wax (record label), 181
mobo-moga life, 4–6
mono (magazine), 203, 211
monpe (farming pants), 11, 14
mook (magazine-book), 106–107
Moonstar (shoemaker), 52, 53
Morita, Gō, 185
motorcycles, 131–132, 141–142
Mr. Bathing Ape (brand), 193
mura-ito (slubby) denim, 207–208
music
hip-hop, 175–176, 179, 181
jazz, 26, 28
new wave, 175
punk, 175
soul, 129
Mystery Train (film), 147

Nagao, Tomoaki, 176
See also Nigo
Nakamura, Hiroki (visvim), 238–239
Nakamura, Shinichirō "Sk8thing", 177–179
Nameneko, 143, 145 (photo)
Nantonaku, Kurisutaru (Tanaka novel), 155
New Academism, 164–165
New Age spirituality, 115–116
New Left, Japanese, 91
New Money, 167–168
New York designers, 152–153
Nigo, 176–179, 181–183, 190, 191 (photo), 241
A Bathing Ape and, 187, 188–189
Busy Work Shop and, 185–186
Feltwell and, 188–189
Nike, 168, 193, 201
1950 Company, 137
Nixon Administration, 92–93
nouveau-riche styles, 167–168
Nowhere (store), 178–179, 181–183, 185, 191–193
nyūtora (New Traditional), 151–152

O'Brien (Lieutenant), 9, 21
Occupation troops, 10, 12
The Official MIE Handbook (Hoichoi Productions), 161
The Official Preppy Handbook (Birnbach), 157–158, 159 (photo)
Ōfuchi, Takeshi (designer), 197, 199, 203–204
"Oh, Mistake" incident, 25–26
Ōhashi, Ayumi (illustrator), 36, 41–42, 42 (photo)
Oil Crisis, 102–103, 150
Ōishi Trading, 79, 81
Ōishi, Tetsuo, 81, 219
Ōkaji, Nobuaki, 177–178
Ōkawa, Teruo (VAN), 6–7, 19
Ōkawa Yōkō (store), 6–9
Okayama Prefecture, 75, 94
Olah, Andrew, 208
Olympic team uniform, Japanese, 49–51, 51 (photo)

Olympics 1964, ix–xii, 45–46
 clean up efforts, ix
 Ivy fashion and, 63
 Ivy League blazer and, 50–51, 51
  (photo)
 VAN and, 49–54
Onward Kashiyama, 152, 167
OPEC oil embargo, 102
Ōsaka Five, 211
Ōshima, Toshio (Big John), 76, 83
Otoko no Fukushoku (magazine), 17–21,
 18 (photo), 27
 See also Men's Club
Ōtsubo, Yōsuke, 109, 195–196,
 205–206
outdoor gear, 108, 110, 113
Oyamada, Keigō, 181–182
Ozaki, Kotarō (Big John founder), 76,
 80, 82, 84, 91–92
Ozawa, Kyō (director), 55, 56–57, 60

Pan Pan Girls, 11–12, 76
pants
 farming, 11, 14
 high-water, 45
 mambo, 126–127
Paris, 164
Parisian style, 165–166
parody, 36, 161, 208, 229
pedestrian paradise, 134, 140–141, *p11*
Pehda, Philip Karl, 95
Pepsi Japan, 70, 187
Pink Dragon (store), 123–125, 124
 (photo), 145, 240
Planet of the Apes (film), 179, 181, 182,
 188
police, x–xii, 5–6, 64–66
 See also riot police
police raids, 46–47
pollution, 102
polo shirts, 112
pompadours, 126, 127, 129, 140
Pottasch, Alan (Pepsi executive), 70
preppy fashion
 end of, 162
 Japanese, 159–160
 lifestyle and, 158, 160–161
 Men's Club and, 156–157, 157 (photo)

prestige, 2, 12–13, 22
Princeton, 21–22, 58, *p1*
prostitutes, 11–12
 See also Pan Pan Girls
protests, 85–86
psychedelic movement, 87

quality, 198–199, 233

radio, 12, 69
rationing, 11–12
Readymade (store), 183–184, 193
ready-to-wear clothing, 14, 19–20
recession, 223
Red Army Faction, 91–92
red suit jacket, 49–51, 51 (photo)
Red Wing boots, *p8*
Renown, 11, 13, 101
replicas
 flight jacket, 212
 jeans, 209–212, 217–218, 219, 239
 vintage clothing, 211–212
retro clothing, 137, 211
right-wing groups (*uyoku*), 142–143
riot police, 86–87
rockabilly movement, 126–127, 148
rock'n'roll craze, 145–146
rock'n'roll style, 123, 125, 139
Roller Tribe, 140 (photo), 141–142, 147
rules, 232, 235
 of Ivy style, 232
 of Japanese fashion, 38–39, 41
 teenagers and, 234
Run DMC, 168, 189

Sadasue, Yoshio (Kamakura Shirts), 37,
 67–68, 67 (photo), 154, 221
sakoku policy ("closed country"), 1
samurai, 1–2
"The Sartorialist," 229, 239–240, *p13*
satire, 155, 156–157, 229
Satō, Ikuya (anthropologist), 125, 143
SCENE (brand), 111
Scha Dara Parr (rap group), 179, 181
school uniforms, xii, 75–76
Scovill, 82
secondhand clothing, 201–205
Seibu, 83, 84–85

Self Edge (store), 217–218
self-expression, 15–16
selvedge, 199–200, 207, 219
sewing machines, 81–82, 93, 213
shibukaji style, 169, 170–173, 170
    (photo), 181, 184
Shibuya, 168–173
Shigematsu, Osamu, 149, 171
    Beams F. and, 152
    European designer imports and, 162
    preppy clothing and, 160
    Shitara and, 150–151
Shinjuku, 133–134
    bōsōzoku in, 139–140
    countercultures in, 86–88
    movement, 88–89
    teenagers in, 87
Shinkō Inc. (Beams parent company),
    149–150
Shiotani, Kenji, 211
Ships, 151, 152, 171, 173
Shirasu, Jirō, 77–78, p5
shirts
    button-down, 28–29, 54, 154
    Hawaiian, 21, 25, 126, 127
Shitara, Etsuzō (Beams founder),
    149–151, 171
shoes
    athletic, 52–53
    Bapesta, 187, 188, 189
    rare, 205
silk, 2
Singapore Night (nightclub), 135
Sk8thing. See Shinichirō "Sk8thing"
    Nakamura
Skateboarder (magazine), 114
skateboarding, 114–115
Ski Life (magazine), 104–106, 105
    (photo)
skiing, 104–106, 161
Slade, Toby, 15–16
Sony, 41, 137–138
soul music, 129
souvenir jackets, 128
spinning technology, 208, 211
sports, 114
    American, 57–58
    outdoor, 101

"Sports American" (sales campaign), 70
    (photo)
stock market, Japanese, 172–173
streetwear, 184, 185–186, 238
student movement, 91, 134
students
    campus style and, 56–57
    Ivy League style and, 21–22
    See also Marxist student movement
Stüssy, 177–178, 193, 228
suits, European, 70–71
sukaman. See Yokosuka Mambo
Sun Tribe, 21, 43, 127
surfing, 115, 231
Suzuki, Daiki, 224, 231, 237, 239
swastika, 143
sweatshirts, logo, 152

tabloids, x, 72
tailor-made clothing, 16, 19
tailors, 28–29
Taishō Era, 3
Takada, Kenzō, xiii, 164
Takagi, Kan (musician), 175–176
Takahashi, Jun "Jonio", 176–179, 183,
    193, 234
Takahashi, Shigetoshi, 78–79
Takarajima (magazine), 112, 177
Take Ivy (film), 54–58, 60
    Tsukiji Police Station screening of,
        64–65
    VAN Jacket Inc. and, 61–63
Take Ivy photo book (Fujingahō), 60–61,
    61 (photo), 62, 156
    Internet and, 226
    rerelease of, 226–227
    T-shirts and, 69
takenoko-zoku (Bamboo Shoot Tribe),
    141–142
Tanaka, Yasuo (writer), 155
Tarumi, Gen (Hollywood Ranch Market
    founder), 213–214
Teamers (chiimaa), 169, 172
tech boom, 225–226
teenagers, ix, xiii–xvi
    American goods and, 116–117
    blue-collar, 125
    button-down shirts and, 54

teenagers (*continued*)
  mambo and, 126–127, 128
  middle-class, 165
  rebellious, x–xii, 87, 126–127, 128
  rules and, 234
  in Shinjuku, 87
  sukaman, 128
  West Coast, 113–114
  See also Miyuki Tribe; tsuppari;
    Vagabond Tribe
Terauchi, Daikichi (critic), 72
Terayama, Shūji (dramatist), 89
Tetoron (fiber), 75–76
textile mills, 92–93
  See also Cone Mills
thinner huffing, 87, 132, 142
*Throw Away Your Books, Run into the
  Streets!* (play), 89
Tianjin, China, 6–8
Tinnie Panx (rap group), 175–176
Tokugawa military government
    (1603–1869), 1–2
Tokyo
  fashion in, 132
  pollution in, 102
  youth in, 73
  See also Olympics 1964
Tokyo Metropolitan Police Department,
    5–6
Tomohito of Mikasa (Prince), 66–67
Toray and Teijin, 75–76
TPO ("time, place, occasion"), 40–41,
    49–50
Trad style, 71
Traditional Ivy Leaguers Club, 29, 30, 31
    (photo), 50
trends
  Ivy style, 67–68
  Preppy, 161
T-shirt, 68–69, 184
Tsujita, Mikiharu (Full Count founder),
    206–207, 209–211, 218
Tsukiji police raids, 46–47
Tsunemi, Yonehachi (Edwin founder),
    83
tsuppari (delinquent teens), 141–142,
    143–144, 145, *p11*

Tsutsumi, Seiji, 164–165
TUKI (brand), 239, 240 (photo)

Uchisaka, Tsuneo (*Popeye* editor),
    120–121
UCLA, 114, 116
Umbrella Tribe, 63
Undercover (brand), 178–179, 181–182,
    193
uniforms
  Army, 138
  gakuran, 23–24, 24 (photo), 25
  for Olympic team, 49–51, 51 (photo)
  school, xii, 75–76
UNIQLO, 219, 222, 234, 241
UNITED ARROWS, 171, 173, 241
United Red Army, 91
University of Pennsylvania, 58
Ura-Harajuku era, 181–183, 184,
    190–193

V6 (music group), 185
Vagabond Tribe, 87
VAN Jacket Inc., 18–20
  bankruptcy of, 118–121, 153–154,
    221
  Brooks Brothers and, 153–154
  customers of, 37–38
  diversification and, 71, 119
  economy and, 66–67
  growth of, 66–67
  Ishizu, Kensuke and, 15–16, 15
    (photo), 18–20
  Ivy League-style and, 22
  Ivy line of, 32–34
  jeans and, 83
  Kurosu, Toshiyuki and, 32–33,
    72–73
  legacy of, 120–121
  logo, 33–34, 33 (photo), 43–44, 44
    (photo), 47, 71
  marketing to youth and, 46–47
  Men's Club (magazine) and, 34–35, 36
  Miyuki Tribe and, 45–46
  Olympics and, 49–54
  rivals of, 68
  shopping bag, 43–44, 44 (photo)

SNEEKERS, 52–53, 53 (photo), 63
success of, 67–68
Take Ivy film and, 61–63
Wrangler Japan and, 94
See also Ivy League style
"VAN Music Break" (TV show), 69
vanity, 15–16
Vietnam war, 99
vintage clothing, 135–136
buyers, 196–197, 200–201, 201 (photo)
demand for, 195–196, 199
imports and, 205
jeans, 198, 205–206
male consumers and, 203
replicas, 211–212
vintage clothing store, 136–137
in America, 200, 202
denim and, 199
See also Cream Soda
vinylon, 75–76
Visvim (brand), 238
V-shape silhouette, 20 (photo), 20–21

"Wanted in Japan" (booklet), 205
Warehouse (brand), 211
Watanabe, Junya (designer), 237–238, 239
Web forums, 225
Westwood, Vivienne, 135, 175
When, Where, What to Wear (Kensuke Ishizu book), 41
Whole Earth Catalog, 97–100, 106, 111
Williams, Pharrell, 189, 190, 191 (photo)

womenswear, xiv, 16, 17, 162
woodblock prints, 36, 106
Woodstock Music Festival, 97
wool jacket, 23–24
World (apparel company), 191–192
World War II, 24
Wrangler Japan, 94, 102
Wrangler jeans, 199

Yale University, 58, 69
Yamagiwa, Hiroyuki (Oh mistake incident), 25–26
Yamamoto, Yohji, 163–164
Yamane, Hidehiko (Evisu founder), 207, 209–210, 211, 216
Yanai, Tadashi, 222
Yankee style, 128–132, 144, 147–148
Yankii culture, 145 (photo), 240–241
bikers and, 145
fashion and, 146, 147–148
Yazawa, Eikichi, 130–132, 131 (photo), 141, 234
yen, Japanese, 55–56, 166
YKK zippers, 93
Yokohama (port city), 128, 151–152
Yokohama Ginbae, 143, 144 (photo)
Yokohama Traditional. *See* hamatora
Yokosuka Mambo, 127–129, 144
sukaman style, 128–129
Yoshida Kaban, 188
Young Plaza: 24 Hours in Harajuku (documentary), 141–142
Yoyogi Park, 141–142, 240

Zephyr productions, 106, 114

W. David Marx is a writer on Japanese fashion, music, and culture. A former editor of the Tokyo–New York street culture magazine *Tokion*, his articles have appeared in *GQ*, *Harper's*, *The Fader*, and *Nylon*. He holds a bachelor's degree from Harvard in East Asian Studies and a master's degree in business and commerce from Keio University. He lives in Tokyo, Japan.